Modern
EAST ASIA

Modern EAST ASIA

AN INTRODUCTORY HISTORY

JOHN H. MILLER

An East Gate Book

LONDON AND NEW YORK

An East Gate Book

First published 2008 by M.E. Sharpe

Published 2015 by Routledge
2 Park Square, Milton Park, Abingdon, Oxon OX14 4RN
711 Third Avenue, New York, NY 10017, USA

Routledge is an imprint of the Taylor & Francis Group, an informa business

Copyright © 2008 Taylor & Francis. All rights reserved.

Library of Congress Cataloging-in-Publication Data

Miller, John H., 1941–
Modern East Asia : an introductory history / by John H. Miller.
    p. cm.
"An East gate book."
Includes bibliographical references.
ISBN 978-0-7656-1822-1 (cloth : alk. paper) — ISBN 978-0-7656-1823-8 (pbk. : alk. paper)
1. East Asia—History. 2. Southeast Asia—History. I. Title.

DS511.M53 2007
950′.3--dc22   2007001675

ISBN 13: 9780765618238 (pbk)
ISBN 13: 9780765618221 (hbk)

Contents

List of Illustrative Materials

Maps

Illustrations

Tables

Preface

This book is an outgrowth of research and teaching over the past several years on the modern history of East Asia. Since East Asia, conceived as a unified region encompassing both Southeast and Northeast Asia, is a relatively new and controversial field of historical study, I have thought it necessary to set forth in the Introduction my reasons for considering it as a coherent region that has persisted over time. Nothing I have to say on this subject should be taken as denigrating the value of area studies or the enormous contribution of historians using this framework. I myself was trained as a specialist in Japanese history and Northeast Asian area studies. One could hardly attempt a book of this sort without standing on the shoulders of these historians, and my indebtedness to them should be evident in the bibliography. Although it relies heavily on the insights of country and area specialists, this book is intended for the general reader and looks at East Asia from the broader perspective of European and world history. It also seeks to use history to shed light on current security issues and concerns in East Asia. As a former U.S. Foreign Service Officer, I spent over twenty years analyzing and reporting on the international politics of the region for an audience of Washington policymakers. I am a firm believer in the view that for history to be truly meaningful, it should help illuminate the problems of the present and provide early warning of new ones that might be coming down the road.

Whether I have succeeded, however imperfectly, in any of these aims and endeavors, I leave to the judgment of readers. I would, however, like to thank Professor Emeritus David D. Buck of the University of Wisconsin–Milwaukee for his insightful and generous comments on an early draft of this book. I have also benefited from extensive discussion of many of the themes in this book with my colleagues and students at the Asia-Pacific Center for Security Studies in Honolulu. Needless to say, all errors of fact and interpretation are my own.

I have used Pinyin phonetic spellings for Chinese words, except where clarity seems to require the older and more familiar Wade-Giles romanization system spellings (for example "Chiang Kai-shek" instead of "Jiang Jieshi"). I have omitted diacriticals from Japanese words.

Introduction
East Asia as a Region

Until the 1990s, most people understood the term "East Asia" to refer to that part of the eastern Eurasian landmass that encompasses the Sinic or Confucian culture area—namely, the contemporary states of China, Japan, Mongolia, Vietnam, South and North Korea, and Taiwan. This definition, which is geographically equivalent to Northeast Asia, was not entirely satisfactory. It included Mongolia, which was never Confucian, and excluded the predominately ethnic Chinese city-state of Singapore in Southeast Asia, which was largely Confucian. Moreover, not everyone agreed that Vietnam belonged in East Asia despite its Confucian cultural overlay. Still, this conception of East Asia worked well enough and acquired near universal acceptance. It also offered a convenient means of differentiating East Asia from other culturally defined world regions, including South, Central, and Southeast Asia. South Asia was united by an "Indic culture" and Central Asia by a "Turkic culture." (Nations of West Asia shared an "Islamic culture.") Southeast Asia's cultural diversity made it more problematic. But for reasons examined below, it, too, was endowed with an underlying cultural unity and designated a region.

These culturally based regions, which are embedded in a larger framework of similarly defined world regions, remain today the basic units of eastern Eurasia above the level of individual nation-states. They are reflected in standard geographical atlases and textbooks, news reports, and everyday parlance. Historians, anthropologists, political scientists, and other academicians are divided into East, South, Central, and Southeast Asian area experts who publish in specialized periodicals like the *Journal of Southeast Asian Studies*. These regions also underlie international organizations such as the Association of Southeast Asian Nations (ASEAN) and the South Asian Association for Regional Cooperation (SAARC). The organizational structures of most foreign ministries are based on these regions, although they group them together differently. The U.S. State Department, for example, deals with Central and

South Asian matters in one geographical bureau. The State Department is unusual in that its Bureau of East Asian and Pacific Affairs has long treated Southeast and Northeast Asia as parts of a larger East Asia, which it links to what some see as the unrelated region of Oceania, or the Pacific Islands.

In the 1990s, the conventional view of eastern Eurasia's regions came under critical scrutiny and pressure for revision. In particular, many questioned the justification for the continued division of Southeast and Northeast Asia into separate regions in light of their growing economic integration. Considered from the latter standpoint, it seemed to make more sense to regard them as forming a single region that, for lack of a better alternative, they dubbed East Asia. The term "East Asia" consequently acquired two different referents—Northeast Asia as the old Sinic culture area, and both Northeast and Southeast Asia as a new economic entity—and it has continued to be employed in both senses, often without explicit recognition or explanation of its dual meaning. (To minimize this confusion, the term will henceforth be used here in its broader sense.) But the revisionist case went further. Some maintained that East Asia was neither new nor based exclusively on economic ties. They argued that it derived its unity as a region from shared "Asian Values" such as respect for authority, hierarchy, and consensus, which were rooted in common traditions stretching far back into history.

The claim that East Asia has a historically based cultural unity elicited considerable skepticism, if not outright derision, from the Western scholarly community. For one thing, it flew in the face of the prevailing orthodoxy, which holds that Southeast Asia has its own cultural identity distinct from the "Confucian identity" of Northeast Asia. For another, there seemed to be no historical basis for a common East Asian culture inasmuch as Southeast Asians had imported most of their higher civilization from South Asia. Critics also charged that the empirical evidence for the existence of Asian Values is flimsy. Survey data show that East Asians differ as much among themselves as they do from Westerners in their attachment to these values. Many noted, moreover, that there is little specifically East Asian or even non-Western about values such as an esteem for social harmony and the priority of group over individual interests. Asian Values, in other words, posit a false dichotomy between Asia and the West. More alarming to critics was the use of these values by some of their proponents to challenge Western conceptions of human rights and democracy, and legitimize authoritarian systems and practices.

A point generally overlooked by critics of Asian Values is that the extent to which such values "really exist" or have any solid historical foundation are secondary questions. The Asian Values movement was, and still is, primarily an exercise in identity building and "consciousness raising." It is little concerned with winning over doubting Thomases in Western academic circles.

The East Asian politicians, bureaucrats, journalists, and intellectuals who are driving this movement are convinced that cultural similarities and common historical experiences make East Asia a distinctive region. For them, this is a given, not something that has to be proven or demonstrated. Their aims are to get this message out to East Asian publics and persuade governments to establish the institutional architecture appropriate to East Asia's status as a major world region. Despite the anti-Western rhetoric of a few, most East Asian regionalists are quite comfortable with Western liberal democracy and the maintenance of close economic, security, and political ties with the United States. They seek greater autonomy and leverage vis-à-vis the West, not the creation of an exclusionary East Asian bloc.

Regions as Social Constructs

Whether or not one agrees with East Asian regionalists that East Asia is, and always has been, a distinctive region, they raise several interesting and important questions, perhaps the most fundamental of which is, what exactly is a region? Regions can be defined as geographically contiguous areas that are thought to have sufficient unity, be it cultural, economic, historical, or political, to set them apart from other, similarly defined areas. The operative part of this definition is the phrase "are thought to have." Contrary to what many people assume, regions are not objective and timeless realities like features of the physical environment. Rather, they are social constructs, or ideas about the world held by particular people, at particular times, for particular reasons. Like nations, they are "imagined communities." Viewed in this light, regions are changeable, since ideas about how people are related change. They are also contested inasmuch as there is rarely unanimity on their boundaries or the extent to which their defining attribute is present. In addition, they are "political" in the sense that they incorporate the often unacknowledged agendas and interests of particular nations and groups.

Consider, for example, the current scheme of culturally defined world regions alluded to above. Far from having always existed and being based on objective realities, this scheme was invented and sold by American social scientists in the years immediately after World War II with the support of the U.S. government. It is, in other words, a Cold War construct that reflected the convergence of interests between the U.S. government and the areas studies establishment. To help fight the Cold War, the former needed a corps of experts conversant with the languages, histories, cultures, social dynamics, and politics of likely battlegrounds, particularly those in the Third World. The emerging field of area studies in U.S. academic institutions was glad to oblige, training generations of scholars and practitioners in return for generous government funding. The Americans were not, of course, the only ones to nurture the development of area studies. The British, Australians, and others followed suit for many of the same reasons. As the West's superpower and standard-bearer, however, the United States led the pack, and its view of the world was adopted by virtually everyone else.

For American area studies experts in the 1950s, the first step in designing a new system of world regions was jettisoning the Europe-centered framework that had prevailed prior to World War II. Europeans conceived of Asia as the East or Orient; that is, everything lying east of Europe, with the Dardanelles and the Ural and Caucasus mountains marking the boundary. They divided Asia into the Near and Middle East, centered on the Ottoman and Persian empires, and the Far East, encompassing the ancient civilizations of India and China and their offshoots. Americans considered this scheme hopelessly "Eurocentric" and out-of-date. They turned to anthropologists' concept of "culture areas" as the building block of a more "scientific" and value-neutral approach. Culture areas, which assume interrelated assemblages of cultural traits that persist relatively unchanged over long periods of time, were ideally suited to remapping postcolonial Asia insofar as they pointed to underlying commonalities that had been obscured by European colonialism. Culture areas were, in other words, in tune with the aspirations of newly emerging nations to recover their cultural identities and heritages.

Reinventing the Far East

In deconstructing the old notion of the Far East into its component culture areas, the Americans were aided by the fact that there was longstanding and universal agreement on the existence of Chinese and Indian civilizational zones. All that was needed was to relabel these zones "Sinic" and "Indic" to disassociate them from the contemporary Indian and Chinese nation-states. Southeast Asia, however, presented a problem. Prior to World War II, hardly anyone thought this area had any cultural unity. Indeed, the term "Southeast Asia" was rarely used. The area's European colonial rulers considered it to be a mélange of Indian, Arab, Chinese, and European influences with no cultural identity of its own. Chinese influence prevailed in Vietnam and among ethnic Chinese immigrants elsewhere. Indian influence, including Sanskrit-based writing systems and Theravada Buddhism, held sway in Burma, Thailand, Laos, and Cambodia. Islam and Islamic culture imported from South and West Asia predominated among the Malay inhabitants of the Malay Peninsula and the Indonesian (or Malay) Archipelago. Filipinos were largely Christians, having been converted to Catholicism by the Spanish.

Reinventing Southeast Asia as a culture area on a par with the widely accepted Sinic and Indic ones entailed heroic and unremitting labor on the part of American area studies experts, assisted by their British colleagues. Many of these experts saw themselves as akin to missionaries, whose task was to rescue Southeast Asia from the obloquy of being dismissed as a mere appendage of higher civilizations, and spread understanding of its cultural autonomy and distinctiveness. Try as they might, however, they were unable to make a compelling case for Southeast Asia as a culture area. The problem, in essence, was that they could not come up with the necessary package of unifying cultural traits. They did, of course, identify a few commonalities such as the relatively high status of women and the prevalence of nuclear families. But religion, language, and other important cultural markers pointed to diversity, not unity. Some sought a way out of this dilemma by asserting a "unity in diversity" that posited a common cultural substratum underlying obvious cultural differences. The difficulty, however, was that the existence of this "substratum" was largely a matter of faith.

Despite the best efforts of the area studies community to establish Southeast Asia as a world region, it might have languished indefinitely in a twilight zone of semi-acceptance. In the 1950s, both its borders and bona fides as a region were contested. But one factor that boosted its claim to "regionhood" was war. Southeast Asia first entered the Western popular lexicon in 1943 with the creation of the South-East Asia Command (SEAC), the British theater of operations in the Pacific War that saw major battles in Assam and Burma in 1944–45. Geographically, SEAC bore little resemblance to what is today thought of as Southeast Asia inasmuch as it included Sri Lanka and northeastern India and excluded the Philippines. However, it implanted the idea that the hitherto amorphous zone south of China and east of India possessed some kind of unity. This idea was reinforced during the 1950s and 1960s when Southeast Asia became an early Cold War battleground and the southern anchor of the U.S. containment line in East Asia. Americans conceptualized it as a row of "dominoes," assuming that the fall of one to Sino-Soviet communism would inevitably lead to the toppling of the others.

Military and geopolitical definitions of Southeast Asia paved the way for its acceptance as a culture area and its induction into the U.S.-designed system of world regions. The lead in this push for regionhood was taken by ASEAN. Established in 1967 by the governments of Singapore, Indonesia, Thailand, Malaysia, and the Philippines, ASEAN took up the cudgels for Southeast Asia's cultural unity and autonomy, which it viewed as a necessary underpinning of the political community it aspired to create and represent. ASEAN governments undertook a massive public relations campaign to sell this idea internationally and among Southeast Asian elites. Western area studies experts joined forces with their colleagues in ASEAN-funded think tanks to flesh it out with a flood of scholarly publications, marginalizing and eventually silencing erstwhile critics of Southeast Asia as a coherent and meaningful region. ASEAN governments used this scholarly outpouring to justify the claim that their so-called "ASEAN Way"—their preference for informality, consensus, and noninterference—was rooted in timeless Southeast Asian values that had reemerged in the postcolonial era.

Today, Southeast Asia is unquestionably a region. It is, however, no more plausible as a culture area now than it was in the 1940s or, for that matter, the 1840s. What makes it a region is the fact that Southeast Asians and the "international community" have decided that it is one. It has been anointed as a region in a manner akin to the conferral of international recognition on an aspiring nation-state. The invention, selling, and legitimization of Southeast Asia as a region should give pause to those who think that there is anything natural or inevitable about Southeast Asia. Its inclusion in the system of world regions created in the 1950s should also inspire skepticism about this system and its claim to rest on objective and immutable cultural realities. As suggested above, the construction of this system was as much a political as an academic exercise, and the realities it reflected were those of the Cold War and decolonization. For example, its architects arbitrarily divided Western and Eastern Europe into stand-alone culture areas less because there were any "objective" grounds for doing so than because Eastern Europe lay within the Soviet Bloc and Western Europe was part of the Free World.

Rethinking Regions

The culture area paradigm is unlikely to be dethroned any time soon as the most widely accepted basis for identifying and classifying regions. Generations have been trained in its verities, and it has behind it the weight of the areas studies establishment, which is deeply entrenched in academia both in the United States and other countries. The end of the Cold War has, however, brought changes. Government and foundation funding for area studies has declined, in part because the demise of the worldwide communist threat has reduced the need for area studies experts. But another, perhaps more fundamental, cause of the current disarray in area studies is the fact that the regions in which they specialize are being eclipsed by the rise of new ones that do not fit into the culture area framework. The post–Cold War emergence of East Asia is only one example. Other new or emerging regions include the "Indian Ocean region," uniting the states surrounding the Indian Ocean, and the "Asia-Pacific region," which is defined in different ways but is usually considered to be based on East Asia, South Asia, and North America.

Studies of regions are moving away from static, "trait-based" approaches toward ones that emphasize dynamic patterns of interaction among otherwise unrelated people. It is recognized, for example, that conflict as well as cooperation can generate regional identities regardless of cultural similarities or differences. More attention is also being paid to the deliberate construction of regions by governments and elites, the invention of Southeast Asia by ASEAN and its collaborators being a case in point. In addition, there is a tendency to give greater weight to the role of ideas in the development of regions and movements to establish regions. Ideas about communities—real or imagined, past and present—are considered particularly important. As noted above, the ASEAN Way is based on the notion of reviving precolonial Southeast Asian cultural tradition. Whether or not such a tradition actually existed is less important than the fact that it is believed to have existed. Relatedly, there is a growing awareness that regions, like nations, can be a significant focus of collective identity and pride. Being a member of a regional community may, in other words, have value to many people.

These new approaches to the study of regions and regionalism have not had much impact on the writing of East Asian history. Indeed, the idea that East Asia has a history to write is not widely accepted. There is a plethora of recent books on the "rise of East Asia," but almost all of these assume that East Asia's career as a region began in the 1980s when Northeast and Southeast Asia came together economically. Some acknowledge earlier precedents and parallels, but they routinely skip over these as being of antiquarian interest and having little to do with what is happening today. As a result of this presumed disconnect between past and present, those who concern themselves with history are largely unaffected by the new conception of East Asia as a single region. They continue to operate in the culture area framework that divides Southeast and Northeast Asia into separate and distinct regions. A few hardy pioneers have written histories of East Asia that transcend this framework. However, their rationale for setting it aside and treating Northeast and Southeast Asia as parts of a coherent historical whole is unclear, being usually assumed rather than spelled out and justified.

The starting point for a history of East Asia is recognition of the fact that its division into separate Southeast and Northeast Asian regions makes little sense. As described above, this division is a post–World War II artifice of American social scientists who tried to shoehorn Southeast Asia into the procrustean bed of their culture area paradigm. The Sinic civilizational zone of Northeast Asia fit this paradigm well enough, but there was nothing remotely comparable in Southeast Asia. Rather than rethinking their model in light of this hard reality, they resorted to the time-honored strategy of model-builders confronted by an anomaly: they wished it away. In practical terms, this meant inventing, virtually out of whole cloth and against over-whelming contrary evidence, a historically based cultural unity for Southeast Asia. ASEAN then appropriated this manufactured cultural unity, using it in the 1970s and 1980s to sell Southeast Asia as a bona fide world region and construct a regional identity around supposedly indigenous Southeast Asian values. ASEAN was successful in both endeavors, but this does not alter the fact that Southeast Asia has no valid historical claim to being a stand-alone culture area.

Neither does East Asia, as critics of the idea of its historical unity often point out. Indeed, East Asia is even more culturally diverse than Southeast Asia, and this was as true in the past as it is today. Proponents of Asian Values, of course, insist otherwise. As previously suggested, however, their claim of unifying East Asian values should be seen as an attempt to build collective identity and pride. It is, moreover, no more fanciful than the contention of Southeast Asian area experts that Southeast Asians share a "substratum" of common values. Both depend less on objective historical fact than on faith and hope. Western academics tend to frown at the idea that East Asians have any cultural unity, while applauding the equally ques-tionable proposition that Southeast Asians do. Apart from the use of Asian Values to sanction undemocratic practices, their double standard reflects the continuing hegemonic sway of the culture area orthodoxy. Admitting the possibility that Southeast and Northeast Asians might not be funda-mentally distinct would undermine this orthodoxy and call into question the rationale for maintaining separate Northeast and Southeast Asian area studies establishments.

If East Asia's historicity depended on its cultural unity, there would be no point in continuing and this book could not be written. But it does not. As noted above, thinking about regions has moved beyond culture areas. It is now widely recognized that a shared culture is only one source of regional iden-tity. Two other factors stand out as being of equal if not greater importance: interactions and ideas. Economic, political, social, and military interactions can create a sense of region among culturally diverse peoples. So, too, can subjective ideas about how people are related irrespective of their objective similarities and differences. Notwithstanding the absence of a unifying culture or civilization, these interactional and ideational factors combined to make East Asia a coherent and meaningful region in both premodern and modern times. Premodern East Asia was integrated around Imperial China, which functioned like the "sun" of a regional "solar system." In modern times, China was ousted from its central position by Japan and the West. But East Asia was held together by pan-Asianism, which posited an underlying cultural unity among Asians and inspired repeated efforts to unify the region.

Premodern East Asia

When precolonial Southeast Asia is viewed on its own terms rather than through the prism of contemporary Southeast Asian regionalists, it is reasonable to see it falling within the sphere of influence of Imperial China. Southeast Asia was oriented culturally toward South Asia, from where it derived its religions, writing systems, art, and much else. But it interacted politically, socially, and economically far more intensely with China. Many Southeast Asians accepted the Chinese "tributary system," an arrangement combining ceremonial vassalage and gift exchanges, which was akin in some ways to a modern business franchising operation. Although Southeast Asian kings were not puppets of China, neither were they fully sovereign in the Western legal sense. Economically, Southeast Asians were tied to southern China by trade networks that dwarfed their long-distance maritime commerce with India. The South China Sea "junk trade," operated by private Chinese merchants, was the lifeblood of island Southeast Asia. In contrast to the near total absence of resident Indians, moreover, Southeast Asia was dotted with enclaves of ethnic Chinese traders, the precursors of later Overseas Chinese.

Northeast Asia, centered on Vietnam, Korea, and Japan, was also closely integrated with China. Northeast Asians enthusiastically embraced China's Sinic civilization, including its Confucian belief system, ideographic writing, political ideals, and artistic and philosophical traditions. But they were no more clones of China than Southeast Asians were knockoffs of India. All jealously guarded their cultural individuality and political independence. There were, however, differences among them. Koreans and Vietnamese were more Sinicized, reproducing Chinese political and social institutions, and accepting tributary relations with China's emperor. The Japanese, isolated in their offshore islands, developed a feudal system based on a warrior aristocracy unparalleled elsewhere except medieval Europe. They refused to kowtow to China, imagining themselves to be a divinely descended people superior to all others. But even the Japanese recognized China's primacy in East Asia, and regarded it as a model. Vietnam, Korea, and Japan were linked to China by Chinese-run trading operations that crisscrossed the East China Sea, with the island kingdom of Okinawa forming a hub.

Inner Asia, comprising Tibet, Xinjiang, Mongolia, and Manchuria, was a third subregion of premodern East Asia. "Inner Asia" is a Sinocentric term since these areas were "inner" only from the perspective of Chinese looking out. It is, however, an accurate label insofar as it points to the fact that they interacted closely with China, differentiating them from Central Asia, which did not. Inner Asians rejected Chinese civilization, which was unsuited to their steppe environment and nomadic way of life. Culturally, they looked to

Central and South Asia for models. For example, the Tibetans and Mongolians adopted a variant of Indian Buddhism, and the Uighurs of Xinjiang borrowed Islam from their Turkic cousins in Central Asia. But China was the focus of their attention. Inner Asians were almost continually at war with China, and two groups, the Mongols and Manchus, conquered it.

Although they did not disrupt China's civilizational or political unity, they left many imprints on China, including a genetic one through intermarriage. When they were not fighting, Inner Asians and Chinese traded with one another, the most important items of exchange being horses, weapons, and luxury goods like silk.

Was there a "regional consciousness" in premodern East Asia? It would be a mistake to project current ideas about regions back into these early times. East Asians were innocent of the concept of Asia until they learned about it from Europeans, and they had only the haziest notions about regional and world geography. They were aware of India and the Indian Ocean littoral, which Chinese fleets explored in the early fifteenth century. But what lay beyond—Africa, Europe, the Pacific, and the Americas—was terra incognita to most. East Asians were better informed about each other, especially China, which was the focus of everyone's attention. The Chinese, on their part, conceived of East Asia as a self-contained world outside of which nothing much mattered. They thought of themselves as representing the summit of human civilization, and looked down on their neighbors as "barbarians." Their preferred mode of dealing with these peoples was the tributary system noted above. The Chinese likened this system to a family of unruly but trainable "children" over which their emperor presided as a stern yet indulgent "father." To this extent, there was an East Asian regional consciousness.

The "European Century"

Even if premodern East Asia enjoyed a degree of unity around Imperial China, it may be objected that the nineteenth-century European onslaught destroyed this unity, consigning the idea of East Asia to the dustbin of history until it was resuscitated in the 1990s. There is some truth in this generalization. The Europeans toppled China from its formerly dominant position and reduced it by the early twentieth century to a condition of helpless impotence. Its tributaries fell away one by one, most being turned into European colonies and protectorates. Some Chinese-run trading networks survived, but East Asia's commerce came under European control and was integrated into a world economic system centered on London, New York, Amsterdam, and Paris. During East Asia's "European Century," which stretched from the 1840s to the 1940s, it was in many ways "de-regionalized," becoming a patchwork of

European-dominated colonies and semi-colonies that were oriented culturally, politically, and economically toward different European mother countries. As noted above, this was the era during which East Asia was absorbed into the European construct of the Far East.

The West's triumph did not, however, obliterate the idea of East Asia as a closely related set of peoples. The champions of this idea were pan-Asianists, mostly Western-educated intellectuals who claimed that "Asia is one" by virtue of underlying cultural commonalities that differentiate Asians from Western-ers. The similarity between this claim and those advanced today by proponents of the ASEAN Way and Asian Values is not accidental. Pan-Asianism in its varied forms has exercised a recurrent hold over the imaginations of East Asians for more than a century. As suggested above, it is the ideational "glue" that gives modern East Asia its coherence as a region despite the centrifugal pull of nationalism. True, pan-Asianists have held divergent conceptions of "Asia," many of which do not correspond with East Asia. But pan-Asianism is primarily an East Asian phenomenon. With the exception of a few prominent Indians, almost all its adherents have been East Asians. Moreover, the chief region-building efforts inspired by pan-Asianism, beginning with Japan's attempt to create a "Greater East Asia" in the early 1940s, have involved all or part of East Asia.

What gave rise to pan-Asianism? Although not all pan-Asianists were anti-Western, it was at bottom a revolt against the West. It is sometimes forgotten that the nineteenth-century encounter between East Asia and the West was a "clash of civilizations" as profound as any claimed to be under way today. Most of the East Asian losers in this unequal contest suffered the double humilia-tion of being deprived of both their political independence and their cultural identity. Even the Japanese, who switched sides and reinvented themselves in the image of the West, could not escape cultural deracination. Indeed, the speed with which they cast off their old Asian identity and embraced a new Western one made their dilemma particularly acute. Westerners applauded their successful Westernization, but never accepted them as equals. For Japanese and other East Asians caught in this no man's land, pan-Asianism offered an appealing identity built on Asian spirituality and communitarianism, which pan-Asianists contrasted with the selfish materialism and individualism of Westerners. Those who embraced this new Asian persona could take pride in being Asian without the stigma of being "backward."

Pan-Asianism is not, of course, unique, being only one of many similar cross-national movements like pan-Slavism, pan-Arabism, and pan-African-ism. Why pan-Asianism has held such a strong and persistent appeal for East Asians is an interesting question to which the answers can only be speculative. It may be that the humiliation of being steamrollered by the West in the late nineteenth century was particularly painful for Asians inasmuch as they had previously considered themselves, with some justification, to be culturally superior to Westerners. This seems particularly true for the Chinese, who equate the European Century with their "Century of Shame." It is also possible that pan-Asianism sank deep roots among modern East Asians because they were predisposed by their past interaction around China to see themselves as forming a "family" of related peoples and cultures. It is perhaps no accident that pan-Asianism developed at the end of the nineteenth century when the Chinese world order was in its death throes. Early pan-Asianists were close enough in time to this world order to have been influenced by it and to have taken over its assumption of East Asia's underlying unity.

There were different sides to Pan-Asianism. As an intellectual movement, it was concerned with identifying an Asian identity and celebrating an "Asian cultural renaissance." Scholars explored the roots of Asian values and speculated on the possibility of reconciling them with Western ones. For many, however, pan-Asianism was a rallying cry for the rollback of Western colonialism and the expulsion of Westerners from Asia. This variant of pan-Asianism, which had strong anti-white overtones and extolled the unity of the "yellow race," came to the fore during the 1930s in Japan, where militarists adopted it as the rationale for a Japanese-led crusade to liberate "East Asia." This term, which they popularized in the mid-1930s, was an elastic one. They initially used to it to refer to the Sinic culture area of Northeast Asia, and went to war with a recalcitrant China in 1937 to try to create a "New Order" there. By 1940, however, they had committed themselves to establishing a "Greater East Asia," which included Southeast Asia. Their pursuit of this goal led them into a collision with the United States in 1941, resulting in the outbreak of the Pacific War and the extension of World War II to East Asia.

For the Japanese, the Pacific War was the Greater East Asia War—a "holy war" to free East Asia from the West and inaugurate a New Order in which East Asians would recover their cultural traditions, realize their national aspirations, and cooperate to achieve "co-prosperity." This idealistic side of Japanese war aims has not fared well in Western historiography, being dismissed by most as mere propaganda designed to dress up what was in fact a Japanese war of aggression and national aggrandizement. But propaganda or not, Japan's call for "Asia for the Asians" struck a chord, at least initially, with many Southeast Asian nationalists, including Burma's Aung San, Indonesia's Sukarno, Thailand's Marshal Phibun, and the Philippines' Jose Laurel. Pan-Asianism was, in other words, not just a Japanese conceit but a widely shared ideology among East Asians. This is true despite the fact that many eventually turned against Japan's New Order or resisted it from the outset. Chinese nationalists, for example, had no interest in playing second fiddle in a Japanese-run

East Asia, and fought an eight-year war of national resistance against Japan to prevent themselves from falling under its domination.

The Cold War Era

Although Japan lost the Pacific War, it also "won" in the sense that some of its war aims were realized. The Japanese smashed the European colonial edifice, ending East Asia's European Century. The Dutch and French tried to put the Humpty-Dumpty of colonial rule back together again in Vietnam and Indonesia in the late 1940s, but they were on a losing wicket and soon gave up. Japan had uncorked the genie of East Asian nationalism, which swept all before it. The United States, propelled to a position of primacy in East Asia by its victory over Japan, presided over decolonization and the emergence of independent nation-states. The Americans had their own vision of a New Order in East Asia, aspiring to create a "Pax Americana" in which Western-oriented liberal democracies would peacefully interact under the benevolent guidance of the United States and its Chinese partner and ally. By the end of the 1940s, however, this vision had foundered on the messy realities of decolonization, the fall of China to Mao Zedong's communists, and the extension of the Cold War from Europe to East Asia. The outbreak of the Korean War in 1950 marked the beginning of the Cold War era.

The conventional wisdom has it that the Cold War represented another phase of East Asia's de-regionalization insofar as it resulted in the bifurcation of the region into competing Sino-Soviet and American blocs. The idea of "One East Asia" could hardly prosper in this setting, and consequently died. In the view of many, moreover, the U.S. hub-and-spoke alliance system based on Japan was a prime obstacle to both regionalization and regionalism. The Americans, in this interpretation, wanted to keep East Asian states divided and dependent on themselves to forestall any challenge to their hegemony. When East Asian regionalism did emerge at the end of the Cold War, Washington consequently opposed it and promoted Asia-Pacific regionalism instead. Broader Asia-Pacific cooperation appealed to the United States because it offered a means to prevent East Asia from spinning out of its grasp and scotch any attempt by East Asians to form an exclusionary bloc. The American nightmare is the emergence of a new "Greater East Asia Co-Prosperity Sphere," particularly one led by a resurgent China bent on reclaiming its historic position as East Asia's "Number One."

While there are important elements of truth in the above interpretative scheme, it is in some ways quite misleading. Consider, for example, the role of the American alliance system. Far from blocking East Asia's regionalization, it was actually its prime mover. The Americans' postwar rehabilitation of Japan,

first as a democratic "peace state" and then as "Asia's workshop," enabled
Japan to reemerge as East Asia's economic dynamo and the chief driver of
its growth and integration in the 1970s and 1980s. Whatever its reservations
about Japan's "unfair trading practices" and increasing regional influence, the
United States cast a benign eye on this process. It is also misleading to suppose that the Americans are fundamentally opposed to emerging East Asian
regionalism, and that East Asia would come together if U.S. obstructionism
could be eliminated. As noted above, most East Asian regionalists have no
intention of forming a bloc that would exclude the United States and other
outside powers. Whether or not the United States has "hegemonic ambitions,"
East Asians have reasons of their own for wanting to keep it involved in the
region, including its usefulness as a counterweight to a rising China.

Another popular myth is that East Asian regionalism sprang to life in the
1990s in an ideological and intellectual vacuum. With a few notable exceptions,
the presentist and ahistorical biases of the political scientists and economists
who study this phenomenon prevent them from seeing its roots in East Asia's
pan-Asianist tradition. The Asian Values movement evolved directly out of
Southeast Asian regionalism led and articulated by ASEAN. As previously
suggested, ASEAN mobilized the idea of Southeast Asian values to support
its region-building project. Although American area studies experts helped
formulate this idea, its wellspring lies in pan-Asianism. Contrary to the belief
of many, pan-Asianism did not die after World War II. Rather, it was reborn
in the Asian Relations Conferences promoted by Indian prime minister Jawaharlal Nehru in the late 1940s and the Afro-Asian solidarity movement of the
1950s. Since ASEAN's founding fathers came out of this revived pan-Asianist
tradition, it was entirely natural that they should have found its central idea
of unifying Asian Values quite congenial and appropriated it to construct a
regional identity for Southeast Asia.

The Plan of This Book

Since this book is about modern East Asia, it does not deal with the full
sweep of East Asian history, which is covered elsewhere in the detail that
it deserves. Still, the stage must be set for the main performance, and this
is attempted in the first two chapters. Chapter 1, "East Asia's Foundations,"
offers an overview of the region's geographical, human, cultural, economic,
social, and political setting as it has evolved over the past several millennia.
It also outlines East Asia's major belief systems, including Confucianism,
Buddhism, and Islam, of which some understanding is essential. Chapter 2,
"East Asia in 1800," presents a panoramic survey of the region as it existed
on the eve of the nineteenth-century European onslaught. It introduces the

"dramatis personae"—the Chinese, Japanese, Koreans, Vietnamese, Thai, Burmese, Indonesians, Filipinos, and others—and describes their interaction with each other and with Imperial China. The Europeans were also on the scene and their influence cannot be ignored. Compared to the Chinese and other "stars" of the East Asian "show," however, they were still bit players in 1800, although this was beginning to change.

The following three chapters deal with the European invasion and East Asians' responses to it, covering the period from the mid-1800s to the early 1900s. "Invasion" is perhaps a misleading term inasmuch as it suggests that the advance of the Europeans into the region was primarily a matter of military conquest. It was that, of course, but more was involved. Chapter 3, "A Clash of Civilizations," makes the case that it was at a deeper level a collision of two quite different kinds of civilization—an inward-looking and tradition-oriented East Asia confronting an expansionist, industrializing, and nationalistic Europe. This chapter argues that, while East Asia was neither static nor incapable of change and adaptation, it was on the whole unable to mount an effective response to the civilizational challenge posed by the West. Chinese and other East Asian elites thought mainly in terms of borrowing Western military technology to defend the existing order. This approach might have worked against a different adversary, but it was a recipe for disaster against the West, condemning these elites to, in effect, go down with the ship of tradition that they were attempting to save.

Chapter 4, "The Development of Nationalism," looks at perhaps the most important long-term effect of the European Century. Although "nations" and "nationalism" are taken for granted today, they are murky and contested concepts. This chapter therefore examines them in some detail. It argues that the idea of the nation as the supreme focus of loyalty is a political construct that was invented in eighteenth-century Europe and later exported to the non-Western world along with other elements of the West's civilizational package. Notwithstanding the existence of "proto-nationalist" movements in East Asia, nationalism proved to be a tough sell there, not least because it clashed with the widely accepted ideal of government based on divine kingship and privileged elites. European colonial rule inadvertently facilitated the triumph of nationalism in East Asia as elsewhere by implanting the notion of national citizenship, initially among Westernized intellectuals and eventually among previously "nonparticipant" peasants. The formation of anticolonial nationalist movements ensued, although these at first posed little threat to European colonial regimes.

Chapter 5, "The Rise of Imperial Japan," addresses one of the major conundrums in East Asian and, indeed, world history—why and how did isolationist and apparently backward feudal Japan quickly transform itself into a powerful industrialized nation-state? One key to this puzzle lies in the fact that Japan was in some ways quite similar to Europe, making it unusually receptive to European models. The Japanese also benefited from strong political leadership, which brushed aside traditionalist resistance and mobilized the entire country behind its relentless quest for national wealth and power defined in Western terms. Japan's success in this endeavor permanently set it apart from the rest of East Asia. As suggested above, the Japanese "quit Asia" and joined the ranks of the Western imperial and colonial powers. Japan's rise made it East Asia's new Number One, eclipsing and humiliating China repeatedly from 1895 onward. By the early 1900s, the region's two strongest powers had thus traded places, with profound long-term effects on their bilateral relations and, as it turned out, the longevity of East Asia's European-dominated colonial and semi-colonial order.

Chapters 6 and 7, "The Turbulent 1920s and 1930s" and "The Pacific War," deal with decline and fall of this order. Here, pan-Asianism enters the story line of modern East Asia in a major way, providing the ideological driver behind Japan's revolt against the West. This revolt began in the 1920s when it was beset by the dilemmas of modernity. But it gained momentum in the 1930s, aided by the economic disruption of the Great Depression, the challenge of rising Chinese nationalism, and the fumbling response of its pro-Western party leaders. Japan's military gradually gained control of the government and mobilized the nation against what it perceived to be the twin threats of liberalism and communism posed, respectively, by the Western democracies and the Soviet Union. The Pacific War was a logical, but not necessarily inevitable, outcome of Japan's pan-Asianist crusade to liberate East Asia from the West. Its 1941–45 "Greater East Asia Co-Prosperity Sphere" restored, albeit fleetingly, East Asia's unity for the first time since the breakdown of the premodern order in the nineteenth century. It also prefigured and contributed to the rise of contemporary East Asian regionalism.

Chapters 8 and 9, "From Postwar to Cold War" and "The Late Cold War," elaborate on themes touched on earlier in this introduction, including postwar U.S. hopes for a "Pax Americana," the division of the region into communist and anticommunist blocs, and the conversion of Southeast Asia into a cockpit of early Cold War rivalry. The Sino-American rapprochement of the early 1970s, a product of the American debacle in Vietnam and the Sino-Soviet conflict, marked a turning point in the character of the Cold War in East Asia, facilitating a regionwide easing of tensions. While conflicts continued in Indochina, the Korean Peninsula, and the Taiwan Strait, regionalism made a comeback, first in Southeast Asia where ASEAN emerged as a region-builder and major diplomatic player. By the end of the Cold War, East Asia as a whole was also coming together as an economic region. Japan was the chief author of the latter trend, providing the model and inspiration for a general shift to export-led industrialization under state-guided capitalism. Even before the Soviet Union's demise, the foundations of the "East Asian miracle" and a resurgence of East Asian regionalism were in place.

Chapter 10, "Post–Cold War Trends," surveys some of the major trends and developments of the 1990s and early 2000s such as the rise of China, the Sino-Japanese feud, and the expansion of ASEAN. It also considers the changing dynamics of the Korean and Taiwan standoffs, and Japan's tilt away from its pacifist isolationism of the Cold War era toward political-military "normalcy." The concluding chapter, "East Asia's Future," attempts to make some predictions about the region's future based on its history, both recent and not so recent. While exercises in crystal-ball gazing are inherently problematical, East Asia's continued growth and economic integration seem good bets. Taiwan and Korea will probably remain "hotspots" at least in the short term, and no end is in sight to the rivalry between China and Japan. Despite the current U.S. preoccupation with the War on Terrorism, Islamic extremism has little future in East Asia. Nationalism and pan-Asianism remain far more important, and the question is which will prevail. Although one cannot be sure, there is every likelihood that current moves to construct a nonexclusionary East Asian regional community will continue.

Modern
EAST ASIA

1

East Asia's Foundations

If one is interested in how an old building came to assume its present form, it is useful to examine its foundations and original layout. So, too, with regions like East Asia. Geography, race, language, ethnicity, subsistence patterns, social structures, political institutions, and belief systems constitute their "ground plan." Unlike buildings, of course, regions are not the product of conscious design, and they lack a clearly defined starting point. There is no single or original ground plan for East Asia. Its architecture was quite different in, say, 500 B.C.E., and 500 C.E., and 1500 C.E., to select random dates on an evolutionary continuum stretching back into prehistory. One can partially get around this difficulty by emphasizing features that remain relatively constant and that are particularly relevant to understanding the modern scene. The result will be a composite sketch weighted toward more recent times. It should be borne in mind, however, that the reality was constant and kaleidoscopic change. The once widespread notion of an "unchanging Asia" is a Western myth that tells more about Westerners and their preoccupations than the societies it purports to describe.

Geographical Setting

Geographically, the most striking feature of East Asia is its relative isolation from the rest of the Eurasian land mass. The Himalayas and Indian Ocean divide it from South Asia, and the steppes and deserts of Central Asia separate it from West Asia. These barriers were never, of course, impenetrable. From early times, the famous Silk Road caravan route across Central Asia linked China with West Asia, and maritime trade across the Indian Ocean connected South and Southeast Asia. Cultural exchange accompanied trade. East Asia appropriated Buddhism and Islam from South and West Asia, along with cotton, refined sugar, and Indian numerals and mathematics. In turn, East Asia transmitted Chinese inventions such as gunpowder, paper, printing, the compass, and porcelain. Nevertheless, East Asia's contacts with other regions were limited before the era of modern transportation and communications. For example, the empires that grew up in China and India had virtually no political or military interaction with one another. In premodern times, West Asia, South Asia, and Europe were more closely linked with each other in a wider range of fields than any of them was with East Asia.

Within East Asia, geography unites as well as divides. One unifying phenomenon is the monsoon, which East Asia shares with South Asia. In summer, moist oceanic air flows inward toward Central Asia, dropping heavy rainfall on Southeast Asia, eastern China, Korea, and Japan. In winter, cool dry winds blow outward from Central Asia. These bring copious amounts of wind-borne dust from the Gobi Desert, which blankets northern China and contributes to the unusual fertility of the soil there. In the age of sail, monsoonal winds largely determined maritime navigation, since ships could move only with the prevailing ones—northeasterly in summer and southwesterly in winter. Monsoonal rainfall patterns also influence agriculture. The coincidence of heavy rains with warm weather permits intensive agriculture and double or even triple cropping. In many parts of island Southeast Asia, however, monsoonal rains leach the naturally poor soils of nutrients. Combined with the heavy forest cover there, this limited agriculture in premodern times, resulting in relatively small and scattered populations.

Climatically, East Asia is highly diverse, with a range of ecosystems similar to the eastern seaboard of North America. In the north, coniferous forests extend from the tundra line in northeastern Siberia to the fringes of Manchuria and Mongolia, encompassing the area Russians call their "Far East." Here winters are harsh and summers short, discouraging agriculture. Inner Asia—the arid steppes, deserts, and plateaus that curve around China from Manchuria through Mongolia and Xinjiang (Chinese Turkestan) to Tibet—is also inhospitable to agriculture and sparsely inhabited. Climatically and to some extent culturally, this area is an eastern extension of Central Asia. Northern and central China, Korea, and Japan comprise East Asia's temperate zone, characterized by mild winters and hot summers. Warm oceanic currents contribute to the mildness of the climate. China south of the Yangzi (Yangtze) River is subtropical, while most of mainland and island Southeast Asia falls within the tropics and has year-round high temperatures with little seasonal variation.

Continental East Asia is dominated by great river systems that rise in the Tibetan massif and flow eastward and southward, forming the region's main centers of agriculture and population. The Yellow (Huang) River turns the fertile soil of northern China into an agricultural breadbasket, although its frequent floods earned it the sobriquet "China's Sorrow." The Yangzi system performs the same function for central China. Because of its milder climate,

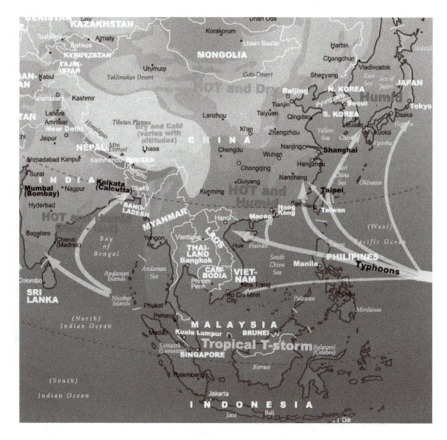

Eastern Asian summer weather patterns.

which permits more intensive agriculture and a greater variety of crops, the Yangzi basin is China's economic and demographic center of gravity. The smaller West River serves China's far south. Together, the Yellow, Yangzi, and West river watersheds comprise the Chinese heartland. Four river systems drain mainland Southeast Asia and set apart its major peoples. The Red (Hong) River valley is the homeland of the Vietnamese. The middle and lower Mekong valley are home to the Laotians and Cambodians (Khmer), respectively. Thailand centers on the Chaophraya valley, while Burma is based on the Irrawaddy basin. The intervening uplands are occupied by many ethnic minorities such as Shans, Karens, and Hmong.

As noted above, the tropical rain forests and poor soils of the Malay Peninsula and Indonesian and Philippine archipelagos kept their populations small and dispersed until recent times. The area's many island habitats also

Eastern Asian winter weather patterns.

contributed to this. Farmers clustered in coastal enclaves, often leaving the heavily forested interior to mobile bands of hunter-gatherers like the Dyaks of Borneo (Kalimantan). Only a few of the larger islands, notably Java, supported agricultural populations comparable to those of Burma, Thailand, and Vietnam. But the islanders were skilled seafarers and traders, and the surrounding seas linked them with mainland Southeast Asia and southern China. In contrast, the Korean Peninsula and Japanese archipelago are well suited to agriculture, and developed large farming populations. Both are also relatively isolated. This is less true of Korea, which is accessible by land from Manchuria. Like Britain, however, Japan is a continental outlier. It was historically a cultural and genetic cul-de-sac, mixing influences from eastern Siberia through Hokkaido, from China and Manchuria mediated by Korea, and from Southeast Asia transmitted through the Ryukyu Islands.

Race, Language, and Ethnicity

Most East Asians are members of the so-called "Mongoloid race," one of the principal racial categories that were until recent years widely employed to classify humankind. The others are the "Caucasoid," "Negroid," and "Australoid" races. Nowadays this racial scheme is looked upon askance in many quarters, in part because of the superficiality and variability of the physical traits on which it is based. Those of "Mongoloids" include straight black hair, sparse body hair, and narrow, fleshy eyelids featuring what is known as the "epicanthic fold." It is hypothesized that people with these characteristics evolved in northern Asia during the last ice age, and subsequently spread into Southeast Asia and across the Bering Strait into the Americas. This hypothesis is supported by the fact that some of their physical traits, such as the epicanthic fold, appear to be cold climate adaptations. It is also consistent with the archaeological record, which points to population movements in post-glacial times from Northeast to Southeast Asia, and the assimilation of pre-Mongoloid, mainly "Australoid" peoples. The Ainu of northern Japan and the Semang of the Malay Peninsula are among the modern survivors of these peoples.

Race offers a crude means of differentiating East Asians from their neighbors. The inhabitants of South and Central Asia are chiefly Caucasoid, while those of Australia and New Guinea are—or in the case of Australia, were—Australoid with some Negroid elements. But the Mongoloid peoples of East Asia are physically diverse, and the divisions between them and other racial groups blur at the edges. Northern Chinese are, for example, generally taller and have sharper facial features than southern Chinese, who more closely resemble Southeast Asian "southern Mongoloids." Some East Asian populations are racially mixed. For example, the peoples at the eastern end of the Indonesian Archipelago exhibit Australoid traits, while those in the Himalayan borderlands and northwestern China display Caucasoid features. Likewise, as one legacy of Spanish colonial rule, the Filipino elite carries a substantial admixture of European genes. Modern population movements further complicate the picture. Until the nineteenth century, the Russian Far East was sparsely inhabited by Mongoloid groups such as the Tungus. Today, however, the area is populated mainly by European Russians.

Language provides another lens through which to examine the peoples of East Asia. Linguists have identified a number of world language families based on structural similarities among seemingly unrelated languages. Given their racial affinities and geographical proximity to one another, one might expect languages spoken by East Asians to belong to the same language family. But this is not the case. There are no less than five families represented in the region: Altaic (including Turkish, Mongolian, Korean, and Japanese); Sino-

Tibetan (Chinese, Tibetan, Burmese); Tai (Thai, Lao, Shan); Austroasiatic (Vietnamese, Cambodian, Mon); and Austronesian (Malay with Polynesian and Malagasay outliers). It is not clear what accounts for this linguistic diversity. A now lost ancestral "super language" may have given rise to some of these families. The common origin of Tai, Austroasiatic, and Austronesian speakers in southern China points in this direction. But it is also possible that the families in question are unrelated and evolved over many millennia in different ecological and cultural settings. This seems to be the case with the neighboring but profoundly dissimilar Altaic and Sino-Tibetan language groups.

The heterogeneity of East Asians is even more striking if the focus shifts to ethnicity or group identities built around real or imagined ties of blood, history, language, religion, and customs. Although there is a large number of such self-defined ethnic groups in the region, the most numerous by far are the "Han Chinese," so named after the Han Empire that politically unified the Chinese heartland some twenty-two hundred years ago. Like most ethnic groups, contemporary Han Chinese assume that they have always existed as a distinct people. In fact, however, the formation of Chinese ethnic identity was a lengthy process that involved the southward expansion of the North Chinese and their assimilation of culturally and physically dissimilar groups in central and southern China. Vestiges of this process include the survival of southern "dialects" like Cantonese and Fukienese, which are closely related to the "Mandarin" tongue of the North Chinese but are separate languages. Similar processes of assimilation and acculturation characterize the evolution of other ethnic groups such as Japanese, Thai, and Javanese.

Although ethnic identities are "constructed" and changeable, they can also be extremely durable. Vietnamese, Mongolians, and Tibetans were at various times incorporated into China, but they never lost their sense of uniqueness or came to see themselves as Chinese. The main exception is the Manchus, who ruled China between the mid-seventeenth and early twentieth centuries, and were absorbed into the Chinese fold through intermarriage and Sinicization. In general, ethnic identities are strongest where geographical barriers, distinctive habitats, cultural differences, or long-standing conflicts keep groups apart. Insularity played a major role in the formation of the Japanese and the many ethnic groups occupying islands in the Philippine and Indonesian archipelagos. River basins unified groups like the Thai, Vietnamese, and Burmese. Differences between uplanders and lowlanders, pastoralists and agriculturalists, and coast and interior dwellers also generated ethnic cleavages. Religion, too, is often a key marker of ethnicity, since it taps deeply held beliefs. Examples include the Islamic faith of the "Moros" of the southern Philippines and the Shinto folk religion of the Japanese.

Like other forms of group identity, ethnicity involves a consciousness of separateness from, and superiority to, outsiders. In premodern East Asia, this "we feeling" was defined in civilizational terms and gave rise to shared traditions and myths. Chinese saw themselves as forming an oasis of civilization in a desert of barbarism, and as the heirs of a timeless and near perfect sociopolitical order. Japanese imagined themselves to be divinely descended and, as such, possessed of peerless virtues and institutions. Koreans prided themselves on their mastery of China's Confucian civilization, which made them equal to the Chinese and superior to the Japanese. Vietnamese also supposed that they had carried Chinese civilization to a pinnacle of perfection and looked down upon their "barbaric" Buddhist neighbors. Cambodians recalled the lost glories of the Khmer Empire, making the depredations of the Vietnamese and Thai all the more humiliating. Mongols, too, looked back to a golden age under their Great Khans when they had ruled China and much of Eurasia. Both Thai and Burmese regarded themselves as martial peoples destined to rule their weaker and less civilized neighbors.

Social and Economic Patterns

The principal socioeconomic divisions in East Asia before modern times were among the nomadic pastoralists of Inner Asia's steppes and deserts, the rice farmers of Southeast and Northeast Asia, and the hunter-fishers of the northern forests. This tripartite division reflects the climatic factors discussed above. The low temperatures and heavy forest cover of the Russian Far East make it unsuitable for farming and herding or, indeed, any mode of subsistence except foraging. The small bands of Altaic-speaking hunters who roamed this area kept largely to themselves. In contrast, Inner Asian pastoralists interacted closely with China and often menaced it. The grasslands of Manchuria and Mongolia, deserts of Xinjiang, and high plateaus of Tibet are too arid for farming. But they are ideal for herding horses, sheep, camels, and yaks. Mongols and other pastoralists who specialized in this way of life moved seasonally in search of pasture and had few permanent settlements. Although not numerous, they were skilled horsemen and archers. Before the sixteenth-century Gunpowder Revolution, their mobile war bands could often outmaneuver and destroy slower-moving Chinese peasant armies.

The agrarian societies of Northeast and Southeast Asia were based on farming of the most intensive sort, which was quite unlike anything practiced by Europeans. The general pattern was irrigated or wet-rice agriculture. Rice is one of the most nutritious cereals, but its cultivation is incredibly demanding and labor intensive. It entails the preparation and maintenance of flat, irrigated fields; the laborious hand-transplanting of seedlings; and their careful weeding and fertilizing. All of this requires many hands and close teamwork. The payoff is much higher yields per acre than dry field crops such as wheat, the European staple. Thanks to the favorable climatic conditions noted earlier, moreover, double cropping is carried out in many areas. Rice cultivation is not confined to East Asians, but their specialization in it is unusual. Its main effect was the creation of dense concentrations of farmers on a scale that boggled the European mind. In 1800, for example, China alone contained about 300 million people, or more than ten times the population of France, then Western Europe's most populous country.

China's agrarian economy was unique in East Asia not only by virtue of its enormous size, but because it was not exclusively based on irrigated rice. The North China Plain around the Yellow River, which is the original homeland of the Chinese, is too cold and dry for rice. It is, however, well suited to wheat and millet, which became the staple crops of the early Chinese. Their labor-intensive farming methods, combined with the area's fertile soil and irrigation systems based on the Yellow River, made for both high productivity and a large population. The flowering of Chinese civilization in northern China in the second and third millennia B.C.E. was no accident. Its agricultural surpluses facilitated class differentiation, the rise of cities, the formation of kingdoms, and the development of metallurgy, art, and writing. As the eastern terminus of Central Asian trade routes, moreover, northern China was exposed to cultural influences emanating from other early centers of civilization in West and South Asia. While these influences are difficult to assess, they probably spurred indigenous trends such as the transformation of Chinese writing from simple pictographs to complex ideographs expressing abstract thought.

Northern China was similar to the rice-growing areas of East Asia insofar as its political and social superstructures rested on a mass of "peasants," or self-sufficient farmers who cultivated small plots of land and spent their lives in village communities consisting of a few dozen to a hundred or more nuclear families. The world of peasants revolved around duties and loyalties to their family and village groups. The individual, as such, was not important and was, in fact, expendable. For most peasants, life was hard and precarious even in the best of times. Flood, drought, famine, and pestilence were ever-present dangers, and there were no safety nets except those provided by family and village. Peasant communities were neither socially undifferentiated nor necessarily harmonious. But survival in an unpredictable environment and the requirements of labor-intensive agriculture dictated the celebration of communitarian values and respect for authority. Periodic festivals and rituals reinforced communal solidarity. Another purpose of these ceremonies was to propitiate the supernatural beings and forces that peasants believed controlled their individual and collective fates.

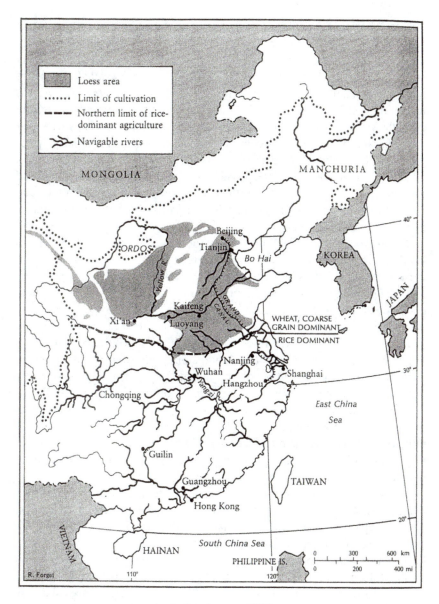

Agricultural zones of China.

In many parts of agrarian East Asia, peasantries formed the base of social hierarchies capped by hereditary aristocracies. Like their counterparts
elsewhere, these aristocracies derived their position from their supposedly
superior bloodlines, monopoly of learning and government office, and con-

trol over the sources of wealth, which usually meant land and the peasants who worked it. The archetypal East Asian aristocrat was a landed magnate who owned vast estates and could call upon the loyalty of large numbers of dependents and hangers-on. Nobilities of this sort prevailed in most of Southeast Asia, including Burma, Thailand, Laos, and Cambodia as well as Java and other Malay societies in the Indonesian Archipelago. To modern eyes, the most striking feature of these nobilities was the wide social gulf that separated them from the peasant masses, and the extraordinary deference they demanded and received from the latter. The noble inhabited a different mental world from the peasant, a world dominated by intrigue and competition with other great families for power, wealth, and preferment. Life at the top had its own hazards, including being on the losing side in family and factional feuds.

The aristocratic ethos had little place for mercantile pursuits. East Asian nobilities generally looked down upon merchants and their activities, as did most peasants. This was less true of Malay aristocrats who, from early times, specialized in trading the pepper, nutmeg, cloves, and other spices grown in the Indonesian islands. Like Scandinavian Vikings, however, they alternated between trading and piracy, and their primary interests lay in plunder and conquest, as in the case of fierce Bugis adventurers who terrorized much of the archipelago in the seventeenth and eighteenth centuries. Warfare and territorial expansion also attracted the Thai and Burmese nobilities, who saw in them opportunities to advance their family fortunes and their standing at royal courts. But these aristocracies did not turn themselves into professional military classes, even though some of their members achieved prominence as military leaders. Like the merchant, the soldier was not widely esteemed or viewed as a role model. The outlook and values of most East Asian nobilities remained nonmartial or civilian.

The great exception was Japan's samurai elite, a class of fighting men unique in East Asia and, indeed, virtually everywhere except medieval Europe. Ancient Japan had a centralized monarchy based on a court aristocracy not unlike those of Burma and Thailand. From the tenth century C.E., however, local warlords and their armed retainers gradually took over, capitalizing on the breakdown of central government, infighting among aristocratic factions, and frontier wars against Ainu aborigines. Since the same processes underlay the evolution of European feudalism, it is unsurprising that samurai resembled European knights and barons. For example, they organized themselves on the basis of lord–vassal ties in which lords granted territorial fiefs to their vassals in return for military service. As occurred in parts of Europe, this arrangement turned Japan by the sixteenth century into a patchwork of autonomous feudal principalities engaged in more or less constant warfare. But the ideal of political unity under the monarchy persisted, preventing Japan's breakup into independent states.

China followed a different course by replacing its aristocracy with a meritocracy unparalleled anywhere outside East Asia. This happened gradually. Until the late first millennium C.E., China remained a fundamentally aristocratic society dominated by great landowning families. Thereafter, however, these grandees were eclipsed by mandarins, or scholar-bureaucrats chosen from the general population by competitive examinations. Mandarins embodied the ideal that only the "best and brightest" should govern, a radical notion in premodern societies where lineage was usually all important. Still, one should be wary of equating them with modern bureaucrats or assuming that their selection was entirely random. They were omnicompetent nonspecialists preoccupied with instilling virtue through precept and example. Most of them, moreover, came from a class of locally prominent families known as "gentry." Although this class was self-perpetuating and was composed of wealthy landowners, it was not a true nobility insofar as admission to its ranks required success in the civil service examinations.

Vietnam and Korea followed China's lead in switching to a meritocracy. But while both created facsimiles of the Chinese mandarinate, transplanting this institution into what were quite different societies entailed problems and modifications. The Korean equivalent of mandarins (called yangban) were, for example, closer to a hereditary aristocracy. This was only to be expected. Korea, like Japan, was overrun in prehistoric times by Altaic-speaking tribal warrior aristocracies from Inner Asia, which bequeathed a tendency to emphasize hereditary authority. The Vietnamese encountered a different problem. Having been ruled by China for ten centuries, one might assume that they would have had less difficulty in adopting its sociopolitical system. As they moved south from their Red River homeland beginning in the sixteenth century into central and southern Vietnam, however, they became culturally and ethnically heterogeneous, resulting in a north-south split and rival political regimes. The reintegration of the Vietnamese into a single people, a precondition for the adoption of the Chinese model, did not occur until the end of the eighteenth and beginning of the nineteenth centuries.

States and Interstate Relations

"States," meaning recognized political entities in which governments claim exclusive jurisdiction over particular territories, existed from early times in East Asia, as they did in many other regions. But these early states were different from their modern counterparts. Despite natural and man-made barriers such as China's Great Wall, borders were usually ill-defined frontier zones with few checkpoints or other controls on movement. The vagueness of state borders was a function of the relative weakness of central governments. The latter might demand obedience to their laws and decrees, but enforcement was another matter. Bureaucracies were seldom large or specialized enough to exercise effective control over the territory they claimed to govern. Even the most despotic regimes relied on the cooperation of local notables and satraps who often enjoyed considerable autonomy. Moreover, many of these regimes were not fully independent, accepting some degree of oversight by other, more powerful states. External and internal sovereignty, the hallmark of modern states, was thus at best embryonic.

East Asia's premodern states were not nation-states. As will be discussed in more detail in a later chapter, the modern idea of the nation as a political body uniting different classes and ethnicities was missing. Peasants, who constituted over 95 percent of the population of these states, were politically "nonparticipant." They did not normally see themselves as playing any role in the governance of the realm or as having a stake in its welfare. They left these matters to elites who jealously guarded their political prerogatives and resisted interference from below. Vertical cleavages between lords and peasants were matched by horizontal ones among ethnic groups. All premodern states were built around a dominant ethnic group whose traditions and ideals they claimed to uphold. But there were usually ethnic minorities that did not see themselves as having anything in common with the dominant group and often resisted it. These political and ethnic cleavages were not, of course, unique to East Asia. Nor were the expedients adopted by state builders to achieve harmony and order.

The key to political unity in premodern states was the institution of monarchy. It provided a transcendent symbol with which everyone, including lowly peasants, haughty lords, and restive minorities, could identify. Kings came in different sizes and shapes. They ranged from princelings governing a few thousand subjects in isolated mountain valleys, to mighty potentates ruling millions of people across vast tracts of territory. All, however, had certain things in common. They invariably invoked the principle of hereditary succession under which eldest sons by legitimate wives inherited the throne. In societies where family ties were of supreme importance to most people regardless of rank or station, there could be no other basis for legitimate authority. Even meritocratic China accepted this principle. As in the case of other monarchies, its emperors were drawn from ruling families or dynasties. Although hereditary succession worked well enough most of the time, it invited occasional problems such as the accession of incompetent or deranged rulers and succession struggles among rival claimants to the throne.

East Asian kings, like those elsewhere, surrounded themselves with pomp and circumstance and often secluded themselves in magnificent palaces such as Beijing's Forbidden City that were designed to inspire a sense of awe and mystery. Kings also invoked religious sanctions to buttress their authority, and many were credited with supernatural powers. Those in Muslim lands, who were known as sultans, acted as defenders and propagators of the Islamic faith. Buddhist kings in Burma, Thailand, and Cambodia upheld Buddhism's teachings and regulated its clergy. Under the variant of Buddhism that prevailed there, they were regarded as figures of exceptional "merit" rather than divinities. But ordinary folk did not make this distinction, seeing them as god-like manifestations of the Buddha who possessed divine powers that ensured the harmony of the cosmos. The Confucian monarchs of China, Korea, and Vietnam performed similar cosmic functions, including controlling the forces of nature and guaranteeing bountiful harvests. But they were also considered indispensable to inculcating morality and proper social behavior on which civilized life depended.

Whether as kingdoms or as empires, dynastic states headed by divinely inspired monarchs proved to be an extraordinarily durable form of political organization in the premodern world. In East Asia, many of these states endured for centuries, surviving civil wars, dynastic changes, foreign invasions, economic breakdowns, and ideological challenges. Some eventually succumbed, like the Khmer Empire, mainland Southeast Asia's preeminent power between the tenth and fourteenth centuries C.E. The roughly contemporaneous Mongol Empire and Srivijayan and Majapahit trading empires, based in Sumatra and Java respectively, were also ephemeral. One common denominator of these relative failures might be the phenomenon of "imperial overstretch," in which the ambitions of rulers outran the human and material resources available to them, resulting in demoralization and disaffection. The Khmer collapse, for example, was linked with the temple-building mania of kings, which diverted manpower from the maintenance of the lower Mekong irrigation systems on which the livelihood of Cambodian peasants depended, leading to the withdrawal of support for the monarchy.

The Chinese Empire stands as East Asia's and perhaps the world's most successful dynastic state insofar as it survived for more than two millennia under six major dynasties. Given China's huge size and diversity, particularly its north-south division, one might expect it to have disintegrated into multiple states. This in fact occurred at times of political disunity that were exploited by nomadic invaders from Inner Asia who set up independent states in the north. Two groups of invaders, the Mongols and the Manchus, even conquered China and created their own dynasties in the thirteenth and seventeenth centuries. Throughout it all, however, the Chinese clung to the ideal of a unitary state under a single all-powerful ruler assisted by mandarin scholar-bureaucrats. One reason for the persistence of this ideal is the fact that the Chinese remained ethnically and culturally homogenous. In contrast to the Roman and other empires, China was never inundated by alien settlers. The steppe nomads were few and their pastoral way of life was not transferable to China's densely populated agricultural heartland. To govern China, moreover, they had to adopt Chinese ways, with the result that most ended up being absorbed or Sinicized.

Given their success in preserving their political system, it is unsurprising that the Chinese assumed that it was timeless and unmatched anywhere else. Dynasties might fall or, in Chinese terms, lose the "Mandate of Heaven." But new ones would always rise to restore the system to its previous prosperity and glory. When operating at peak efficiency, China's mandarin government approximated what some nowadays might regard as "good governance." Despite draconian punishments and the brutal suppression of dissidents, it was by premodern standards relatively benevolent. Most emperors and mandarins took seriously Confucian injunctions to morally uplift and nurture the common folk. To modern eyes, however, the government they provided was curiously superficial. District magistrates, the lowest rung of the mandarin hierarchy, were responsible for administering an average of several hundred thousand people assisted by only a few clerks. They therefore depended on the voluntary cooperation of the gentry. Indeed, the latter informally ran government at the local level, settling disputes, allocating taxes, subsidizing schools, organizing charities, and raising militias.

China's gentry-based mandarin government exerted a powerful attraction throughout the Confucian world of Northeast Asia. As noted above, Koreans and Vietnamese reproduced it with varying degrees of success. More surprisingly, feudal Japan also looked upon China as a model. It is difficult to imagine more antithetical figures than the refined and learned Chinese scholar-bureaucrat and the rough-and-ready samurai swordsman and war fighter. In contrast to China's centralized monarchy, moreover, Japan's emperor was a powerless figurehead whose only political function was to legitimize the rule of autonomous feudal lords. Still, the samurai had no other civilizational ideal than China, and they were sensitive to the charge leveled at them by both Chinese and Koreans that they were barbarians. While they never abandoned their martial ethos and warrior code, many samurai gradually took on some of the attributes of a Chinese-style Confucian "gentleman," such as a fondness for learning, poetry, and calligraphy. Eventually, they also began to see themselves as the equivalents of mandarins, dispensing benevolent government and moral instruction to Japanese commoners.

The Chinese political model made no headway in Inner and Southeast Asia, where Buddhism and Islam held sway. In Inner Asia, the agricultural economy that this model presupposed was missing. Mongol and Turkish "khanates" were loose tribal federations held together by kinship ties and the charisma of war leaders. Buddhist monks operated what amounted to a theocracy in Tibet. The Buddhist monarchies of mainland Southeast Asia resembled their Confucian counterparts insofar as they were based on peasant rice farmers, but they were less centralized and bureaucratized. As noted above, they were dominated by landed aristocrats who regarded high office as a hereditary right and treated outlying provinces as their personal satrapies. Royal authority depended on conciliating the aristocracy and the Buddhist clergy or "sangha," the other major power center in these kingdoms. Except in Java, where intensive rice agriculture permitted the rise of large kingdoms, most Malay sultanates were mini-states with rudimentary central governments. Sultans rarely exercised much control over nobles and Islamic teachers or "ulamas" did not constitute a clergy capable of backing them.

Interstate relations in premodern East Asia were founded on "suzerainty," or the overlordship of superiors over inferiors. There was nothing like the early modern European state system with its professional diplomats, rules of conduct, and periodic conferences. The European system rested on the idea of a community of sovereign and theoretically equal states. This idea was alien to East Asians. They took for granted hierarchy and subordination as unalterable facts of life. Their societies and states were structured on these principles, and it was only natural to apply them to relations among rulers. Where suzerainty did not apply, as between states of roughly equal power, conflict and rivalry were the norm. Examples include the protracted struggle for dominance among Vietnam, Thailand, and Burma. Temporary alliances and truces were not unknown, but these rarely developed into sustained cooperation or even regular diplomatic contact. The alternative to conflict was wary coexistence. The Koreans, for instance, sent occasional "goodwill" missions to Japan in hopes of detecting hostile intentions, while barring Japanese emissaries from Korea as potential spies.

China sat atop the multiple pyramids of suzerain relationships that defined East Asia's interstate order by virtue of its enormous size, central location, military power, economic attraction, and cultural brilliance. Although the Chinese were at times expansionist, their primary aim was to surround themselves with docile and compliant states. They were chiefly concerned with the military threat posed by Inner Asian nomads, and employed fortifications, diplomacy, and force in a millenia-long struggle to neutralize this threat. The danger in the east and south was less acute. The Japanese, who tried to invade China through Korea in the 1590s, were a potential menace, but one that Beijing could safely ignore after Japan retreated into isolationism in the early 1600s. China enrolled Korea, Vietnam, Burma, Thailand, and other states as tributaries mainly to enhance its emperor's prestige as a universal ruler. These states accepted Chinese overlordship for a variety of reasons, including securing commercial privileges, acquiring legitimization from China's "Son of Heaven," obtaining his protection from hostile neighbors, or merely maintaining amicable relations with the regional superpower.

Belief Systems and Religions

Animism, or belief in nature and ancestor spirits that control human affairs for good or ill, formed the core of peasant folk religion throughout East Asia, defining ethnic identities, shaping conceptions of kingship, and influencing higher religions. Animism was not, of course, unique to East Asian peasants, being, rather, the earliest human belief system and, as such, universal. For animists, the unseen spirit world is an omnipresent reality pervading all aspects of daily life. Spirits are less "gods" than benevolent or malevolent forces that inhere in natural objects and phenomena as well as people and animals. Although animism generates elaborate mythologies and prescribes rigorous taboos, it entails no ethical code and lacks a concern with personal salvation or an afterlife. Believers seek to influence spirits to gain material benefits, particularly good harvests, and avoid misfortunes such as illness. They suppose that this can be achieved through rituals and prayers. Animism dispenses with churches, clergy, scriptures, and other trappings of organized religion. But there are often holy places where worshippers congregate, and shamans or mediums who assist in communicating with the spirits.

In premodern East Asia, animism defined group identities and legitimized political authority. Families, clans, villages, tribes, and even ethnic groups worshipped tutelary or protective spirits whom they equated with common ancestors. Leaders derived their authority from their putative descent from these ancestors, and often claimed shamanistic powers in communicating with them. Shinto, the Japanese variant of animism, offers an example. Japan's monarchy evolved in prehistoric times from a line of chieftains who purported to be lineal descendants and living embodiments of their tribe's tutelary spirit and progenitor, Amaterasu or the "Sun Goddess." They combined the function of tribal leader with that of high priest or shaman of the sun cult. When these chieftains converted themselves into the rulers of Japan in the fifth and sixth centuries C.E., they extended the sun cult to embrace all Japanese and assumed the role of their priest-king. Even though Japan subsequently came under strong continental cultural influences, its emperor never lost this original role, which invested him with inviolable political authority as the divine paterfamilias of the Japanese people.

Confucianism, the dominant belief system in Northeast Asia, was less a religion, as this term is ordinarily understood, than a philosophy of life. It called upon its adherents to turn away from the supernatural and concentrate on perfecting themselves and their societies through moral self-cultivation. For Confucianists, the key problem is bringing human behavior into conformity with "heaven" or the cosmic forces that control nature. They believe that the solution to this problem lies in ordering behavior on the basis of the seniority and gender relationships in the family. Filial piety or reverence for parents is the most important of these relationships and the one that binds the Confucian moral system together. Confucianists assume that if everyone internalizes such "family values," society will come into tune with heaven, and harmony, contentment, and prosperity will ensue as a matter of course. In the Confucian view, responsibility for guiding ordinary people to this happy state lies with "sages," or men of superior virtue and wisdom. The sage acts primarily through moral instruction and example, and his virtue is such that lesser mortals will spontaneously wish to follow his lead.

For the Chinese and their emulators, Confucianism offered a compelling vision of the "good society" that could be realized if power was entrusted to sages. Confucian kings and their mandarin assistants invariably presented themselves to their subjects as embodying sagely rule, even when these kings fell short of personifying sagehood in their private conduct. In a Confucian political system, the real or perceived moral failure of rulers was a serious matter, since it undermined the legitimacy of governments, although not necessarily that of the system itself. Inasmuch as rulers were responsible for the moral condition of society, which was equated with cosmic balances, moreover, natural disasters assumed great significance as signs of heavenly dissatisfaction with a ruler's performance. Despite these double-edged swords, which could justify protest or rebellion, Confucianism provided a persuasive rationale for authoritarian, albeit paternalistic, government. This rationale was, however, convincing only in societies where Confucian assumptions were widely accepted, particularly the notion that existential questions such as the meaning of suffering and death are irrelevant.

The spiritual void at the heart of Confucianism was partially filled in China by Taoism, which urged the pursuit of mystical union with nature. Taoists derided Confucianists as officious busybodies whose didactic moralizing interferes with the natural impulses of people that link them with cosmic rhythms and forces. Confucian efforts to inculcate morality, they argued, have the paradoxical effect of spreading immorality. Taoism extols spontaneity, intuition, and relativism, which puts it at odds with Confucianism's emphasis on self-discipline and conformity. Nevertheless, many Confucianists embraced Taoism when "off duty," finding in it a welcome release from the rigorous demands of Confucian moralism.

Among elites, Taoism's major impact was in arts such as poetry and painting. But it also spoke to the hopes of many to overcome the ineluctable miseries of the human condition, particularly old age and death. Taoists were preoccupied with the search for immortality through elixirs and dietary and exercise regimes. This quest entered Chinese folk religion, contributing to it the notion that invulnerability to infirmity and even bullets could be gained by magical incantations and yoga-style exercises.

Buddhism, an import from South Asia, was a more influential competitor of Confucianism in East Asia as a whole. Buddhism also addresses the problem of suffering, attributing it to human cravings and desires which condemn people both to eternal misery and endless reincarnations or cycles of death and rebirth. For Buddhists, the ultimate goal is escape from this condition through the attainment of salvation or Nirvana, a beatific state in which the self is extinguished and the soul becomes one with the Absolute. They believe that the way to Nirvana is revealed in the "Four Noble Truths" and "Eightfold Path" set down by the historic Buddha, who lived some twenty-six centuries ago in what is now Nepal. Although the Buddha prescribed a rigorous code of right conduct and thought, he put salvation potentially within the reach of all regardless of gender, social position, or educational attainment. In this respect, Buddhism differs from Hinduism, a related South Asian religion, which holds that people are locked permanently into unequal castes or hereditary occupational groups, and that only a small priestly elite has any hope of glimpsing the Absolute either through esoteric rituals or ascetic practices.

Buddhism filtered into East Asia during the first millennium C.E., eventually achieving wide popularity virtually everywhere. Its appeal derived largely from its egalitarianism and eclecticism, which enabled it to adapt to local religious traditions. In Tibet, for example, it fused with animism and shamanism to produce Lamaism, or belief that the spirit of the Buddha could possess people, turning them into transcendent beings. The Dalai Lama, the spiritual and temporal head of Tibet, is revered as such a being in Tibet and Mongolia. In China, Buddhism blended with Taoism and Confucianism to generate a large number of sects that made their way into Japan, Korea, and Vietnam. In Southeast Asia, Buddhism was appropriated in combination with Hinduism, which gave rise to syncretistic Hindu-Buddhist faiths. Hinduism, however, ultimately lost out. It was primarily a court religion concerned with deifying kings as incarnations of Siva and Vishnu, the Hindu gods of destruction and regeneration. It never sank deep roots among peasants, many of whom were glad to see it go. Such disaffection played into the breakdown of the "Hinduized" Khmer Empire in the fourteenth century.

Buddhism in East Asia was no more homogenous than was Christianity in Europe. Its principal division, comparable to the split between Catholic and

Orthodox Christianity, was between its Mahayana and Theravada branches. For Mahayana or "Greater Vehicle" Buddhists, Buddhism remained a religion of practice, but by opening a pathway to salvation by faith, Mahayana sects gained an enormous popular following. Many preached reliance on the saving grace of "bodhisattvas," Buddha-like figures such as the Goddess of Mercy who were thought to have stopped short of Nirvana to help others reach this blessed state. In contrast, Theravada or "Lesser Vehicle" Buddhists emphasized salvation through individual effort unaided by external agency or help, which they regarded as the Buddha's original teaching. But the Theravada faith also inspired popular fervor and sank deep roots among peasants through village temples and monks who ministered to their spiritual and educational needs. The Theravada tradition still prevails in Burma, Thailand, Laos, and Cambodia, while the Mahayana branch dominates in Tibet, Mongolia, China, Korea, Japan, and Vietnam.

Although Buddhism remained a powerful spiritual force in China, it was eclipsed there by the resurgence of Confucianism between the eleventh and thirteenth centuries C.E. One reason for this resurgence was the success of Confucian scholars in co-opting Buddhist metaphysical speculation about the ultimate nature of reality, which restored Confucianism's prestige among the educated. "Neo-Confucianism," as this synthesis is called, became the new orthodoxy throughout Northeast Asia. Another reason for the Confucian revival was elite dissatisfaction with Buddhism. In China, Buddhist egalitarianism and sectarianism created disorder which invited invasions by Inner Asian nomads. The incorporation of Buddhism into folk religion produced waves of popular enthusiasm and millenarian revolts aroused by hopes that bodhisattva saviors would inaugurate a paradise on earth. Confucianism, with its stress on order, hierarchy, and duty, provided an antidote to such unrest. Korean, Japanese, and Vietnamese elites, all of whom took their cue from China, also found Buddhism disruptive and followed the Chinese lead in making Confucianism the dominant belief system of their societies.

Islam, a West Asian monotheistic religion akin to Christianity, triumphed among the Malays of island Southeast Asia. Like Buddhism, Islam considers earthly existence a vale of tears and offers salvation to all. Unlike Buddhism, however, it equates salvation with an afterlife in paradise and demands submission to the will of an all-powerful God (Allah) as revealed by his prophet Muhammad in the Koran. The Islamic faith was spread among Malays by Arab and Indian traders in the middle centuries of the second millennium C.E., roughly the same period in which Theravada Buddhism, borne by monks from Sri Lanka, achieved dominance in mainland Southeast Asia. The egalitarianism of Islam and Buddhism enabled them to capitalize on a reaction against the elitism of earlier Hindu court religions. In addition, both were relatively tolerant. Although Islam requires the exclusive loyalty of its followers and enjoins strict adherence to its "sharia" or Holy Law, its success among Malays was due to its syncretism. It adapted to Malay folk religion and customary law and, like Theravada Buddhism, accepted elements of Hindu belief and ritual, especially in Bali, which remained only partly Islamized.

In contrast to their Buddhist and Confucian counterparts, Islamic sultans could not claim personal divinity, which would have been sacrilegious in the eyes of pious Muslims for whom there is but one god. On the other hand, there was no place in Islam for a secular conception of kingship, since all aspects of life were regulated by the Holy Law as interpreted by ulamas. As noted above, the latter did not constitute an organized clergy comparable to the Buddhist monkhood. The strongest Islamic states, such as those in Java and Aceh in northern Sumatra, were based partly on the support of ulamas. In general, however, sultans lacked a clerical prop. Islam posits a sharp distinction between believers and nonbelievers, sanctioning "holy war" (jihad) against the latter and unity among the former. Holy wars against infidels enabled sultans to gain stature among their subjects and created the potential for broader alliances. In practice, this potential was negated by ethnic divisions and rivalries. Nevertheless, many Muslims were attracted to the ideal of Islamic unity and were influenced by Middle Eastern intellectual trends through the institution of the hajj, or pilgrimage to Mecca, required of all believers.

One might conclude from the foregoing survey that Southeast, Northeast, and Inner Asia formed separate and fundamentally unrelated worlds despite commonalities like race, animism, rice agriculture, peasant communalism, hereditary aristocracy, and divine kingship.

Southeast Asians were oriented toward South and West Asia. Their religious beliefs, political institutions, law codes, writing systems, literary tastes, monumental architecture, and artistic traditions were modeled on imports from the west, particularly India. In contrast, China acted as the civilizational fountainhead of the Northeast Asian or "Sinic" culture area, providing political, social, and cultural prototypes for Korea, Japan, and Vietnam. Culturally, Inner Asians were closer to Central and South Asia than China. Pastoralism and tribalism tied them to Central Asia, while Lamaism linked them with India. The isolated hunter-gatherers of the far north were even more detached and idiosyncratic. This picture of heterogeneity is, however, only partly accurate. As will be argued in the next chapter, East Asians were more closely interconnected and East Asia more coherent as a region than these cultural differences suggest.

2
East Asia in 1800

What was East Asia like on the eve of the nineteenth century European invasion? The year 1800 offers a convenient vantage point from which to consider this question. By then, the major dynastic states that were shortly to face the European onslaught—such as Qing China, Tokugawa Japan, Choson Korea, Chakri Thailand, and Konbaung Burma—were firmly established, and some were at the height of their prosperity and power. An examination of them sheds light on the cultural, political, social, and economic baselines from which modern East Asia has evolved. In terms of the architectural analogy introduced in the previous chapter, the East Asian "house" in 1800 represents the last stage of the traditional order, the culmination of successive refurbishments and remodelings stretching back for millennia. To modern eyes, this "house" is archaic and alien, seemingly having little connection with the present. East Asians in 1800 were embedded in states and societies quite different from their modern counterparts, and acted on beliefs and world views difficult for us to comprehend. Still, as will become clear below, there are also ways in which East Asia in 1800 prefigures East Asia today.

Qing China

In 1800, China functioned as East Asia's geographical, political, economic, and, to a lesser degree, cultural center, a role that it had played for more than 2,000 years. There were, however, several remarkable features of China at this time. Perhaps the most striking is that it was ruled by a non-Chinese group, the Manchus. The latter originated from semi-nomadic pastoral peoples who inhabited the grasslands of Manchuria and were linked culturally to the Mongols and linguistically to the Tungusic hunter-fishers of the northern forests. Manchu ethnic identity crystallized only in the late sixteenth century when they began to expand south, taking advantage of disorders that accompanied the decline of China's Ming dynasty. They employed their army of horsemen to capture Beijing in 1644 and install themselves in power as the Qing ("Pure") dynasty, but they did not gain full control of southern China until

Table 2.1

Estimated Population of East Asian Countries, 1800, 1900, and 2000
(in millions)

Country	1800	1900	2000
China	300	470	1,262
Indonesia	13	40	225
Japan	30	44	127
Philippines	2	8	81
Vietnam	5	14	79
Korea	7	14	70*
Thailand	3	8	61
Burma	3	11	42
Taiwan	—	3	22
Malaysia	.4	2	22
Cambodia	.5	1	12
Laos	.2	.6	6
Singapore	—	.2	4
Mongolia	—	.6	2.4

Sources: Various.
*Includes South Korea (48) and North Korea (22)

they crushed the last Ming loyalists in the 1680s. In a move foreshadowing the flight of Nationalists from the mainland after the Communist victory in 1949, some of these loyalists took refuge on Taiwan and used sea power to fend off Manchu attacks for several decades.

Because the Manchus were alien conquerors, their ascendancy over China might be regarded as a foreign occupation similar to that imposed by the Mongols in the thirteenth century. Unlike the Mongols, however, the Manchus succeeded in winning the loyalty of most of their Chinese subjects. This was no small feat considering the fact that Chinese looked down upon nomadic peoples as "barbarians." But the Manchus were an exception. They embraced the Chinese system of government by mandarin scholar-bureaucrats, and most Manchu emperors strove to embody the Confucian sage-king ideal. They operated a "dyarchy," or dual government, in which Manchu nobles shared power with Chinese mandarins. They endeavored to conciliate their Chinese subjects, particularly the wealthy elite of the lower Yangzi Valley who reciprocated by declaring their fealty to the Qing. The Manchu elite was an Altaic-speaking tribal nobility that differed from Chinese in speech, dress, comportment, pastimes, and attitudes. Despite Manchu efforts to preserve their separate identity, these distinctions gradually eroded, and Manchus became in the end virtually indistinguishable from Han Chinese.

Considered as a "Chinese" dynasty, the Qing holds the distinction of extending the sway of Imperial China over vast territories never before occupied. Previous Chinese dynasties, notably the Han and T'ang, conquered parts of Vietnam and Korea and sent expeditionary forces deep into Central Asia. But the Sino-Manchu armies of the Qing, armed with cannons and muskets, finally brought the Tibetans, Uighurs, and Mongols to heel, and incorporated them into the empire as closely supervised dependencies during the late seventeenth and eighteenth centuries. The Qing meanwhile maintained control over their sparsely populated Manchurian homeland, which they used for recreational purposes and kept off limits to Chinese immigration until the 1870s. The Qing conquest and annexation of Inner Asia was one of the great turning points in China's history, finally ending the age-old nomad threat to the Chinese heartland. Although many Tibetans, Mongols, and Uighurs would disagree, it also established the frontiers of the modern "nation" that Chinese nationalists today seek to uphold and defend. In this and many other ways, Imperial China under the Qing is the progenitor of modern China.

Qing society, like others in East Asia and elsewhere, was an agglomeration of different ethnic groups. The Han Chinese, concentrated in the zone of arable land in the Yellow, Yangzi, and West river watersheds, were numerically dominant, constituting well over ninety percent of the total population. Even in this zone, however, there were minorities who neither considered themselves Chinese nor necessarily welcomed Beijing's rule. In the south and southwest, peoples ethnically related to Thai, Laotians, and Vietnamese maintained their separate identity, as did Muslims of Turkish origin in the northwest. Beyond the area of direct Chinese administration, Manchus, Mongols, Uighurs, and Tibetans carried on their pastoral way of life under their own leaders. Although the Qing did not attempt to Sinicize them, they asserted control over their political affairs through resident Chinese officials backed by garrisons, turning Tibet, Mongolia, and Xinjiang into Chinese protectorates. These peoples generally did not welcome Chinese rule and would have broken away if they could. In modern times, the Mongols succeeded in doing so, and the Tibetans and Uighurs tried to follow suit.

Like their predecessors, Qing emperors styled themselves the rulers of "all under heaven," which theoretically included the entire world. In practice, however, they were concerned only with states and peoples near at hand, especially those that affected the empire's security. Once they had subjugated the Inner Asian nomads, the Qing perceived few external threats and generally took little interest in the outside world. For example, they ignored the contemporary Mughal Empire across the Himalayas in India. Beijing paid more attention to its immediate neighbors, particularly Korea, Vietnam, Thailand, and Burma, which it enrolled as tributary or "vassal" kingdoms. Unlike Tibet and Mongolia, these states were not required to submit to Chinese military oc-

Qianlong Emperor in Court Dress, eighteenth century China.

cupation or political supervision, and enjoyed almost complete independence. China reserved the right to intervene only when civil war or obstreperous kings imperiled the stability of its border provinces. As noted in the previous chapter, the Chinese viewed these tributaries as enhancing the prestige and authority of their emperors, and likened their vassals to benighted children sitting at the feet of their benevolent Chinese "parent."

There was another important side to Qing China's relations with its East Asian neighbors—the movement of Chinese goods, merchants, and settlers into the region, particularly Southeast Asia. Trade was conducted partly through tributary relationships under which it was treated as the ritual exchange of "gifts" between suzerain and vassal. But there was also extensive unofficial trade based on Chinese luxury goods that was carried out by Chinese merchants centered in east coast port cities like Guangzhou (Canton). Some of these merchants took up residence in Southeast Asia and developed close ties with the ruling classes there. They were joined by a stream of peasant immigrants seeking to make their fortune in the "South Seas," as Southeast Asia was then known. The Qing, holding commerce and merchants in low esteem like other Confucian rulers, at first tried to ban this unofficial overseas trade as disruptive. Still, they recognized that trade brought prosperity and eventually tolerated it. Trade also offered officials opportunities for extralegal exactions or "squeeze" from merchants, which they used both for personal enrichment and to finance government projects.

Qing administration over the eighteen provinces of China Proper continued the pattern of centralized bureaucratic government established by the Ming and previous dynasties. Jesuit missionaries and other European observers during the seventeenth and eighteenth centuries were favorably impressed by this system, which they considered a model of "enlightened despotism." But few of these observers perceived that China's myriad peasant villages largely governed themselves under the supervision of local gentry. Corruption or incompetence on the part of mandarin officials could cause serious problems, but the proper functioning of the Chinese system ultimately depended on the stability and cohesion of these villages and peasant acceptance of gentry authority. European admirers of China also failed to recognize that many of their own governments were becoming more efficient and centralized than China's. Early modern European monarchies such as those of France, Sweden, and Prussia developed specialist bureaucracies, professional militaries, and tax and legal systems that enabled them to "reach out and touch" their citizens in ways that Chinese mandarins could not.

The eighteenth century was Qing China's "golden age." Peace and order provided a setting conducive to economic and demographic growth, and the flourishing of trade, handicrafts, cities, and the arts. China's population doubled, rising from about 150 million in 1650 to an estimated 300 million in 1800. This increase was accompanied by stable or rising living standards for most peasants. The introduction of new crops from the Americas such as maize and sweet potatoes enabled them to bring previously marginal land under cultivation and feed more mouths than was possible through exclusive reliance on rice and wheat. Another driver of China's growth was foreign trade, especially with Europeans. The latter coveted Chinese silk, porcelain, and tea. As the British became tea drinkers during the 1700s, China became a major supplier and dominated the world tea trade well into the nineteenth century. Europeans, initially having little to offer that interested Chinese, paid for their purchases with silver, which flooded into China, becoming the standard currency and fueling an inflationary boom. Eighteenth-century China thus struck many observers as being a relatively wealthy and "advanced" country.

Around 1800, the sands began to run out on the Qing. Official corruption became a problem and the once formidable Manchu army had lost its fighting edge. A more fundamental difficulty was a growing Malthusian crunch. Although the economy had reached its absorptive capacity under existing technology, population continued to expand, rising to approximately 430 million by 1850. The resulting demographic crisis unfolded slowly and with regional variations. But increasing numbers of peasants were forced to the wall and became highly vulnerable to natural disasters. Village solidarity and gentry authority eroded under the strain, producing signs of social breakdown and demoralization, including widespread opium addiction and the mushrooming of antidynastic secret societies and religious cults. A large-scale peasant rebellion in the 1790s based on one of these cults foreshadowed worse disorders to come. The Confucian outlook of Qing officials predisposed them to see such problems as arising from moral decline and ideological deviance. Their prescriptions for reform consequently emphasized heavy doses of moral indoctrination and the quashing of dissidence.

Tokugawa Japan

Developments in Japan during the seventeenth and eighteenth centuries resemble those in China insofar as civil war gave way to domestic peace, economic growth, and, by 1800, serious socioeconomic problems. But these similarities conceal major differences between the two societies. In Japan, internal order was achieved by freezing the feudal status quo as it existed in 1600 and closing the country to foreign contact except for a few carefully supervised "windows" on the outside world. The architect of these arrangements was Tokugawa Ieyasu, Japan's most powerful feudal lord, who was preoccupied with creating political stability and perpetuating his family's dominance. The fundamental problem he faced was the tendency toward anarchy inherent in Japan's division into several hundred warring feudal principalities. One solution was replacing them with a centralized bureaucratic government such as had existed a thousand years earlier. But this course was a nonstarter, since

Ieyasu was not strong enough to impose it. His best remaining option was to leave the feudal lords in place, while asserting sufficient control over them to neutralize their capacity to make political trouble.

One prop of the Tokugawa system of "centralized feudalism" was their assumption of the title of shogun, or military deputy of the emperor, clothing them with the mantle of imperial legitimization. This mattered to the samurai ruling class, but hardly at all to Japanese peasants. The latter were only dimly aware of the significance or even the existence of the emperor, who was sequestered under virtual house arrest in the ancient capital of Kyoto.

Another pillar of the Tokugawa political system was the requirement that feudal lords maintain expensive residences in the shogunal capital of Edo, modern Tokyo, and spend part of their time there. This obligation, combined with periodic levies on them to contribute to expensive building projects, saddled lords with heavy financial burdens and kept them under the watchful eyes of the Tokugawa. These burdens fell disproportionately on a number of large feudal domains in southwestern Japan that had opposed Ieyasu's rise to power and were consequently viewed as potential rebels. In contrast, the Tokugawa granted special privileges and exemptions to their most trusted vassals, who were concentrated in central and northern Japan.

Perhaps the most unusual feature of the Tokugawa system was the withdrawal of samurai from the countryside and their concentration in the "castle towns" of their lords, a move dictated by Ieyasu's desire to prevent them from acquiring power bases among the peasantry. Previously rustic farmer-warriors, the samurai now became an urban class of salaried bureaucrats. Nothing like this occurred in Europe, where the knightly class generally remained on the land, slowly transforming itself into a petty nobility that lived cheek by jowl with its peasant dependents. The separation of samurai from the peasantry had several important effects. One of these was to make Tokugawa Japan a relatively urbanized country dotted with sizable castle towns containing samurai and their families as well as new groups of merchants and artisans to serve their needs. Another result was that Japan, while by no means a "police state," became East Asia's most regimented and disciplined society. Samurai soldier-bureaucrats were ubiquitous and armed with swords that symbolized their absolute authority. They exercised tighter control and supervision of peasants than any other ruling class in East Asia.

A final element of the Tokugawa system was Japan's isolation. Until Ieyasu's accession in the early 1600s, Japan was relatively open to foreign cultural influences, including Christianity, which was introduced by Spanish and Portuguese missionaries. Japanese pirates and adventurers ravaged the China coast and ranged into Southeast Asia. Ieyasu and his successors ended all of this, proscribing Christianity, forbidding Japanese to travel overseas,

Tokugawa Yoshimune, early eighteenth century Japan.

and clamping tight controls on foreign contacts. Among Europeans, only Protestant Dutch merchants were permitted entry and they were confined under
prison-like conditions in the southern port city of Nagasaki. The Tokugawa
saw these "Seclusion Edicts" as necessary to seal Japan from divisive foreign
creeds like Christianity, and prevent feudal lords from amassing wealth and
power through overseas trade. The Tokugawa had nothing against trade, which
flourished with China and Korea, but they were intent on monopolizing it.
The net effect of Tokugawa isolationism was to turn the Japanese inward,
reinforcing their insularity and tendency to see themselves as a unique people
fundamentally different from their neighbors.

The Tokugawa political system was highly successful to the extent that it ended the feudal anarchy of earlier centuries, and gave Japan some 260 years of unbroken peace and order. But it generated unintended consequences that were unwelcome to the feudal class. Foremost among these was the development of a thriving commercial economy. Despite the restriction of overseas trade, the concentration of samurai and their dependents in towns created a large pool of consumers whose needs stimulated the growth of agriculture and handicrafts. Domestic trade expanded, moving along a combination of coastal waterways and overland roads centered on Edo and Osaka, the commercial emporium of western Japan. The "winners" from these trends were merchants whose wealthier members formed a new urban elite given to conspicuous consumption. The "losers" were samurai and their lords whose income, derived from taxes in kind on peasants, failed to keep up with their expenses. By the late eighteenth century, most lords were heavily in debt to merchants. Their low-ranking samurai retainers fared even worse, many sinking into genteel poverty.

Japan's feudal rulers never found a way to tap the wealth produced by the growing commercial economy around them. Neither did Chinese mandarins, but they had less incentive to try to do so. The responsibilities of the imperial government in Beijing remained fixed and there was no need to increase revenues. The ultimate solution to Japan's dilemma lay in abolishing feudalism and moving toward a fully centralized government. Autonomous feudal domains made little sense in a unified national economy, especially since most were too small to be viable. The unproductive and underemployed samurai class was also anachronistic, constituting a drain on government finances. Still, few considered systemic reform. Lords and samurai tried to muddle through by belt tightening and merchant loans. A more promising approach followed by larger domains was teaming up with merchants to market specialty products like sugar and cotton. Raising taxes on peasants was also attempted but often provoked protests that were embarrassing insofar as they signaled the failure of benevolent Confucian government that samurai claimed to represent and took seriously.

Such protests raise the question of how Japanese peasants fared under centralized feudalism. Japan's population doubled between 1600 and the early 1700s to about 30 million, only gradually increasing thereafter. This pattern is susceptible to different interpretations. Periodic famines and mass uprisings against profiteering merchants and corrupt officials in the late eighteenth and early nineteenth centuries suggest a pattern of dynastic decline like that which was overtaking Qing China. The spread of messianic faith-healing cults reinforces this impression. One might conclude that many peasants were living close to the margin of subsistence and that village solidarity was breaking down. In contrast to Chinese peasant revolts, however, Japanese protests took the form of ephemeral "riots" that involved little loss of life and challenged neither samurai nor village leaders. There were, moreover, signs of rising expectations such as the diffusion of basic literacy, the spread of rural schools, and the practice of voluntary family limitation. Japanese peasants were becoming attuned to market incentives and the possibility of individual advancement through diligence, thrift, and education.

The late Tokugawa period also saw the development of "national" allegiances among samurai that prefigure modern nationalism. This is at first glance surprising. In a feudal polity, one might expect the loyalty of retainers to focus on their lords and domains. This was the case in seventeenth-century Japan, but by 1800 many samurai identified with emperor and country. One factor behind this shift was the unifying effect of the Tokugawa system, which brought samurai together in Edo and subjected them to common shogunal decrees and demands. Another was the weakening of the lord-vassal bond as lords evolved from the leaders of war bands into "board chairmen" willing to sacrifice their more expendable "employees" to enhance the corporate bottom line. A third factor was Chinese influence. Although the Tokugawa rejected Qing overlordship as an affront to the authority of their own emperor, they admired China as a model. Samurai thus confronted the humiliating fact that their feudal system made them "barbarians." In reaction, they turned to a "National Learning" school that glorified Japan's indigenous Shinto values and traditions, and the shadowy figure in Kyoto who embodied them.

Korea and Vietnam

Although Korea and Vietnam were quite different societies in other respects, both enthusiastically emulated China. They adopted its ideographic writing, its art and architecture, and its Mahayana Buddhist and Neo-Confucian belief systems. Unlike Japan, moreover, they reproduced key features of the Chinese state, including rule by Confucian sage-kings and mandarin scholar-bureaucrats. It is therefore tempting to label them "miniature Chinas." As noted in the previous chapter, however, this is a misleading characterization. Chinese institutions did not operate the same way in Korea and Vietnam as they did in China. The meritocratic principle was, for example, undercut by aristocratic traditions, especially in Korea. Moreover, neither Koreans nor Vietnamese saw themselves as "Chinese" and were in fact proud of their separate identities. As much as they accepted their own rulers' deference to China, they resented Chinese interference in their internal affairs and were prepared to resist by force. The Vietnamese were particularly wary of China, which had occupied Vietnam for a thousand years, and which they suspected of harboring ambitions to "recolonize" them.

Notwithstanding occasional tensions between Korea and China, their relationship was relatively close and harmonious. Beijing, impressed by the Korean elite's deferential posture and assiduous efforts to appropriate Chinese civilization, regarded Korea as a "model tributary." Koreans, for their part, generally viewed China as a benevolent cultural mentor and military protector. Unlike the Vietnamese, they did not undergo a prolonged period of Chinese domination, or have to fight for their independence. China occupied part of northern Korea in the early centuries of the Common Era, but subsequently withdrew and never again attempted to invade the peninsula. China and Korea were natural allies against the tribal pastoralists who periodically swept out of Manchuria in search of plunder and conquest. Korea anchored the eastern end of China's "containment line" against the northern nomads, functioning as an extension of North China's Great Wall. Korea and China also shared a common interest in checking the depredations of Japanese pirates and ma-rauders who roamed the East China Sea during the height of Japan's feudal anarchy in the fifteenth and sixteenth centuries.

The high point of Sino-Korean cooperation came in the 1590s when they combined to repel an invasion of the peninsula by Japanese feudal armies led by Hideyoshi Toyotomi, Japan's paramount warlord, who aimed to use Korea as a stepping-stone for conquering Ming China. Although this invasion failed and the Japanese retreated, it was a catastrophe for Korea, resulting in the despoliation of the country and the mass slaughter of Koreans. Stories, myths, and images of this traumatic event are fixed in the minds of Koreans today. Many see it as a great national calamity and an illustration of Japanese brutality and rapacity, but also as a source of pride insofar as it inspired heroic resistance. Korean loyalty to the Ming led to another invasion in the 1630s, this time by the Manchus, who did not want a hostile state on their flank as they prepared to overthrow and replace the tottering Ming dynasty. Korea accepted the suzerainty of Qing China and maintained correct tributary rela-tions with it. Mindful of the "barbarian" origin of the Qing, however, Koreans never regarded them as fully legitimate, and imagined themselves to be the true heirs of the Ming and the chief upholders of Chinese civilization.

The Choson or Yi dynasty that ruled Korea during the transition from Ming to Qing times was one of the most durable in East Asia, surviving for more than five centuries (1392–1910). Perhaps the main reason for this dynasty's longevity was its symbiotic relationship with Korea's powerful elite, the *yangban* (literally, "two groups," which refers to its civil and military branches). Although similar to Chinese mandarins in that they took pride in their Confucian learning and held "degrees" based on civil service examina-tions, the yangban were in fact a court aristocracy composed of a handful of great families that held large provincial estates. Relations among these families were marked by continuous factional infighting, the object of which was to gain control of the king and use him as a figurehead. Usurpation was neither necessary nor part of the "rules of the game." Since Choson kings lacked a power base of their own, most were creatures of yangban factions and sat on the throne at the pleasure of those factions. By the same token, strong leaders rarely emerged from the ranks of the yangban. No single family or faction was powerful enough to completely dominate the others or dispense with their cooperation.

Korea's Sinicized court aristocracy was not unique—Japan was governed by a similar one between the ninth and twelfth centuries. While civil war was always a potential danger to these regimes, their stability depended ultimately on the ability of great families to preserve their provincial power bases and turn back challenges from groups seeking to take over local government. Unlike their Japanese counterparts, who were eventually overthrown by provincial samurai, Korea's yangban elite proved extremely successful in maintaining control. One way it perpetuated its dominance was by isolating the country from disruptive foreign influences and restricting trade to official channels. Late Choson Korea pursued a policy of national seclusion as rigorous as that enforced by Tokugawa Japan, earning it the sobriquet of "Hermit Kingdom" among Western observers. Another expedient employed by aristocratic families to forestall discontent and rebellion was opening their ranks to local notables. Eventually, almost everyone who mattered in Korean society gained yangban status by virtue of their membership in extended lineages that centered on the court aristocrats in Seoul, the royal capital.

The restoration of peace in the mid-seventeenth century facilitated agricultural and demographic growth. Korea's population rose from perhaps 5 million in 1650 to around 8 million in 1800. But this growth mainly represented recovery from the devastation of the Japanese and Manchu invasions, and the expansion of subsistence agriculture. There was no blossoming of trade, handicrafts, and cities comparable to that in eighteenth-century Japan and China. In socioeconomic terms, Korea remained relatively backward. This suited the yangban elite inasmuch as it underpinned stability and its continued ascendancy. By the early 1800s, however, there were signs of increasing peasant distress arising from population pressure. A particularly serious peasant rebellion in northern Korea in 1811 pointed to the fact that central control by Seoul aristocrats was weakening. There was no lack of tinder for further explosions. Provincial yangban were restive, seeing themselves discriminated against and excluded from power. Dissident Buddhist cults grew, joined by underground Christians who had been converted by Catholic missionaries from China and who had become targets of persecution.

There were some calls for reform among the Confucian-educated Korean elite. The school of "practical learning," an offshoot of a similar movement in Qing China, criticized the arid scholasticism of official Neo-Confucianism and urged greater attention to shoring up the livelihood of peasants through flood control and other public works projects. In general, however, such calls went unheeded. The problems confronting late Choson Korea were variations of those that had long been present and seemed manageable with a business-as-usual approach. There was consequently little sense of crisis among Seoul officialdom. Like Qing China, the Korean royal government concentrated on rooting out and punishing ideological dissidents. These efforts rarely met with much success, since the bureaucratic apparatus was too small and inefficient to exercise effective "thought control." But insofar as order was maintained and taxes collected, the yangban great families saw no need for change and pursued their customary factional feuding. Dazzled by the continuity of the Confucian system in China and their own country, they assumed that it would survive all challenges as it had for centuries.

Vietnam, the other major variant of Chinese-style Confucian government, was in 1800 regaining its unity after several hundred years of division and civil wars. Vietnam's long struggle for political unity stemmed largely from its lack of geographical cohesion. It was split into three distinct regions: Tonkin (the Red River basin around Hanoi); Annam (the narrow central waist centered on Hue); and Cochin China (the Mekong delta area based on Saigon, today's Ho Chi Minh City). Tonkin was the original heartland of the Vietnamese and the most populous and productive part of their country. But its control over the central and southern regions was impeded by the difficulty of communication and transportation except by sea. Moreover, as Vietnamese settlers moved south into Annam and Cochin China, they mixed with ethnically distinct Khmers and Chams, a seafaring Malay people who had embraced Islam. Regional cleavages consequently deepened and the early Vietnamese monarchy, which was based in Hanoi, gradually lost control. In the sixteenth and seventeenth centuries, Tonkin and Annam developed into rival power centers, each of which was headed by princely families.

Significantly, neither of these families asserted its independence, claiming, rather, to rule on behalf of the powerless monarchy in Hanoi. While the ideal of political unity persisted, translating it into reality proved difficult. Economic growth and integration during the eighteenth century slowly reduced the north-south division. As long as the separate Tonkinese and Annamese regimes survived, however, political reunification was next to impossible. In the 1770s, a large-scale peasant revolt swept away both of these regimes and replaced them with a new monarchy claiming jurisdiction over the entire country. But civil war continued, complicated by a brief and unsuccessful Chinese military intervention in support of the old Hanoi ruling line. Resistance was also mounted by the scion of the deposed Annamese princely family, the Nguyen. The latter received support from French Catholic missionaries who had made their way into Vietnam in the seventeenth century and built up a sizable following of converts. In 1802, the Nguyen pretender prevailed and established a dynasty that ruled all of modern Vietnam from the Annamese capital of Hue.

Nguyen Vietnam more closely resembled Qing China than Choson Korea. The Vietnamese counterparts of China's Confucian mandarins were selected by competitive civil service examinations and formed a true meritocracy. But there was no exact equivalent of the Chinese gentry, particularly in the southern frontier region of Cochin China. Given Vietnam's relatively small population of some 5 million, the state bureaucracy was extraordinarily large and expensive to operate, requiring heavy taxes on the peasantry that provoked peasant unrest and occasional uprisings. This oversized administrative apparatus was needed because Vietnam's continuing regional and other cleavages made centralized government difficult. Not all ethnically mixed southerners were reconciled to their incorporation into the Nguyen state, and both Buddhists and the large Catholic minority resented its insistence on strict adherence to Neo-Confucian orthodoxy as defined by Hue. Catholics were particularly difficult to control and their French connection made them suspect in the eyes of the authorities. So, too, were ethnic Chinese immigrants, who dominated the country's domestic and foreign trade.

The Buddhist Kingdoms

Vietnam simultaneously looked north to Qing China and west to the Theravada Buddhist kingdoms of mainland Southeast Asia. Hue accepted Beijing's suzerainty and sent regular tribute missions. Like Korean kings, Nguyen rulers needed consecration by China's Son of Heaven to legitimize themselves in the eyes of their Confucian-educated elite. But they distrusted the Qing, less because they were of barbarian origin than because they were Chinese. Vietnamese never forgot or forgave China's "imperialist" record and were convinced that it sought to subjugate them again. They also resented what they took to be China's condescending view of them as barbarians. Ironically, however, they themselves looked down on Cambodians, Laotians, Thai, and Burmese. To Vietnamese, these peoples were only semi-civilized inasmuch as they were ignorant of Confucianism, overly deferential to Buddhist monks, willing to entrust government to nobles unfit to govern, and given to "primitive" superstitions such as the notion that their kings were "living Buddhas." In addition, Vietnamese saw the Thai and, to a lesser extent, Burmese as rivals for dominance over the Cambodians and Laotians.

Thai King Rama III.

By the eighteenth century, earlier Cambodian and Laotian kingdoms had declined, turning the Mekong Valley into a battleground between Vietnam and Thailand. Laos was divided into the rival principalities of Vientiane, Luang Prabang, and Champassak, the main centers of population and irrigated rice farming. The forested uplands were sparsely inhabited by "slash-and-burn" or swidden agriculturalists of various ethnicities who were organized into small tribal groups. The kingdom of Cambodia, heir of the once mighty Khmer Empire, was based in the rich rice-growing area around Phnom Penh, its capital, in the lower Mekong valley. The Cambodian monarchy was riven by feuds within its royal family and nobility, and exercised only nominal control over its outlying provinces. Both the Thai and the Vietnamese viewed the weak Laotian and Cambodian states as tempting targets for dynastic aggrandizement, and repeatedly sent armies against them with the aim of reducing them to tributary status. These states survived as semi-independent entities in part by playing off the Thai and Vietnamese, but this was a dangerous game insofar as it invited annexation by one or the other.

Thailand, or Siam as it was then known, was emerging in 1800 as the strongest of the Theravada Buddhist kingdoms. The foundations of Thai power were laid five centuries earlier with the establishment of the first Thai kingdoms in the fertile Chaophraya River valley. However, these kingdoms were prone to aristocratic infighting, which invited civil war and foreign invasion. In 1767, the Thai monarchy underwent a near-death experience at the hands of Burmese conquerors who sacked the royal capital of Ayudhya and carried off its inhabitants into slavery. Like the Hideyoshi invasion of Korea, this calamity passed into Thai folklore and myth as a seminal event in the formation of modern Thai national identity. The Thai nobility rallied to drive out the Burmese and reestablish the monarchy in 1782 under a new dynasty, the Chakri, who moved the capital to Bangkok. Although the Chakri did not create a centralized bureaucratic state comparable to that of Vietnam, they conciliated the nobility and focused the kingdom's resources on external expansion eastward against the Laotians and Cambodians, westward against the Shans, and southward against Malay sultanates on the upper Malay Peninsula.

Burma, Thailand's arch-rival in the west, was quite similar to Thailand. The Burmese were centered in the rich rice-growing area of the middle Irrawaddy valley, which formed the base of a number of powerful kingdoms that dominated neighboring peoples such as the Mon in the south and Shans in the northeast. Like their Thai counterparts, these kingdoms were vulnerable to succession disputes and noble revolts. One particularly devastating revolt in the 1750s extinguished the existing monarchy and destroyed its capital near Mandalay. Prefiguring the later Thai response to the sack of Ayudhya, however, the Burmese rebounded under the Konbaung dynasty. This line produced a series of remarkable military leaders who nearly succeeded in conquering Thailand in the 1760s, threw back Qing punitive expeditions in the same decade, annexed the previously independent kingdom of Arakan in the southwest, and brought the Tenasserim coast in the southeast under Burmese control. Rebuffed in repeated attempts to overcome Chakri Thailand, Konbaung kings were in 1800 shifting their attention westward toward India, where they projected the conquest of Assam and British-ruled Bengal.

Burma and Thailand were expansionist multiethnic empires with roughly the same population (3 to 4 million) and core rice-growing areas of about the same size and productivity. They accepted Chinese suzerainty mainly to secure commercial privileges but, unlike Vietnam, did not regard China as a political and cultural model. Their governments were less centralized and bureaucratic than Vietnam's Confucian monarchy, and more dependent on the charisma of their kings. The latter relied on wars of conquest to burnish their prestige and obtain booty and territory with which to reward their nobilities. While they were sensitive to the benefits of trade and accepted foreign merchants, both Chinese and European, they presided over subsistence economies that generated little in the way of cities and merchant and artisan classes. Thailand, with its capital closer to the sea, was more oriented toward maritime commerce. Konbaung kings founded Rangoon (Yangon) in hopes of developing overseas trade and the Irrawaddy delta, but Burma remained an inland agrarian state whose manpower and resources were stretched thin by continuous wars with its neighbors.

The Malay World

Peninsular and island Southeast Asia was dotted in 1800 with relatively small Islamic sultanates that relied primarily on maritime trade, sometimes combined with piracy. The more important included Aceh in northern Sumatra; Brunei in northern Borneo; Johor on the tip of Malay Peninsula; Macassar in southern Sulawesi; and Sulu in the southern Philippines. These states were the heirs of earlier empires that employed naval power to impose loose suzerainty over parts of this area and dominate the Strait of Malacca, which was from ancient times the key artery and transshipment point of trade between India and China. The most celebrated early example was the Hindu-Buddhist Srivijayan Empire, centered on the port city of Palembang in southern Sumatra, which flourished from the seventh to tenth century. The last indigenous trading empire was that of the Islamic sultanate of Melaka (Malacca) on the west coast of the Malay Peninsula, which was destroyed by the Portuguese in 1511. During the seventeenth and eighteenth centuries, the Dutch used their heavily gunned warships, which outclassed smaller Malay craft and Chinese junks, to establish themselves as the dominant regional power.

Like the Portuguese and Spanish before them, the Dutch were drawn to East Asia by the lure of spices, which were grown chiefly in the Maluku Islands (Moluccas) or "Spice Islands" in the eastern Indonesian Archipelago. Spices were in high demand among European elites as a food preservative and ingredient of perfumes. The Dutch prevailed over their Iberian rivals in the spice trade primarily because they were better organized and financed, and because their objectives were more limited. Their East India Company represents one of the premier examples of how capitalist enterprise led early modern Europe's overseas expansion. The Dutch company operated what amounted to a private navy and army which it used to cow local rulers and carve out bases and spheres of influence. Since the company's aim was to maximize the return on investment of its Dutch stockholders, it avoided assuming expensive administrative responsibilities or unnecessarily antagonizing indigenous peoples. In contrast to the Spanish and Portuguese, for whom expanding the dominions of their kings and converting heathens to Christianity were of major importance, the Dutch concentrated on trade and profits.

The Dutch trading empire in the Indonesian Archipelago was based on a string of fortified bases and local alliances that stretched from Melaka in the west to Ambon in the Malukus. This system was anchored on Java, where the Dutch established their headquarters at a port on the northern coast that they renamed Batavia. In Java, they encountered the rising power of the sultanate of Mataram, which was intent on recreating the glories of the fifteenth-century Hindu-Buddhist Majapahit Empire, a state that many Indonesian nationalists today consider to be the precursor of their modern nation-state. Mataram might have succeeded in this project had it not fallen victim to succession disputes and power struggles, which the Dutch exploited to increase their political influence, eventually becoming the power behind the Mataram throne. In the mid-eighteenth century, they split the sultanate into rival princedoms that they could more easily manipulate. Java was by then a dependency of the Dutch company. Javanese princes and nobles enjoyed substantial autonomy, but only to the extent that they accepted Dutch trading monopolies and the ultimate authority of the company's representatives in Batavia.

Outside of Java and a few other islands, the Dutch presence in the archipelago was relatively unobtrusive, involving commercial agreements and alliances with rulers who remained independent in fact as well as name. Moreover, some sultans chose not to deal with the Dutch and regarded them as interlopers. This was the case, for example, with the sultanate of Aceh, which competed with them for control over the pepper-producing areas of central Sumatra. Bugis merchant-pirates also operated independently of the Dutch and defied their attempts to pacify them. In addition, Chinese junks plied the waters of the South China Sea, linking the islands to southern China and bringing Chinese merchants and immigrants. As in mainland Southeast Asia, the Chinese attached themselves to local rulers, performing useful commercial and artisanal functions that their own people often disdained. The Dutch, too, acted as their patrons, and Batavia acquired a large ethnic Chinese community. While such communities generally coexisted with the Malay majorities around them, there were tensions and occasional anti-Chinese pogroms, foreshadowing future problems in modern Southeast Asia.

The European impact on the Malay world was strongest in the Philippines, which the Spanish conquered and colonized in the late seventeenth century. The Philippines presented the Spanish with a tabula rasa. Except in the Islamized south, it was inhabited by animists who were fragmented into many ethnic groups and lacked any form of political organization above village headmen. Although the islands did not produce spices, the Spanish nevertheless viewed them as a useful addition to their empire. They offered a field for proselytization, a task entrusted to Franciscan and other Catholic missionary orders, who succeeded in Christianizing the Filipinos. Equally important, the Philippines provided the Spanish with a base to tap into the lucrative China trade. Chinese merchants brought silk, porcelain, and other luxury goods to the colonial capital of Manila, which the Spanish purchased with silver from their mines in the Americas. Since the Spanish were few in number, Hispanicization was superficial among Filipino peasants, who adopted neither their language nor customs. Nevertheless, the Spanish presence set Filipinos apart from other Malay peoples in 1800 and continues to do so even today.

Europe and East Asia

If one's focus shifts to East Asia as a whole, the Spanish Philippines and Dutch-controlled Java stand out as exceptions. Prior to the nineteenth century, Europeans rarely tried to take over major states or govern large populations. Most sought trading opportunities rather than territorial dominion, and backed off when they encountered serious resistance. The Spanish, for example, stood by as the Japanese massacred their Catholic missionaries and converts in the early 1600s; the Russians withdrew when Qing armies challenged them for control of the trans-Amur region in the 1680s; and a French expeditionary force fled Thailand in the same decade when a filibustering scheme went awry and Thai armies massed against them. European warships ruled the waves, but their land forces were small and highly vulnerable. These forces enjoyed no great technological advantage over the similarly armed peasant levies that East Asian states could deploy against them in vast numbers. Although the military balance shifted in favor of Europeans in the eighteenth century as they developed disciplined professional armies, neither side at first appreciated the significance of this change.

Since East Asia faced Europe from a position of strength, it dictated the terms of their interaction during the seventeenth and eighteenth centuries. With the notable exception of Korea, which excluded virtually all foreigners,

East Asian states generally welcomed trade with Europeans inasmuch as it brought prosperity and precious metals, above all silver. In an age innocent of the idea of free trade, East Asian governments sought to restrict this trade to official channels and monopolize its profits. The Qing, for example, insisted that European merchants deal only with officially licensed Chinese merchants in the southeastern port city of Guangzhou. The "Canton System," as this arrangement was known, entailed irksome restrictions on Europeans, including their confinement in a virtual prison and the prohibition of their contact with ordinary Chinese. As previously noted, the Japanese imposed similar restrictions on the Dutch in Nagasaki. From the perspective of the Chinese and Japanese, these controls served the dual purposes of funneling the profits of trade into official coffers, and preventing Europeans from spreading their disruptive customs and beliefs, especially Christianity.

Tokugawa Japan ruthlessly persecuted Christians, both European and Japanese, whom it regarded as fifth columnists of European empire builders. The Japanese were not alone in their suspicion of Christianity. Although the Qing tolerated the presence of Sinophile Jesuit missionaries at court, they proscribed Christianity as a faith and tried to stamp it out. French Catholic missionaries had more success in Vietnam, but they eventually ran afoul of the Nguyen government, which persecuted them and their converts. In general, East Asian rulers, whether Confucian, Buddhist, or Islamic, viewed Christianity and its European adherents as posing a political and ideological threat. This view acted as a strong disincentive to look upon Europe as a political or cultural model. Once East Asians had imported sixteenth- and seventeenth-century European military technology, chiefly cannons and muskets, they closed the door on further borrowing and ignored developments in Europe. Proponents of "Western learning" faced a brick wall of indifference and suspicion. Surprisingly, only the Japanese paid any attention to Europe, keeping themselves apprised of happenings there through the Dutch.

The example of European empire builders was not entirely ignored by East Asian rulers. The Qing conquest of Inner Asia, for example, was inspired partly by their desire to keep pace with and preempt the advancing Russians. However, Europe's impact on East Asia was more economic than political or cultural. European long-distance sailing ships tied the region into a global trading system encompassing Europe, Africa, the Americas, West and South Asia, and eventually the Pacific. East Asia's terms of trade with Europeans were tilted in its favor, resulting in an inflow of gold and silver that stimulated economic growth and commercial development. The Europeans also introduced new crops from Africa and the Americas such as maize, peanuts, tobacco, and potatoes, which boosted agricultural production and permitted populations to rise. Qing China was the main beneficiary, its eighteenth-century prosperity being largely the result of its integration into this global system. But since China functioned as the hub of East Asia's own political-economic system through its tributary and trading networks, it diffused the benefits to its neighbors, including even isolationist Korea.

Prior to 1800, Europeans generally accepted their subordinate position in East Asia's Sinocentric order. This was in part a matter of necessity inasmuch as the alternative to playing by East Asian rules was not playing at all. Even the Dutch overlords of Java conformed to local prejudices, avoiding proselytization and keeping out of sight behind their Javanese collaborators. The Dutch also acquiesced in being treated as tributaries by China and Japan. They and other Europeans rarely manifested attitudes of cultural and racial superiority that became so common in the nineteenth century. Indeed, many admired East Asian states and considered China to be in some respects more advanced than their own. As previously mentioned, European Enlightenment thinkers held up Qing China as a model of benevolent autocracy and meritocratic government. By the end of the eighteenth century, however, these favorable views were giving way to more critical ones. Lord Macartney, who journeyed to Beijing in 1793 on behalf of the British king to plead for free trade and "normal" diplomatic relations, was put off by what he saw as China's arrogance, backwardness, and obscurantism.

3

A Clash of Civilizations

The imposition of Western control over East Asia during the nineteenth century can be seen as a straightforward conquest achieved by superior fire-power and military organization. But at another, deeper level it was a "clash of civilizations"—a collision between fundamentally incompatible cultural systems. Behind the West's military superiority lay its novel, science-based industrial civilization and nation-state ideal. East Asian states and societies were based on older and quite different principles and assumptions. Like other non-Western peoples, East Asians were slow to recognize the nature of the Western challenge or devise effective responses to it. They assumed that they could hold the West at bay by borrowing bits and pieces of its civilization, especially its military techniques. This approach had worked in the seventeenth century when Europe and East Asia were more similar, but it was futile in the nineteenth century when the cultural gap between them had become a chasm. The only alternative to being subjugated by the West was embracing its civilization. Most East Asian rulers and elites balked at the latter course and chose, in effect, to "go down with the ship" of tradition.

Europe's New Civilization

The Europe that East Asians confronted in the nineteenth century was quali-tatively different from the one they had faced earlier. It was, in fact, a new kind of civilization unprecedented in world history. At its heart was modern science, or the use of mathematics and experimentation to explain, predict, and control natural phenomena. The roots of Europe's Scientific Revolution go back to the sixteenth-century Renaissance and the groundbreaking work of figures like Leonardo da Vinci and Nicholas Copernicus. But the pace quick-ened in the seventeenth century when a host of practitioners of the "scientific method" began applying it to biology, medicine, astronomy, and other fields. A turning point came in 1687 with the publication of Isaac Newton's laws of planetary motion, which transformed educated Europeans' understanding of the natural world. Newton showed that phenomena previously regarded as the unfathomable workings of divine Providence were explicable in terms of natural forces that operated much like a clock. If this was true of the planets, it was also potentially true of all other natural phenomena, opening the way for the abandonment of supernaturalism and the embrace of rationalism.

One might ask why the Scientific Revolution occurred among Europeans and not East Asians. China produced many marvelous inventions such as paper and the compass. Moreover, Chinese Taoists used experimentation in their search for life-prolonging elixirs, sometimes hitting upon revolutionary concoctions like gunpowder. Chinese were no less practical and inventive than Europeans, and equally intent on understanding and controlling the natural world. Like medieval European alchemists and astrologers, however, their outlook was "pre-scientific" insofar as it rested on untested and unverifiable assumptions about the way this world operates. Early modern European scientists shifted to a new paradigm in which knowledge was grounded on proof and demonstration employing mathematical reasoning. This paradigm shift was closely related to the contemporaneous European Reformation. The breakdown of the absolute authority of the Roman Catholic Church and the rise of Protestantism, in which individuals were responsible for their own salvation, created an intellectual environment conducive to the skepticism and rationalism on which modern science depends.

Europe's Scientific Revolution stimulated a parallel Technological Revolution in which the scientific method was applied to the solution of practical problems ranging from boosting crop yields to driving machinery. The lead was taken by artisans and capitalists in northwestern Europe who were interested in turning a profit from their inventions. Eighteenth-century Britain, a relatively open society hospitable to entrepreneurs and commercial enterprise, was the center of this movement. The most important British invention was the coal-fired steam engine which became the foundation of another transformation, the Industrial Revolution. The British initially used steam engines in mining but later in the century they hit upon the idea of using them to mechanize textile manufacturing, particularly cotton spinning and weaving. The mechanization of other industries, previously the domain of handicraft workers, proceeded apace, as did the development of factories and mills to house such operations. In the early 1800s, steam engines were adapted to overland and sea transportation. The first practical steamboat was introduced in 1807 and railroads soon followed.

The Industrial Revolution was still in its infancy at the beginning of the nineteenth century even in Britain, where it was most advanced. But it was already producing striking social and political changes. The shift from handicraft to factory production gave rise to an industrial proletariat, concentrations of factory operatives recruited from displaced farm laborers and tenant farmers. Many of these "proletarians" lived in conditions of appalling overcrowding and poverty in slums that arose in factory towns. At the same time, however, a new urban middle class took shape, composed of managers, professionals, and small businessmen. The "captains of industry" put themselves at the head of this class and agitated for policies they deemed appropriate for the new industrial age. Foremost among these was the aggressive pursuit of overseas markets and raw materials to keep their factories humming. They also demanded more representative government. To the new business class, it seemed intolerable that kings and aristocrats should continue to monopolize power. In the view of this class, the "people" deserved a greater voice in the governance of the realm.

Nationalism and Nation-States

Another aspect of Europe's emerging industrial societies that made them even more formidable was the rise of nationalism and nation-states. Nations as cultural or ethnic communities are timeless and universal. But nations as political communities of citizens sharing equal rights and duties are more unusual. The germ of such political communities existed in classical antiquity in Greek city-states and the Roman Republic. However, citizenship in these ancient states as well as their medieval Italian successors was restricted, typically excluding women, slaves, and the "rabble." Most were oligarchies in fact if not name. The idea that the "political nation" should be built on universal citizenship was quite radical in Europe. Seventeenth- and eighteenth-century absolute kings such as those of France, Prussia, and Austria welcomed the loyalty of the "lower orders" but resisted their participation in government and rejected the notion that they might be responsible to them. Although the famous dictum of France's Louis XIV, *L'etat c'est moi* (I am the state), exaggerates royal control, it accurately reflects the determination of these rulers to govern unconstrained by popular interference.

The triumph of the ideal of universal citizenship and its concomitant, popular sovereignty, resulted from the diffusion of the political theories of Enlightenment thinkers like John Locke and Jean-Jacques Rousseau. Seeking a rational basis for government, they imagined the existence of a "Social Contract" between ruler and ruled in which the latter delegates limited power to the former and can legitimately reclaim it through rebellion if the ruler oversteps his bounds. Rousseau went further, arguing that absolute and inalienable sovereignty lies in the "General Will" of the people, including all citizens high and low, who have the right to depose rulers whenever they see fit. Spread by propagandists of the "Rights of Man" like Tom Paine, these ideas gained a wide following in France, the center of Enlightenment thought and agitation. But their revolutionary potential first became evident in the 1775–83 American War of Independence in which American colonists broke away from their British "mother country," defining themselves simultaneously as a sovereign people and new nation. This was the prototype of a wave of similar anti-colonial nationalist rebellions in Spanish America in the 1810s and 1820s.

In Europe, the French Revolution of 1789 inaugurated an age of nationalism in which one European people after another discovered itself as a nation, forcing dynastic states to become nation-states. The rickety French monarchy was the first and most important domino to fall. Its royal government was replaced by a series of regimes that claimed to embody the will of the French nation and successfully mobilized mass support for its defense and the spread of its ideals of "liberty, equality, and fraternity." Nationalism fired France's citizen armies with an élan that the hired soldiers of dynastic states could not match. Napoleon used these armies to try to conquer Europe and almost succeeded until he was finally brought to bay and defeated in 1815. Napoleon's conquests inspired an abiding fear of France. But they also implanted French-style nationalism among Germans, Italians, Spanish, Czechs, and other ethnic groups. Previously content with their status as passive subjects of absolute monarchs, these groups now began to see themselves as political communities of citizens that enjoyed inalienable rights and deserved representation by governments of their own choosing.

In the aftermath the French Revolution and Napoleonic Wars, reactionaries hoped to restore the status quo ante. With nationalism on the rise throughout Europe, however, old-fashioned dynastic states headed by absolute monarchs faced growing political unrest. Some rulers, such as those of Russia and Austria, presided over multiple ethnic groups that pressed for independence as separate nations. Others, like those in Germany and Italy, governed fragments of ethnic groups that viewed themselves as single nations. Even kings of ethnically homogenous realms confronted demands from their heretofore inert subjects for political rights and liberties befitting their new status as citizens. In short, European ancien régimes faced a crisis of legitimacy. Many responded with police repression, but this only intensified mass discontent, resulting in uprisings throughout Europe in the 1848 "springtime of nations." In the end, most rulers accommodated demands for national and popular sovereignty by transforming themselves into the symbolic representatives of nations, and opening up government to popular participation through elected national assemblies.

Europe's new nation-states were stronger and more cohesive than their dynastic predecessors inasmuch as they tapped the primary loyalty of their citizens. For the latter, national and ethnic identity merged, so that ethnicity and nationality became equivalent and interchangeable concepts. Not surprisingly, governments encouraged nationalism and national myths, such as notions that nations were united by ties of blood and common ancestry; that they had glorious histories stretching far back into the past; and that they embodied special virtues superior to those of all other nations. But mass nationalism was a double-edged sword for governments, introducing an explosive new element into domestic politics and international relations. Real or perceived insults to the nation's honor triggered popular demands for redress that politicians and statesmen ignored at their peril. By the same token, policies that enhanced the nation's prestige and competitive standing attracted strong support. With the onset of peace in Europe after 1815, European nation-states directed their rivalries outward to the conquest, exploitation, and "civilization" of the non-Western world, including East Asia.

Europe's New Imperialism

Nineteenth-century Europe's imperial thrust into non-Western lands was new insofar as it was driven by nationalism and industrialization, and based on overwhelming technological superiority that made the conquest of previously formidable opponents relatively easy. True, the revolt of British and Spanish colonies in the Americas at the end of the eighteenth and beginning of the nineteenth centuries temporarily diminished the appeal of empire building. Some Europeans saw overseas possessions as more trouble than they were worth, especially in an era of free trade when raw materials and markets could be obtained without them. But there were countervailing forces at work in European societies that pushed them toward imperial expansion. Christian missionaries anticipated a rich harvest of converts and wanted unimpeded access to them. Nationalists argued that the acquisition of empire was essential to burnish the nation's prestige and get a leg up on national rivals. Capitalists favored colonies as a means of efficiently exploiting the agricultural and mineral resources of the non-Western world. And soldiers promised quick and relatively painless victories over militarily outclassed non-Westerners.

There was a glaring contradiction at the heart of European imperialism. Having recently secured their own rights and liberties as citizens of nation-states, Europeans now aimed to deprive non-Western peoples of these same rights by turning them into colonial subjects. If the Rights of Man were indeed universal, as Enlightenment thinkers had proclaimed, why should they be restricted to Europeans and people of European descent? The answer offered by imperialists was summed up in the idea of "the white man's burden," which was the theme of a famous 1899 poem by Rudyard Kipling, the bard

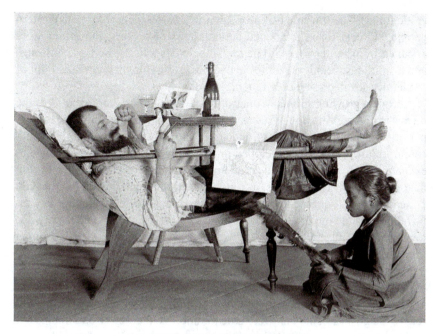

Colonial life in French Indochina, 1903.

of British imperialism. Kipling and other imperialists argued that nonwhites were racially and culturally inferior to the "white race" and, as such, in need of prolonged colonial tutelage to bring them up to European standards. Most Europeans found this argument persuasive since it provided a moral as well as seemingly scientific justification of colonialism. Scientific theories of race-based behavioral traits were in vogue in the late nineteenth century, as was social Darwinism, which suggested that "inferior breeds" had fallen behind in the struggle for survival because they were "less fit."

Europeans were confident of the superiority of their industrial civilization and regarded its worldwide triumph as inevitable. The nineteenth century was an age of progress and improvement in Europe. Science and technology produced a flood of discoveries and inventions that gave Europeans unprecedented control over nature, and it seemed only a matter of time before they unraveled its remaining mysteries. Beginning with Britain's 1851 Great Exhibition, Europeans celebrated their accomplishments with periodic international expositions. The underside of industrial capitalism was addressed by public health measures, factory legislation, and self-help initiatives by workers. Constitutional and representative government became the norm, and emerging liberal democracies in Britain, France, and other countries pointed to a democratic future. The flip side of European pride was contempt for non-Western peoples. Except for scholars and connoisseurs of exotica, Europeans were appalled by what they took to be the archaic despotisms, barbaric customs, and primitive superstitions of these peoples. Dragging them into the light of modernity seemed to be doing them a favor.

Europe's growing military superiority gave would-be empire builders the means to conquer the non-Western world with relative ease. Initially, this superiority was as much organizational as technological. During the eighteenth century, European states developed professional armies that were trained to exchange volleys of musket and cannon fire and overwhelm opponents with bayonet charges. Their navies, meanwhile, acquired larger and more heavily armed warships equipped with better navigational devices. Another key innovation was the improvement of military engineering skills and supply and logistical systems. "Scientific soldiers," turned out by new officer training schools, made their appearance. Together, these developments added up to a quantum jump in European military capabilities, or a "revolution in military affairs" in today's parlance. Behind the new armies and navies lay Europe's scientific and technological revolutions as well as increasingly elaborate bureaucratic governments that were able to mobilize the wealth and manpower of their societies through efficient tax systems, comprehensive law codes, and local administrations controlled from the center.

The proving ground of Europe's new military capabilities was the Indian subcontinent, where the British succeeded in the late eighteenth century in taking over the decaying Mughal Empire and transforming it into "British India." This takeover was accomplished by the British East India Company, the counterpart of the Dutch company of the same name.

From its establishment in the early seventeenth century, the British company concentrated on India, which offered spices and high-quality textiles. The British situated themselves in small enclaves and at first remained content with trade. But the breakdown of the Mughal Empire in the early 1700s amid succession disputes, domestic revolts, and foreign invasions created opportunities for political intervention, which the British were quick to exploit. Warring Indian princes welcomed their military assistance and formed alliances with them. The British used these alliances to eliminate their French rivals and extend their territorial holdings. Backed by "sepoys," or British-trained Indian troops, they won the 1757 Battle of Plassey, enabling them to gain control of the large northeastern state of Bengal, which became their main base in India.

The British subjugation of India, which was completed in the early 1800s, demonstrated the feasibility of conquering and occupying large non-Western countries with a relative handful of European soldiers. Some Indian princes resisted and their troops fought bravely, but they were no match for the British. The latter governed India with a small civil service staffed by Britons, which administered some areas directly and elsewhere supervised semi-autonomous "princely states." Control of India proved highly advantageous to the British, compensating them for the loss of their American colonies. They diverted Indian land tax revenues into their own coffers and set up a powerful British-officered sepoy army. They also reorganized the Indian economy to suit British industrial interests, quashing competing Indian textile producers and encouraging Indian raw cotton exports to supply British textile mills. In return, the British offered the benefits of European civilization. They imposed British law codes and procedures; curbed "barbarous" customs such as widow burning (*suttee*); built roads, ports, and railways; and made available British education to the Indian elite.

Britain's successful exercise in empire building in India did not immediately inspire similar ventures elsewhere. Europeans were distracted by the Napoleonic wars until 1815 and, as noted above, the subsequent revolt of Spain's American colonies temporarily dampened enthusiasm for overseas imperial expansion. As Europe's preeminent naval and colonial power, Britain might be expected to have taken the lead in such expansion. But the British had their hands full in India and were, in any case, attracted to free trade, which did not require colonies. In the post-Napoleonic period, moreover, Britain and other European states were preoccupied with domestic political reform necessitated by the rise of nationalism and popular demands for representative government. To the extent that they looked outward, they focused on the nearby Ottoman Empire, whose disintegration offered opportunities to seize territory, stimulating European rivalry. France grabbed the Ottoman dependency of Algeria in 1830, while Austria and Russia competed to pick up the pieces from the gradual breakdown of Ottoman rule in the Balkans. Russia also expanded into the Caucasus area, Central Asia, and across the Pacific to Alaska.

The pace of Europe's imperial advance quickened from mid-century, and within four or five decades virtually all of the non-Western world passed under its direct or indirect control. In the Middle East, the Ottoman and Persian empires survived, but both were a shadow of their former selves and subject to strong European influence. A "scramble for Africa" in the 1880s turned the entire continent into European colonies or protectorates, the only significant holdout being the Abyssinian (Ethiopian) Empire. Southeast Asia suffered the same fate with the exception of Thailand, which maintained its independence by serving as a buffer state between the expanding British and French. Northeast Asia fared somewhat better. Although the Chinese Empire lost its trans-Amur territories to Russia, it remained intact until the 1890s, when the Europeans and Japanese began to carve it up into spheres of influence. Korea and Japan also escaped colonization or reduction to protectorate status, mainly because they lay outside the main path of the European advance. By 1900, the Europeans and Americans had taken over all of the Pacific islands, including the previously independent Hawaiian kingdom.

One factor behind the expansion of European empires was the development of even better weapons, including repeating rifles, accurate long-range artillery, and steam-powered warships. Improvements in medicine and hygiene made tropical military operations and residence less hazardous for Europeans. In addition, new incentives for acquiring colonies and dependencies came into play. Europe's industrialization and emerging consumer societies created an insatiable demand for tropical commodities and raw materials, and the imposition of European political control seemed necessary to organize their efficient production and export. Plantation agriculture, a European specialty originally developed in the Americas in the seventeenth and eighteenth centuries, spread to Africa, South Asia, Southeast Asia, and the Pacific. The nineteenth-century Transportation Revolution, resulting from the introduction of railroads and steamships and the opening of the Suez Canal in 1869, created a more integrated global economy in which far-flung colonial producers played a vital role. "Globalization," assumed by many to be a present-day phenomenon, was already a reality in 1900.

Europe's imperial expansion was also driven by domestic politics and national rivalries. The unification of Germany and Italy in the 1860s created new German and Italian nation-states, both of which wanted a place in the imperial sun and thus joined the race for colonies. Even the United States, a reluctant and ambivalent imperialist, eventually participated. Empire building was popular among newspaper-reading publics, producing international celebrities like David Livingstone, the intrepid explorer of "darkest Africa," and "Chinese" Gordon, who died a hero's death defending Khartoum against attacking "native hordes." For many, imperial expansion was a measure of national greatness irrespective of the economic benefits it brought or burdens it imposed. Britain, France, Russia, Germany, and other imperial powers squared off in a global competition for territory in which the stakes were national prestige. They often seized real estate for no better reason than to deny it to a rival. But they also acquired dependencies haphazardly or even accidentally, as when expansionist zealots in the field acted independently of home governments, or local rulers petitioned them for protection.

The Assault on East Asia

Signs that the Europeans posed a potentially serious threat to East Asia were apparent by 1800 to the few able to read them. But most East Asians ignored the storm warnings. Had Chinese mandarins been attentive to developments in Europe and the significance of Britain's conquest of Mughal India, they might have regarded the 1793 Macartney mission as a wake-up call for reform. They instead viewed his rebuff and withdrawal as evidence that the "Western barbarians" could be contained indefinitely in the straightjackets of the Canton System and tributary relations. They were not alone in such complacent views. The Thai, Burmese, Vietnamese, and Koreans were equally oblivious to the mounting danger. Only a handful of officially subsidized Japanese scholars of "Dutch learning" had any inkling of the European threat. They warned that the Europeans, equipped with powerful new armies and navies, were closing in and would have to be met on their own terms, which would require drastic reform. But the Tokugawa authorities largely ignored these warnings. They were committed to maintaining Japan's isolationist stance and the political system set up in the early 1600s.

The Burmese and Javanese were the first East Asians to confront the European military juggernaut. As noted in the previous chapter, Burma's Konbaung kings, repulsed by the Thai in the east and west, turned west to exploit seemingly easy pickings in northeastern India. This brought them into conflict with the British in Bengal. Although a diplomatic settlement might have been worked out, the Burmese underestimated the military capabilities of the British and supposed that they could defeat them. Burmese armies therefore moved into Assam in the early 1820s with plans to invade Bengal. This was a fatal mistake. The British countered by landing their Indian army in Rangoon and overrunning southern Burma. Although Burmese peasant levies fought doggedly, they were overwhelmed by British firepower, discipline, and logistics. The 1824–26 Anglo-Burmese war ended in a humiliating defeat for Burma. It was forced to pay a large indemnity, cede its Arakan province, and accept the presence of British diplomats and merchants. But the Konbaung monarchy remained defiant and believed that it could defeat the British in a second round.

The 1820s also marked the end of the relative autonomy of Javanese aristocrats under Dutch suzerainty. The Netherlands, nearly bankrupt and reduced to the status of a minor European power, was determined to make Java a paying proposition and boost its prestige as an imperial player. To these ends, the Dutch set about converting Java into a giant coffee and sugar plantation. Javanese peasants and aristocrats rebelled, resulting in the 1825–30 Java War. A Dutch army, backed by auxiliaries from Madurese and other peoples that had no liking for Javanese, eventually prevailed at the cost of several hundred thousand Javanese lives. As in the Anglo-Burmese war, the key to victory was superior European discipline and firepower, which more than compensated for their small numbers. The Dutch followed up their triumph by turning

Java into a full-fledged colony. Javanese aristocrats became the front men of a Dutch-run administration that required peasants to grow and deliver cash crops as taxes. Although many peasants were driven to the edge of starvation, this system was highly profitable for the Dutch, making Amsterdam a center of global trade and finance.

China became East Asia's first victim of British "free-trade imperialism" in the 1839–42 Opium War. This conflict grew out of Britain's long-standing dissatisfaction with the Canton System and its determination to open China to free trade on British terms. Opium brought the issue to head. Grown in Bengal under British East India Company license, this drug enjoyed a growing demand among Chinese addicts and was highly profitable since the Qing government banned its import. British merchants smuggled it into China around Guangzhou with the help of Chinese middlemen and corrupt officials. The Qing were alarmed by the rapid expansion of this illicit trade in the early 1800s, which undermined public morals, promoted official corruption, and resulted in the outflow of Chinese silver currency, reversing China's previously favorable trade balance with the British. The latter ignored official Chinese requests to curb the trade, so the emperor ordered a crackdown. Modern Chinese nationalists view "Commissioner Lin," the mandarin charged with this task, as a hero for taking the British bull by the horns, confiscating and publicly destroying their opium stocks in Guangzhou.

The British government responded by declaring war on the grounds that China's action violated the property rights of its citizens and insulted the British nation. But London's primary motivation was to coerce Beijing into giving it unrestricted access to the supposedly limitless Chinese market for British manufactured goods, particularly cotton textiles. The British dispatched a powerful naval task force equipped with shallow-draft steamships. Qing China, like other East Asian states, proved incapable of offering effective resistance to such modern forces. The British fleet ranged along China's east coast, blasting forts, sinking "war junks," and scattering Chinese troops. The coup de grâce came when the British sailed up the Yangzi and besieged the city of Nanjing, threatening to sever the vital inland canal system supplying northern China. The Qing threw in the towel and accepted British peace terms. As set forth in the 1842 Treaty of Nanjing, these included the payment of a large war indemnity, the cession of Hong Kong Island off the southeastern coast, and the opening of five "Treaty Ports" where British merchants could reside and trade immune from Chinese law and interference by Chinese officials.

The Nanjing Treaty was the first of a series of "Unequal Treaties" that the British and other Europeans imposed on East Asian states. They were unequal insofar as they granted Europeans nonreciprocal rights that they themselves would have regarded as unacceptable infringements on their sovereignty.

British warships destroying Chinese junks in the First Opium War, 1839–42.

One of these was "extraterritoriality," or the right of Europeans to operate under the jurisdiction of their own laws and courts. In the European international system, only diplomats enjoyed this immunity. Another right secured by Europeans was the power to limit import duties on goods they wished to sell. No European state would have considered giving up such a fundamental attribute of sovereignty. A third concession extracted from East Asians was their acceptance of "most-favored-nation" clauses under which any rights and privileges they might give one country automatically applied to all. European states rarely signed treaties with these clauses, since they deprived them of bargaining leverage. For example, the French gained the right to spread Christianity in China, forcing Beijing willy-nilly to extend the same right to all Westerners despite its aversion to doing so.

China's defeat and submission to Britain sent a shock wave through East Asia. If the Western barbarians could humiliate the regional superpower, they might be more dangerous than earlier had been thought. Japanese and others began to bolster their defenses, some even buying European weapons. But the Chinese initially were confident that they could hold the West at bay without reforms. To China's mandarins, the Nanjing Treaty was regrettable but hardly a disaster. Since they did not accept the European international system or aspire to join it, they were unconcerned by its "unequal" aspects. What troubled them, rather, was that it tarnished the Qing dynasty's prestige and enabled Europeans to spread what mandarins saw as the twin poisons of opium and Christianity. Still, it could have been worse. The British might have attempted to conquer China like earlier nomadic invaders. The fact that they did not try to do so and seemed content to go about their business in a few coastal enclaves suggested to mandarins that it might be possible to contain them and perhaps even reimpose the defunct Canton System when China had recovered its strength.

The European Noose Tightens

As noted above, the European imperialist advance accelerated in the 1850s and 1860s. In East Asia, its main focus was China. Europeans saw China's hundreds of millions of people as potentially eager consumers of their Christian religion and manufactured goods. But no European power made a full-scale attempt to conquer China or split it up into colonies. By the 1850s, the British were joined by two strong rivals, France and Russia, resulting in an imperialist stalemate. London, Paris, and St. Petersburg were at loggerheads as to which of them should dominate China or how it might be divided among them. As in the case of the Ottoman and Persian empires in West Asia, they tacitly agreed to keep the Chinese Empire intact and use the Unequal Treaty system to pursue their individual interests. There were, however, several problems with their "cooperative imperialism." Beijing refused to abide by its Unequal Treaty obligations and, in fact, tried to throw them off. Moreover, the Qing dynasty seemed to be on its last legs, being assailed at mid-century by multiple peasant rebellions, including the Taiping revolt, one of the most remarkable mass insurrectionary movements in East Asian history.

The ideology of the Taipings will be examined in the next chapter. Suffice it to say here that it was based on Chinese folk religion with some Christian elements. While not Christians, the Taipings were revolutionaries. Their 1850–64 uprising came close to toppling both the Qing dynasty and China's gentry-based Confucian sociopolitical order. It turned the lower Yangzi basin, China's rice bowl, into a battleground of clashing armies on which tens of millions of lives were lost, dwarfing the death toll of the contemporaneous American Civil War. The Qing eventually rallied and crushed the Taipings and other rebels with gentry support. The dynasty was, however, permanently weakened. Although runaway population growth soon resumed with its attendant social and economic ills, central China only slowly recovered from the carnage and devastation. During the rebellion, moreover, power gravitated into the hands of regional officials who took the lead in suppressing it with the aid of European volunteers and weapons. Beijing never succeeded in fully restoring its control over the country. China's political system and Confucian civilization survived the Taiping assault, but both were debilitated.

Despite the mortal threat posed by the Taipings, the Qing opted to defy the European powers in hopes of inducing them to quit China. But this only led to another humiliating military defeat. In the Second Opium War of 1856–60, a joint Anglo-French expeditionary force marched on Beijing and burned the emperor's magnificent summer palace as he fled to Manchuria. Although peace was restored in 1860, European terms were onerous. The Qing were obliged to hand over to Russia the trans-Amur region, a sparsely populated but vast area that is today's Russian Far East. They were also compelled to accept the establishment of a large number of new Treaty Ports, including some located far inland along the Yangzi. Europeans could now trade and proselytize in the Chinese hinterland protected by extraterritoriality and gunboats. In addition, the Europeans secured the right to station their ambassadors in Beijing and deal with the Son of Heaven as the equivalent of a European head of state. All of this was a bitter pill for the Qing and China's mandarins to swallow, but they reluctantly accepted it as the price that had to be paid to keep the Western barbarians at arm's length.

In Southeast Asia, the advancing European imperialists had no compunction about conquering and annexing kingdoms, especially since these offered promising areas for plantation agriculture. In the 1860s, the French moved into Vietnam, where their missionaries had long been active. They forced the Nguyen king to cede Cochin China, the Mekong delta area around Saigon, which became a French-administered colony. This concession bought time for the Nguyen but not security, since it led to increasing French pressure and interference in their affairs. The end of the line for independent Vietnam came in the mid-1880s when civil disorder in the Tonkin region in the north provided the French with the pretext for military intervention and the imposition of full political control over the country. Although they preserved the fig leaf of continued Nguyen and mandarin rule, they governed Vietnam directly and began developing it as a producer of rubber, rice, and other commercial commodities. The French rounded out their takeover of Vietnam by establishing protectorates over Cambodia and Laos, grouping all three in a new colonial entity they called the "Union of Indochina."

The British meanwhile absorbed Burma. In 1852, the government of British India, angered by Konbaung recalcitrance, launched another seaborne punitive expedition against Burma. This second Anglo-Burmese War of 1852–53 was militarily a repeat of the first insofar as British-Indian forces easily crushed Burma's outclassed peasant army. The British compelled the defeated Kongbaung to cede all of their southern provinces, including the Irrawaddy delta around Rangoon, and accept what amounted to a British protectorate. Konbaung kings chafed under these terms and flirted with the French in hopes of securing arms and aid. This was the last straw for the exasperated British, who did not want a hostile pro-French state near India. In 1885–86, they launched a third and final military strike against the Burmese, seizing the capital of Mandalay and capturing the Konbaung king, whom they packed off to exile in India. Since they could find no suitably compliant successor, the British abolished the monarchy and incorporated Burma into India. Under British rule, Burma experienced an influx of ethnic Indian immigrants who helped make it a major exporter of rice, teak, and eventually oil.

Chakri kings managed to preserve Thailand's independence thanks to adroit diplomacy and Anglo-French rivalry. Observing the fate of Konbaung Burma and Qing China's defeat in the Opium War, they concluded that accommodating European demands offered the only hope of escaping conquest and colonization. At Britain's insistence, they accepted an Unequal Treaty in 1855 that fully opened Thailand to European trade, merchants, and missionaries. Under King Chulalongkorn (r. 1868–1910), the monarchy took the lead in creating a Western-style state, including a professional bureaucracy, modern army, and European legal system. While peasant and noble resistance forced Chulalongkorn to proceed slowly and cautiously in building this state, his reforms helped convince Europeans that Thailand was endeavoring to become a "civilized" country meriting lenient treatment. But Thailand's political survival depended ultimately on its good fortune in lying at the juncture of the expanding British and French, who agreed to preserve it as a neutral buffer state between their colonial empires. Even so, they stripped it of its Burmese, Laotian, Cambodian, and Malay dependencies.

The formation of "British Malaya" beginning in the 1870s was an unplanned outcome of the convergence of British and Malay interests. In the late 1700s and early 1800s, the India-based British East India Company moved into the Strait of Malacca, establishing footholds in Penang and Singapore. The British aimed to control this choke point in the sea lanes between India and China, and expand their commercial activities in the area. Malay sultans on the peninsula welcomed their presence as a check on both the Thai and the Dutch.

In the mid-1800s, a tin-mining boom in the western part of the peninsula brought the sultans and British closer together. Both profited from this boom and wanted to keep it going. But feuding among ethnic Chinese miners, who entered in large numbers through Singapore, created problems. So, too, did ethnic tensions between Chinese and Malays, and rivalry among sultans. The solution lay in the imposition of overall British political control. The formula employed—the stationing of British "residents" with broad administrative powers at the courts of sultans—replicated arrangements in Indian princely states and proved acceptable to both sides.

The late-nineteenth-century integration of the Indonesian Archipelago into the "Dutch East Indies" was a more contested and protracted process. As the Dutch moved out from their base in Java, they often encountered rulers unwilling to accept their rule. The Balinese and Achenese offered the fiercest resistance. In the 1870s, for example, Aceh declared a holy war (jihad) against the Dutch, beginning a forty-year guerrilla struggle. Even modern weapons and military organization had limits against these tactics, but the Dutch persevered and devised effective countermeasures. Like the British in India, moreover, they benefited from the archipelago's many ethnic rivalries, which enabled them to play off groups against each other and recruit substantial numbers of loyal mercenaries. They employed carrots as well as sticks, offering sultans generous subsidies and respected ceremonial positions in the Dutch-run administration. By the 1880s, they had overcome most resistance and begun exploiting the archipelago's mineral and agricultural riches. The Dutch East Indies, centered on Java and Sumatra, became a major producer of coffee, sugar, rubber, tobacco, and other plantation crops.

Compared to China and Southeast Asia, Korea and Japan offered few economic attractions to European imperialists, who consequently accorded them a lower priority. It fell to the Americans to "open" Tokugawa Japan in the 1850s, employing gunboat diplomacy to force the Tokugawa to accept an Unequal Treaty in 1858. Ten years later, a new government came to power in Japan led by a group of samurai reformers who, like Thailand's King Chulalongkorn, set about creating a European-style state. For reasons examined in later chapters, this government proved highly successful not only in establishing a modern state, but remaking Japan's society and economy on the model of the West, a process well under way by the 1880s. In contrast, Choson Korea continued to resist all contact with Westerners and was not brought under the Unequal Treaty system until 1876. Curiously, Japan, rather than a Western power, imposed this system on Korea, using the same gunboat methods it had earlier experienced at the hands of the Americans. This was an early sign that the modernizing Japanese intended to "join the West" and distance themselves from their Asian neighbors.

East Asian Responses

Even with their invincible armies and navies, Westerners might have found imposing their will on East Asia difficult and costly had they not encountered many willing allies and collaborators. The French move into Indochina, for example, was facilitated by the fact that Cambodian kings and Laotian princes welcomed French protection against the Vietnamese and Thai, whom they regarded as far more dangerous "imperialists." As mentioned above, Malay sultans voluntarily accepted British political control, since it brought law and order and economic prosperity, while leaving them with the trappings of power and control over Malay customary law and matters pertaining to Islam. The Dutch employed the same formula in the Indonesian Archipelago where they also played on long-standing ethnic animosities and rivalries. A united front against the Dutch was never in the cards inasmuch as sultans distrusted and disliked one another more than they resented the Dutch as alien interlopers and "infidels." The British used similar divide-and-rule tactics in Burma, courting "hill tribes" and other ethnic minorities that nurtured traditional grievances against what they perceived to be Burmese oppressors.

East Asians, for their part, attempted to exploit rivalries among European imperialist powers with varying degrees of success. The Thai, for example, played the French against the British in hopes of preventing either from dominating them. The Chinese also practiced divide-and-rule diplomacy which they had long used to break up potentially hostile combinations of nomadic tribes in Inner Asia. Chinese mandarins naturally assumed that it would also be effective against the Western barbarians. In this, however, they were largely disappointed. The Europeans' preference for "cooperative impe- rialism" made it difficult for Beijing to play them off against each other, and their insistence on the "most-favored-nation" principle meant that concessions granted to one had to be extended to all. There were also dangers in invoking the assistance of imperialist power inasmuch as it could be an invitation to a takeover. As the Burmese discovered when they sought French help against the British, moreover, it could backfire by provoking military action by one while the other stood by, seeing the risks of intervention as outweighing the potential gains.

The alternative to diplomacy was armed resistance. Given the Europeans' military superiority, confronting them in set-piece battles with outmoded weapons and organization was a recipe for disaster. Guerrilla warfare might keep alive the flame of resistance, but it could not defeat the Europeans. Moreover, the Dutch, French, and others soon developed effective, albeit brutal "counterinsurgency" methods. Another more promising approach was what the Chinese called "self-strengthening," or appropriating Western weapons and military technology to strengthen the ability of existing states to defend themselves. This approach was appealingly simple and had a long tradition behind it. East Asians had applied it successfully in the sixteenth and seventeenth centuries when they borrowed then state-of-the-art European armaments and used them to hold the Europeans in check. There seemed to be no reason why they could not do so again. In the mid-1800s, Qing China, Tokugawa Japan, Choson Korea, Konbaung Burma, Chakri Thailand, and Nguyen Vietnam all embraced self-strengthening, creating at least rudimentary Western-style armies and navies.

The forces built up by Qing China in the 1870s and 1880s illustrate the limitations of self-strengthening. These forces looked formidable, leading some Western observers to suppose that China was making a comeback as East Asia's superpower. They included a large fleet of steam-powered warships equipped with the latest German-made guns, as well as sizable Western-trained military units armed with repeating rifles and modern artillery. But China's new army and navy performed poorly when put to the test. Problems became apparent during the Sino-French War of 1883–85 when Beijing intervened to try to prevent France's takeover of its Vietnamese tributary state. Although Chinese infantry inflicted heavy casualties on French troops in jungle fighting along the Chinese-Vietnamese frontier, the French navy caught the Chinese southern fleet at anchor and destroyed it virtually without opposition. This debacle foreshadowed an even worse disaster in the Sino-Japanese War of 1894–95 which was fought over Korea. Chinese forces were cut to pieces by the Japanese who had adopted not just Western military forms, but their substance and spirit as well.

Qing China's Western-style armed forces were poorly trained and led, and suffered from pervasive corruption and low morale. These problems arose from the fact that they were set up by powerful regional officials who, while loyal to the Qing and committed to defending China's Confucian system, treated them as their personal creations. They used them as a source of "squeeze" and to provide sinecures for incompetent followers and relatives. This situation reflected the Chinese elite's disdain for the West and its ways. The Qing court and most mandarins were ideologically hostile to Westernization and disinclined to use central government revenues to finance it. True self-strengthening, in their view, was more a matter of Confucian "moral rearmament" than imitating the despised West. They assumed that the Western barbarians, faced by a morally strong and united China, would spontaneously submit or withdraw. Mandarins consequently saw little need to increase the power of the Chinese state beyond the level required to perform its traditional functions of promoting public morality, suppressing "false doctrines," and relieving peasant distress in times of famine and natural disasters.

Resistance to Westernization was common to all East Asian elites. They were not averse to adopting Western weapons and techniques, but only to the extent that these did not interfere with their traditional prerogatives and could be financed by customary methods. Efforts by reformers to set up Western-style centralized governments evoked strong opposition. For example, Thai nobles tried to depose King Chulalongkorn when he attempted to impose such a system in the 1870s, and the Korean elite quashed like-minded reformers in the 1880s. Self-strengthening programs throughout East Asia consequently remained underfunded and superficial, producing only token Westernized forces that European armies and navies brushed aside with ease. These forces were of no help to the kings of Burma and Vietnam when they made their last stands against the British and French in the mid-1880s. Even in the case of Thailand, which Chulalongkorn gradually transformed into a modern state, they were useless in deterring Western exercises in gunboat diplomacy, as in 1893, when a French fleet threatened to level Bangkok unless the Thai agreed to territorial concessions in Laos.

The basic difficulty with self-strengthening was its assumption that Western military techniques could be grafted onto traditional states with minimal changes. In fact, though, the development of effective Western-style armies and navies necessitated radical reforms, beginning with the establishment of modern states. In other words, countering the West militarily required becoming like it politically, socially, economically, and culturally. Most East Asian rulers and elites shrank from this course. They sought to resist the West, not remake themselves and their societies in its image. This dilemma was not, of course, peculiar to East Asians, nor were they unique in electing to go down fighting in defense of the old order. There were several exceptions. Although Thailand remained a tradition-oriented peasant society with a quasi-colonial plantation economy, Chulalongkorn's reforms produced a Western-style state run by a small, Westernized elite. Japan went in a different direction. In the 1870s, it discarded self-strengthening and embraced all-out Westernization under a government that by 1900 had turned it into East Asia's and the non-Western world's first industrialized nation-state.

4

The Development of Nationalism

An unintended consequence of the establishment of European empires in the non-Western world was the rise of indigenous nationalist movements that eventually made these empires untenable at the price Europeans were willing to pay. This was a predictable and perhaps inevitable development. Successful anticolonial nationalist revolts in the Americas in the late eighteenth and early nineteenth centuries showed that European nationalism was "contagious" and could not easily be contained within the framework of colonial rule once it had taken hold. But the spread of nationalism was not automatic or immediate. As pointed out in the previous chapter, the response of East Asian elites to nineteenth-century European imperial encroachments was to strengthen their states by borrowing the West's military technology. Except for the Japanese, few supposed that it might also be necessary to adopt the European idea of the nation. This idea was poorly understood and what was known about it suggested that it was subversive of traditional political and social arrangements. Its eventual triumph consequently came slowly and only in the face of considerable resistance and apathy.

The Idea of the Nation

Nations are taken for granted in today's world. Most people regard them as "givens" akin to natural phenomena or the physical landscape. Few stop to consider where they came from or exactly what they are. Yet nations, like the family, are the focus of strong loyalties and emotional attachments, as is reflected in the phrase "my country, right or wrong." Asked to define a nation, the average person is apt to be at a loss. The usual answer is that it is a collectivity united by ties of religion, language, customs, blood, and history. But these characteristics also define ethnic groups. The question then becomes what differentiates ethnic groups from nations, or are they one and the same? Confronted with this question, many run out of patience. They often reply that nations and ethnic groups may be different but are so closely related that trying to distinguish them smacks of hairsplitting and pedantry. This complaint is not unjustified. As previously suggested, nationality and ethnicity became intertwined in eighteenth- and nineteenth-century Europe, where modern nationalism arose. Still, nations and ethnic groups are distinct, and conflating them is a source of endless confusion and misunderstanding.

To recapitulate points made in the last chapter, modern nations are basically political communities built around universal citizenship, or equal rights and duties for all members regardless of differences in age, gender, wealth, status, race, or even ethnicity. Political communities of this sort existed embryonically in ancient and medieval republics, but citizenship in them was usually restricted to privileged groups. A breakthrough to the ideal of universal citizenship came in the eighteenth century when European Enlightenment thinkers introduced theories of "the social contract," "the Rights of Man," "the General Will," and "popular sovereignty." The political nation was now seen as a body of free and equal citizens, one that theoretically embraced everyone and collectively exercised sovereignty. The next step was the identification of these bodies with ethnic groups that were united by language and other cultural commonalities. The "French nation," for example, was imagined simultaneously as a political community of equal citizens and a cultural community of people who spoke the French language, practiced French customs, and shared a common French history and ancestry.

As the French case illustrates, the new idea of political nationhood was grafted onto ethnic groups, many of which had existed for centuries. Europeans were often strongly attached to these groups. In sixteenth-century Tudor England, for example, many took pride in being "freeborn Englishmen," venerated "Good Queen Bess" as the personification of England, and looked with suspicion on Scots, Irish, French, and other foreigners. But no one in Tudor England imagined it to be a community of free and equal citizens from whom its kings and queens derived their authority to govern. Although the germ of this idea may have existed, it took England's "Glorious Revolution" of 1688 to topple its divine right monarchy and replace it with one beholden to the English "people" acting through Parliament. Even then, England remained essentially an oligarchy dominated by landed aristocrats through the eighteenth century. A move toward full popular sovereignty did not come until the nineteenth century when voting rights were extended to those previously excluded. This process was accomplished in a relatively peaceful and orderly manner in England, but it was more violent elsewhere.

The French Revolution was Europe's first nationalist revolution and the inspiration for a wave of similar if less bloody upheavals in subsequent decades. "Liberty, Equality, and Fraternity" the watchwords of revolutionary France in the 1790s, encapsulate the dynamic behind these upheavals. Hitherto "nonparticipant" subjects became conscious of themselves as free and equal citizens who collectively possessed supreme political authority. For many, particularly those earlier regarded as "rabble," acquiring citizenship rights was a liberating and empowering experience insofar as it put them on par with aristocrats and made them the ultimate arbiters of the fate of kings. The French ideal of "fraternity," or the brotherhood of citizens, was also highly appealing. It lifted people out of their parochial attachments to village, workplace, locality, and status group, and gave them a new identity as members of a larger "national family" in which all citizens held a respected place. For European nationalists, loyalty to this national family took precedence over all other allegiances. At the same time, it imposed heavy demands on them, including the obligation to lay down their lives in its defense.

Unlike the apolitical ethnic groups on which they were based and soon absorbed, Europe's emerging "political nations" posed serious problems for dynastic states, hereditary aristocracies, and absolute monarchs. As noted in the last chapter, nationalists opposed alien rule, demanding to be "masters of our own house." They also challenged royal absolutism and hereditary privilege, which they considered to be an affront to popular sovereignty and citizen equality. It is easy to equate nationalists with liberals, especially since they often made common cause against reactionary regimes and joined in agitating for governments responsive to the popular will. But they were quite different. Liberals viewed representative government as essential to the defense of individual liberties against tyranny. Nationalists, however, were comfortable with dictators like Napoleon, who made himself the "emperor" of revolutionary France. Despots were acceptable to nationalists as long as they embodied the "General Will" and upheld the honor and interests of the nation. Nationalists were, in other words, collectivists for whom the nation, not the individual, was the overriding concern.

The triumph of nationalism in nineteenth-century Europe is partly attributable to publicists and activists such as Johann Herder in Germany and Giuseppe Mazzini in Italy, who sold the idea of the nation through propaganda and agitation. They claimed that Europe was divided into political nations, which, far from being new, had existed from time immemorial and were rooted in ethnic groups bound together by indissoluble ties of blood, language, and history. They imagined these nations as akin to "Sleeping Beauties" that had slumbered for centuries, waiting to be discovered and brought back to life. Skeptics might argue that European ethnic groups had never considered themselves to be nations and, indeed, could not have done so inasmuch as the idea of the political nation was a post-Enlightenment construct of the European intelligentsia. But nationalists were unfazed by such arguments. Drawing on folklore, memory, and history, they invented plausible national traditions and "mytho-histories" that seemed to demonstrate that Poles, Germans, Italians, Czechs, Norwegians, and others were nations-in-waiting. Nationalists urged these peoples to rise and realize their national destinies.

Nationalists could not have gained large followings without rising standards of literacy and the emergence of mass-circulation newspapers, which provided them with a vehicle to disseminate their ideas. The popular press also enlarged the horizons of its readers by acquainting them with happenings on the national, European, and world stages. In addition, the nineteenth-century Transportation Revolution facilitated the growth of a "national consciousness" among Europeans. Steamships, railways, canals, and better roads crisscrossed Europe, knitting together previously isolated regions, and encouraging people to think of themselves as forming larger groups. European states, having co-opted nationalism, began to propagate it both as a means of inspiring loyalty and of "homogenizing" their populations, which were often divided along class and ethnic lines. Kings reinvented themselves as embodiments of nations and claimed to govern in the name of the "people" rather than by divine right as in the past. Military conscription, compulsory schooling, and national elections gave nation-states new instruments to inculcate nationalism and blot out competing loyalties.

East Asian "Proto-Nationalism"

Nationalism was a tougher sell among East Asians. There was little in their history or traditions that prepared them to accept the European idea of the nation as a political community. Few among the elites that confronted the onrushing tide of Western power during the nineteenth century were well enough informed about the West to recognize that its strength was closely linked to nationalism. Fewer still were willing to undertake reforms necessary to implant nationalism in their own societies. Universal citizenship and popular sovereignty were alien and subversive concepts that challenged aristocratic privilege and royal prerogatives. With the important exception of Japan's samurai, moreover, East Asian elites considered the political and social systems over which they presided to be fundamentally sound and in no need of restructuring along Western lines. As pointed out in the previous chapter, they were willing to adopt only those elements of the West's civilizational package that seemed useful in defending these systems and that could be appropriated with minimal disruption. Reformers with broader agendas, like Thailand's King Chulalongkorn, faced an uphill struggle.

East Asian peasants were no less resistant to nationalism. Sun Zhongshan, the father of Chinese nationalism better known as Sun Yat-sen, once

Thailand's King Chulalongkorn.

compared the Chinese people to a "heap of loose sand," meaning that they were incapable of seeing themselves as a nation. Sun's observation applies equally to other East Asian peasantries. Peasant loyalties centered on their families, villages, regions, or ethnic groups. As in pre-national Europe, moreover, peasants played no meaningful role in the governance of realms and rarely concerned themselves with it. They left politics and government

China's Sun Yat-sen.

to kings and elites, asking only to be left alone in their self-contained and self-governing village communities. The European concept of the nation as a body of equal citizens consequently struck them as being both incomprehensible and threatening. The notion that peasants and nobles enjoyed equal political rights and duties seemed preposterous. It challenged the principles of hierarchy and subordination which peasants and elites alike accepted as the foundation of orderly social life. In the view of peasants, it also opened the way for the imposition of unwelcome new burdens and exactions from above.

Although East Asian peasants normally accepted their subordinate position and obeyed directives from their kings, they sometimes erupted onto the political stage in mass movements that can be considered "proto-national" insofar as they were based on ideas and beliefs that in some ways prefigure modern nationalism. The most common were rebellions against rulers whom peasants saw as flouting customary law by levying onerous tax or labor requirements. In Confucian societies, such uprisings were rationalized as "righteous rebellions" against kings or officials perceived to have failed in their duty to provide benevolent government. Chinese peasants also believed that they could legitimately make or unmake dynasties through such rebellions. The Ming dynasty, for example, came to power in the fourteenth century on the back of a large-scale peasant rebellion. The "rights consciousness" underlying these insurrections overlaps with the modern concept of popular sovereignty. But it was different insofar as the protests it inspired were sporadic and ephemeral, and rarely challenged the institution of absolute monarchy, much less the sociopolitical order.

Some peasant rebellions, especially those based on millenarian beliefs drawn from folk religion, were more "revolutionary," seeking to overturn existing social and political structures and create egalitarian utopias. Perhaps the most spectacular example is the Taiping Rebellion in mid-nineteenth century China, touched on in the previous chapter. The Taipings aimed to establish a "heavenly kingdom" founded on the equality of all men and women. To this end, they abolished gender and social distinctions, pooled wealth in communal treasuries, and distributed equal plots of farmland. Not surprisingly, some modern Chinese communists, notably Mao Zedong, saw the Taipings as prefiguring their own movement. Be that as it may, Taiping egalitarianism does seem to echo the Liberty, Equality, and Fraternity of the French Revolution. But the Taipings would not have understood either the patriotism or idea of liberty espoused by citizens of revolutionary France. Like other peasant millenarians, they sought no rights or liberties recognizable as such to Europeans, being intent, rather, on recreating the harmony and togetherness of idealized village communities.

Another type of peasant uprising that foreshadows modern nationalist movements is that inspired by xenophobia, or hatred of foreigners. Nationalists and xenophobes are alike insofar as both seek to defend their groups against threatening aliens. But they conceive of these groups differently. Nationalists uphold nations, that is, sovereign bodies of free and equal citizens. The citizen-soldiers of revolutionary France who rolled back foreign invaders in the 1790s thought of France primarily in these terms. On the other hand, xenophobes protect ethnic or cultural communities. Irish resisters of English invaders from the twelfth through eighteenth centuries were of the latter sort.

However laudable or heroic one might consider Irish or other prenational "resistance fighters" against alien oppressors, they were not nationalists and wishing otherwise does not make them so. True, many Irish viewed Ireland as a political entity that deserved to be independent of English rule. Likewise, some French fought for France as an ethnic community besieged by despised foreigners. But this does not diminish the importance of the contrast between them. The French were basically nationalists while the Irish were not.

Premodern East Asia gave rise to many xenophobic movements directed against other East Asians. Some of these grew out of dynastic quarrels that communicated themselves to ruling elites and eventually to entire ethnic groups. Examples include the feuds between Thai and Burmese, Koreans and Japanese, and Cambodians and Vietnamese. The island habitats of the Indonesian Archipelago were fertile breeding grounds of ethnic rivalries such as those among the neighboring Javanese, Madurese, Makassarese, Buginese (Bugis), and Balinese. Other conflicts arose from different ways of life. As noted in the first chapter, perhaps the most important of these was the cleavage between pastoral nomads and settled agriculturalists. But there were others. "Hill tribes," or tribal groups practicing slash-and-burn agriculture in the mountains of mainland Southeast Asia, like the Hmong in Laos, Kachins in Burma, and Montagnards in Vietnam, were at odds with lowland rice farmers. Chinese immigrants in Southeast Asia who specialized in trade sometimes became the targets of pogroms not unlike those directed against Jewish communities in late medieval Europe.

Prior to the nineteenth century, Europeans were rarely objects of popular xenophobia. They were few in number, ensconced in fortified enclaves, and largely restricted their activities to trade. One notable exception was Tokugawa Japan's extirpation of Christianity and expulsion of Catholic missionaries in the early 1600s. This was less a popular movement than a deliberate act of policy by Tokugawa shoguns who aimed to insulate Japan from what they considered to be divisive European influences. The Tokugawa exclusion edicts and proscription of Christianity implanted strong anti-Western sentiment among the samurai, though not among Japanese peasants, for whom Westerners were curiosities. The Muslim *moros* in the southern Philippines, as the Spanish called them, waged a holy war with broad popular support against the invading Spanish conquistadors. Beginning in the late sixteenth century, the *moros* rallied behind their sultans to defend their religion, lands, and identity. Unlike their present-day successors, however, they were not conscious of fighting a "war of national liberation" and, indeed, would not have understood the meaning of this phrase.

The *moros'* intermittent war against their would-be Spanish colonizers was the prototype for similar anti-European resistance movements that sprang up in some parts of East Asia during the nineteenth century as European imperialists stepped up their encroachments. Many of these movements were built around the idea of expelling Western intruders and restoring indigenous rulers to power. Examples include the 1825–30 Java War and the longer Aceh War, which began in 1873 and dragged on into the early 1900s. Restorationist revolts, led by elements of the traditional elite, also broke out in Burma and Vietnam after the British and French takeovers in the mid-1880s. The Dutch, British, and French eventually quashed these uprisings with a combination of repression and conciliation. They were aided by the fact that most monarchist rebels, outgunned, disorganized, and demoralized, simply gave up. But the equation of the defunct monarchy with a lost pre-European "golden age" persisted among Burmese peasants, inspiring the 1930 Saya San uprising led by a former Buddhist monk who claimed to be divinely empowered to drive out the British and make himself king.

By far the most spectacular eruption of mass anti-Western feeling in East Asia was the 1899–1900 Boxer Rebellion in China, which involved massacres of European missionaries and their Christian converts in northern China and the siege of Western diplomats in Beijing. This uprising grew out of the long-simmering resentment of Chinese peasants toward Christian missionaries, who the peasants felt were undermining their folk religion and the harmony and integrity of their village communities. The Boxers, a traditional antidynastic secret society that specialized in Taoist immortality rituals, provided a loose organizational framework for this resentment. The Boxers at first called for the overthrow of the Qing, but soon shifted to the slogan "Support the Qing, Destroy the Foreigners." This turnabout resulted from the decision of reactionaries at the Qing court to back the Boxers in hopes of using them to compel Westerners to quit China. In the event, the Boxers melted away before an avenging Western multinational expeditionary force. The failure of their uprising marked the beginning of the end both for the Qing dynasty and, as it turned out, China's millennia-old Confucian system.

Japanese Nationalism

Xenophobia did not necessarily lead to nationalism in East Asia or elsewhere. Indeed, xenophobes typically resisted nationalism because, as a Western ideology, adopting it meant in effect selling out to the enemy. Nevertheless, some overcame this obstacle by accepting the necessity to become "like Westerners" as the price of survival in a Western-dominated world. Emulating an adversary that otherwise could not be resisted might seem an obvious and inevitable solution to the problem posed by the West's overwhelming power. As previously noted, however, most East Asian ruling classes were understandably averse to following this course. The Western idea of the nation as a sovereign body of equal citizens challenged these elites' privileged position and required them to accept lowly peasants as political equals. Nationalism, in other words, meant their own elimination and the overturning of hierarchy and subordination, which they equated with the natural order. Not surprisingly, they recoiled from this prospect, opting instead to try to prop up their traditional states with Western guns even though it soon became apparent that this expedient would not save them.

The chief exception was Japan's samurai, who during the 1860s converted themselves from violent anti-Western xenophobes into ardent nationalists. Why and how did this metamorphosis occur? At first glance, it is difficult to imagine a more inhospitable setting for the embrace of the Western idea of the nation than Tokugawa Japan. Under Japan's Seclusion Policy, contact with Westerners was banned and intruding Western ships were routinely driven off with gunfire. Xenophobia was not just official policy; fear and loathing of Westerners, or "Southern Barbarians" as they were called, were widespread among samurai, in part because of their association with Christianity, which samurai perceived as a deadly threat. Moreover, Tokugawa Japan seemed to have little political unity, being divided into several hundred autonomous feudal domains that maintained their own armies and bureaucracies, and competed with one another economically. Such unity as Japan had derived was from the Tokugawa shogun, who functioned as a kind of feudal primus inter pares, and the shadowy and secluded figure of the emperor in Kyoto who held ultimate authority but no power.

This picture of disunity and hostility to the West is, however, in some ways misleading. As suggested in a previous chapter, the primary allegiance of late-Tokugawa samurai had shifted from their domains and lords to emperor and country, making it natural for them to see Japan as a unified realm governed directly by the emperor without the aid of feudal intermediaries. Moreover, reverence for the emperor, or imperial loyalism, was something of a cult among many samurai, stimulated by a nativist reaction against the overwhelming cultural prestige of China. The flip side of loyalism was dissatisfaction with the feudal system, which impoverished lower-ranking samurai and denied them opportunities for advancement. Although this dissatisfaction was held in check by the military discipline of samurai, the potential for disaffection or even rebellion existed. Furthermore, samurai were well enough informed about the West to understand that Japan had fallen far behind it technologically and was in mortal danger. This knowledge was widely available because Tokugawa Japan was the only East Asian country that officially subsidized the study of the West.

The forced opening of Japan by the Americans in the 1850s triggered a samurai revolt against the Tokugawa that culminated in the overthrow of the shogunate and the restoration of direct imperial rule. Samurai loyalists were outraged by the decision of the Tokugawa to bow to American demands and allow the hated Southern Barbarians entry into Japan. In their view, the Tokugawa had forfeited all claims to loyalty by failing to defend the emperor and his "divine land." Under the slogan "Revere the Emperor, Expel the Barbarians," they took matters into their own hands by assassinating Tokugawa officials and Western diplomats. Imperial loyalists also plotted the overthrow of the shogunate and the return of power to the emperor. In the 1860s, they found allies among several large feudal domains in southwestern Japan that nurtured longstanding grudges against the Tokugawa and welcomed the opportunity to oust them. Backed by the military forces of these domains, the samurai loyalists prepared for civil war against the Tokugawa shogun and his supporters. They also used these forces to step up their attacks on Westerners, including bombarding Western ships entering Japanese waters.

In the mid-1860s, the aim of anti-Tokugawa activists shifted from expelling Westerners to learning from them. Erstwhile samurai xenophobes were impressed by demonstrations of the West's military might, such as the leveling of a Japanese city by Western warships, which convinced them of the futility of further armed resistance and the necessity of discovering the secrets of its wealth and power. Travel and study in European countries and contact in Japan with Western missionaries, teachers, and diplomats revealed to them that the West's military prowess was built on novel political, economic, and social arrangements, including nation-states and nationalism. They resolved to appropriate and replicate these in Japan even if it meant jettisoning their feudal system and its hierarchy of hereditary social classes. In contrast with other East Asian elites, they were willing to tread this revolutionary path because they were not wedded to their system and considered it expendable. What mattered to them was defending the emperor and his divine land, and they were prepared to resort to any and all means to this end. In their view, the top priority was transforming Japan into a Western-style nation-state.

In 1868, they seized power following a brief civil war with the Tokugawa and proclaimed the restoration of direct imperial rule after a thousand-year hiatus. The emperor, a boy of sixteen, moved from Kyoto to Edo, now renamed Tokyo, and took up residence in the shogun's former castle at its center. Like his predecessors, he took a Chinese-style reign name, which in his case was Meiji, or "enlightened rule." The Meiji Restoration, as this political change is known, was not what it seemed to be insofar as the emperor was not the real decision maker in the new government. His role, rather, was to legitimize policies worked out by his advisors, a group of several dozen lower-ranking and relatively young samurai who had engineered the overthrow of the Tokugawa.

Japan's Emperor Meiji in 1873.

Backed by the military forces of the southwestern domains, this group set about remaking Japan into a nation-state on the model of what they took to be the most advanced Western countries of the day—Britain, France, the United States, and Germany, which was unified by Prussia in 1871. This course was dictated less by their liking or admiration for the West than by the imperative of national survival in a Western-run world and their determination to free Japan from the stigma of inferiority symbolized by the Unequal Treaties.

Their first and most important task was building a strong central government, without which nothing else could be achieved. This required abolishing

Japan's feudal system and centralizing power in Tokyo. Feudal lords, most of whom had long been bankrupt, offered no resistance to the Meiji government's demand that they hand over their domains to the emperor, especially since they were rewarded with generous pensions. Getting rid of the samurai class posed a more serious problem. Pensioning them off like their former lords was not an option, since they were far too numerous. On the other hand, the government could not afford to continue to subsidize them in idleness, and their military skills were obsolete. The only solution, adopted in the mid-1870s, was to cut them adrift with small severance payments in the form of bonds. Some ex-samurai found employment in the army, police, civil service, schools, and other Western-style institutions that the government was setting up. But many did not, becoming farmers, merchants or even clerks. Although individual families took pride in their samurai heritage, the samurai disappeared as a social class within just a few years.

The abolition of the traditional ruling class was perhaps the Meiji government's most revolutionary step. This would have been unthinkable elsewhere in East Asia, where it would have provoked civil war and the probable overthrow of the government. As it was, this move split the Meiji leadership group and triggered sporadic revolts by disgruntled samurai, the last and most serious of which was the 1877 Satsuma Rebellion. But the government's new peasant conscript army crushed this "last stand," ending further challenges to its authority. What is most noteworthy about samurai rebellions is that they were not larger and more determined. Part of the explanation lies in the fact that few samurai were committed to preserving a system that had reduced many of them to penury in late-Tokugawa times. Still, samurai values such as honor, pride, and "face" might be expected to have generated stronger resistance. That they did not do so is largely attributable to their loyalty to emperor and country. The emperor appeared to favor stripping them of their privileges for the "good of the country." Most samurai therefore raised no objection and stoically accepted their fate.

Although the samurai faded away, their loyalist ideology and martial ethos lived on, becoming the basis of the Meiji leaders' attempt to turn Japanese peasants into loyal citizens of the new nation-state they were building. This attempt faced formidable difficulties. In contrast to samurai, late-Tokugawa peasants were largely unconcerned by the intrusion of Westerners, and felt no loyalty to the emperor and the "divine land" he embodied. Having never seen Europeans and knowing nothing about them, peasants regarded them as nonthreatening but bizarre creatures akin to space aliens. Peasants did not know who the emperor was or what he represented, but since samurai venerated him, they assumed that he must be a human incarnation of an unusually potent folk deity similar to those they worshipped in their Shinto rituals and festivals. They watched as curious but disinterested spectators the momentous happenings of the 1850s and 1860s, including the arrival of U.S. warships in 1853, the antiforeign activities of samurai zealots, the punitive bombardments of Japanese cities by Western fleets, and the overthrow of the Tokugawa in the civil war of 1867–68.

In the first years of the 1868–1912 Meiji era, many peasants wanted no part of Japan's emerging nation-state. They were bewildered by the government's abolition of traditional class distinctions and announcement that all were now equal before the law. Moreover, they resented Tokyo's interference in their village affairs and resisted its demands for new taxes and obedience to national laws. The 1870s were consequently punctuated by peasant riots much like those of the late Tokugawa period. Gradually, though, the Meiji government attracted peasant support and loyalty. As in Europe, military conscription and compulsory education provided indispensable tools of indoctrination. But other factors also promoted the development of a national consciousness. The abolition of feudal jurisdictions and elimination of restrictions on travel and residence enabled peasants to see themselves as part of a national community. Already relatively literate in late Tokugawa times, peasants became avid readers of Western-style newspapers that sprang up throughout the country and brought them in touch with national and international developments. By the 1880s, mass nationalism had begun to take hold in Japan.

Chinese Nationalism

While Meiji Japan remade itself into a Western-style nation-state in the 1870s and 1880s, Qing China remained committed to preserving and, in fact, strengthening its Confucian system of government. Despite defeats by the West in the Opium Wars and the imposition of the nettlesome and humiliating Unequal Treaty system, the mandarin elite regarded these as mere pinpricks compared to the near-death experience China's traditional sociopolitical order had undergone at the hands of the Taipings and other rebels. For mandarins, the top priority was restoring Confucian government to its former vigor so that such rebellions would not recur. If this could be done, they reasoned, the problem posed by the West would take care of itself and Westerners would eventually resume their proper place as respectful tributaries of the Son of Heaven. In the meantime, they supposed that China could control the West by adopting its weapons and diplomatic practices, including its notions of international law. But the Qing court and most mandarins accepted even limited Westernization grudgingly and looked upon those who strongly advocated this course with suspicion.

As suggested in the previous chapter, the impetus for self-strengthening or military modernization came primarily from powerful regional officials who built up political-military machines based on cliques of local gentry, merchants, and soldiers who were personally loyal to them. These figures were not nationalist reformers. Unlike the leaders of Meiji Japan, they did not accept the need to remake China into a nation-state, nor did they seek to mobilize China's politically inert peasant masses behind the idea of the nation. Their aims, rather, were to protect the dynasty and the existing order and to enhance their personal power within it. They perceived no contradiction between these goals, and there seemed to be none inasmuch as they followed orders from Beijing and were deferential to the emperor. However, the development of quasi-autonomous regional satrapies with what amounted to private armies and navies spelled future trouble. Political-military power was devolving from the center to the provinces and Beijing was losing control. Late-Qing China was, in other words, gradually falling apart and the seeds of what later would be called warlordism were sprouting.

Self-strengthening produced military forces that were effective against domestic rebels but no match for Western armies and navies. This had become apparent in the Sino-French War of 1883–85, but the clincher was China's lopsided defeat at the hands of Japan in 1894–95. Mandarins were shocked and dismayed. It was one thing to be vanquished by a major European power but quite another to be humiliated on the battlefield by a small neighboring country that Chinese had always viewed as culturally inferior. To make matters worse, the revelation of China's military impotence set in motion a "Scramble for Concessions" by the Europeans imperialist powers, who proceeded to carve up the country into spheres of influence based on leased territories and exclusive economic concessions. The Russians moved into Manchuria, the British staked out central China, the French wanted southern China as their preserve, and the Japanese, having seized Taiwan, eyed Fujian Province across the Taiwan Strait as their sphere. In the late 1890s, it seemed only a matter of time before the imperialists converted these spheres of influence into outright colonies or protectorates.

In this crisis, mandarins cast about for new approaches. In 1898, a small group of Westernized officials won the support of the emperor for an attempt at top-down reform based on the model of Meiji Japan. But this "Hundred Days' Reform" was quashed by reactionaries. As noted above, the latter then tried to use the Boxer Rebellion to drive the Western imperialists out of China, with disastrous results. China's demoralized and discredited mandarins now came to the realization that the ancien régime could not be saved. They offered no resistance to a last-ditch effort by the Qing in the early 1900s to convert the empire into a Western-style nation-state. The Qing abolished the Confucian examination system and replaced mandarins with Western-trained bureaucrats. They also set up elected provincial assemblies and, following the lead of Meiji Japan, sought to reinvent themselves as a constitutional monarchy. But it was too late. The provincial gentry had lost confidence in the monarchy and were attracted to republican ideas spread by anti-Manchu Chinese nationalists. No one rallied to the dynasty's defense when it was toppled by a series of military mutinies in 1911.

The Chinese Revolution of 1911 and the subsequent proclamation of a republic marked the triumph of nationalism in China. The Chinese elite embraced the idea that China should be a nation-state with a republican form of government. But nationalists were divided, disorganized, and lacked broad support. The most prominent of them, Sun Yat-sen, was a Western-trained medical doctor who drew his backing mainly from Overseas Chinese. Realizing that Sun and other nationalist politicians were too weak to govern, provincial army commanders shunted them aside and set up autonomous regimes based on their private armies. Although a nominal central government functioned in Beijing and the ideal of national unity was never abandoned, these "warlords," the heirs of the regional bosses of the self-strengthening period, became the real rulers of Republican China for the next sixteen years. As China fell into warlord anarchy, the outlying parts of the Qing Empire—Mongolia, Tibet, and Manchuria—spun out of Chinese control and passed under the influence, respectively, of Russia, Britain, and Japan. Japanese imperialist encroachments on China continued and intensified during World War I.

Sun Yat-sen's main goal was to reunify China under an effective central government. To this end, he established the Guomindang, or National People's Party, and sought help from friendly warlords and sympathetic foreign powers. But warlords proved unreliable and no assistance was forthcoming from the West or Japan. In the event, only the Soviet Union offered aid, seeing Sun's "bourgeois nationalist" movement as a stepping-stone to an eventual Communist takeover of China. Although Sun never became a Communist, he formed an alliance with the Soviets in the early 1920s under which he received Soviet money, arms, advisors, and the backing of the tiny Chinese Communist Party. With Soviet help, he rebuilt the Guomindang on the model of the Russian Bolshevik Party with its own military force. Sun died in 1925 before the party-building process was complete. But his successor, Chiang Kai-shek (Jiang Jieshi), led the Guomindang in a "Northern Expedition" in 1926–28 that resulted in the establishment of a new national government in Nanjing. Even then, national unity remained elusive, since Chiang broke with the Communists, who began a peasant-based guerrilla insurrection.

Anti-Colonial Nationalism

In most Southeast Asia countries—Burma, Vietnam, Laos, Cambodia, Malaya, Indonesia, and the Philippines—nationalism evolved in opposition to

Western colonial regimes. The general pattern was similar to the earlier rise of anticolonial nationalist movements in the Americas. Although colonial governments were almost always hostile to these movements and tried to suppress them, they unwittingly created conditions that favored nationalists. Europeans, a small minority, needed help in running their colonies, including policemen, schoolteachers, engineers, and other specialists. These could only come from "natives," who made up new Westernized elites that inevitably acquired the tastes, values, and ideas of their colonial masters, including nationalism. Indigenous nationalists, harried by colonial police and alienated from the traditional societies around them, often found it difficult to attract mass followings. In many cases, however, "colonial modernization" implanted a wider receptivity to nationalism by promoting literacy and a popular press, unifying people under uniform administrative and legal systems, and drawing them together through improved transportation and communications.

The Spanish Philippines offers an early example. By the 1870s, 300 years of Spanish colonial rule had produced an Hispanicized elite, the *ilustrados* (enlightened ones). Although of mixed Spanish, Malay, and Chinese ancestry, this elite saw itself as "Filipino" and, influenced by Spanish nationalism, as the leaders of an emerging Filipino nation that deserved self-rule. *Ilustrado* appeals for mass support struck a chord with peasants who were also beginning to define themselves as Filipinos, thanks to the homogenizing effects of Christian proselytization, a uniform Spanish colonial administration, and the spread of plantation agriculture, especially sugar production. José Rizal, the central figure in *ilustrado* agitation, died a martyr's death at the hands of the Spanish colonial authorities in 1896, triggering East Asia's first anticolonial nationalist revolt. U.S. intervention flowing from the Spanish-American War of 1898 enabled Filipino nationalists to declare a Philippine Republic. But this republic was crushed in 1901 by the United States, which decided that the Philippines was not ready for independence and required a lengthy period of colonial tutelage in American-style democracy.

Westernized elites emerged later elsewhere in Southeast Asia, where the imposition of European colonial rule was more recent. By the early 1900s, however, they appeared in Burma, Vietnam, and Indonesia, and began to agitate for the revival of traditional values and belief systems that seemed to be threatened by Westernization. In the Dutch East Indies, for example, the Sarekat Islam (Islamic unity) movement, founded in 1912, quickly attracted several million followers by promising a solution to local discontents through the revival of Muslim piety and unity. In Burma, the Young Men's Buddhist Association, established in Rangoon in 1906 on the model of the Young Men's Christian Association, pursued similar revivalist goals in the context of Therevada Buddhism. In Vietnam, intellectuals extolled Vietnam's cultural and

José Rizal of the Philippines.

historical traditions in hopes of bolstering Vietnamese pride and identity in the face of Gallicization. Although some of these movements called for self-rule, colonial authorities generally tolerated them, since their preoccupations were educational and cultural rather than political, and they lacked a clearly defined conception of the nation.

In the 1920s, overtly nationalist movements came to the fore in Vietnam, Burma, and Indonesia. These were composed of a new generation of West-ernized students, many educated in Europe, who demanded national inde-pendence. Indonesia's Sukarno, a Dutch-trained engineer who became the leader of the Indonesian Nationalist Association (PNI) in 1927, was typical. He assumed that the artificially constructed Dutch East Indies embodied a timeless Indonesian nation—"one land, one people, one language"—that was crying out for liberation from Dutch oppression. The expression of such views brought him to the attention of the Dutch colonial police, who soon jailed him and many of his followers. Vietnamese nationalists met the same fate. But police repression was not the only problem faced by Vietnamese, Burmese, and Indonesian nationalists. They were relatively few in number, poorly organized, and ideologically divided. Communists feuded with noncommunists, gradualists vied with proponents of "direct action," and secularists tilted with those who believed that Islam or Theravada Buddhism should serve as the foundation of national identity and unity.

In Vietnam, non-Communist nationalists influenced by China's Guomindang were virtually wiped out by the French after they attempted a popular uprising in the late 1920s. This left the field to a handful of Communists led by Ho Chi Minh, a veteran activist in the Soviet-backed "Comintern" (Communist International) who established the Indochina Communist Party in 1930. In Indonesia, on the other hand, Sukarno's non-Communists dominated the nationalist movement after their Communist rivals were decimated in an unsuccessful insurrection against the Dutch. However, neither Ho nor Sukarno posed a serious threat to the Dutch and French inasmuch as the parties they headed lacked both a mass following and the means to acquire one. The same was true of Burmese nationalists, who were even more fragmented and ideologically diverse than their Indonesian and Vietnamese counterparts. The British co-opted many of them in the 1920s by offering limited self-rule under a dual government arrangement modeled on British India, in which a popularly elected assembly shared power with the British-appointed governor. The Americans set up a similar system in the Philippines.

There were few stirrings of nationalism in Laos, Cambodia, and Malaya. In contrast to their heavy-handed behavior elsewhere, the British and French trod gingerly in these dependencies, leaving the authority of traditional rulers largely intact, avoiding interference in local customs, and limiting disruptive commercial activities. In Malaya, the British oversaw the development of rubber plantations and tin mining, but these operations relied on imported Chinese and Indian labor, and did not directly impact Malay villagers. For the majority of Malayans, Laotians, and Cambodians, life under the British and French went on much as before. Although small Western-educated elites emerged, they viewed European overlordship as a source of stability and security rather than an infringement of their national rights. Indeed, the idea that there were Malayan, Cambodian, and Laotian "nations" to defend made little headway among these elites, perhaps because it was so clearly at odds with the tradition-bound societies around them. The nondevelopment of nationalism in these colonial settings is a reminder that there was nothing automatic about the triumph of the national idea in East Asia.

Thai and Korean Nationalism

Thailand resembles Meiji Japan insofar as it remained independent and underwent top-down modernization under royal auspices. In fact, however, Thailand's experience is closer to the colonial pattern in that nationalism developed there first among a small Westernized elite and only gradually spread to the rest of the population. King Chulalongkorn, Thailand's "modernizing monarch," did not have the power to implement anything like the Meiji political revolution of the 1870s and 1880s. The royal government he inherited in 1868 was dominated by a landowning nobility averse to changes that would undermine its control over the peasantry and provincial administration. Under these circumstances, Chulalongkorn had to proceed slowly and cautiously in building a strong central government staffed by Western-trained bureaucrats loyal to himself. His chief allies in this project were members of his own family, royal princes who traveled and studied abroad in search of foreign models and oversaw their adaptation. The models most appropriate to Thailand's needs were those offered not by Europe or Meiji Japan, but by neighboring colonies such as British Burma and French Vietnam.

By the time of Chulalongkorn's death in 1910, Thailand had become an absolute monarchy presiding over a Western-style central government that exercised effective control over the hinterland. As in nearby colonies, nationalism was restricted to a tiny Westernized elite dominated by army officers and civil servants who were concentrated in Bangkok. In contrast to colonial nationalists, this elite was concerned with the question of who should control the national government, and many were dissatisfied with the royal absolutism created by Chulalongkorn. Under his less able successors, their discontent exploded in a 1932 coup that converted Thailand into a constitutional monarchy run by competing bureaucratic and military factions. Thai peasants were largely indifferent to these events. They remained innocent of any conception of national citizenship and did not see themselves as participants in the political affairs of the realm. They continued to look upon their kings as semi-divine beings who ensured cosmic harmony and embodied Thai ethnic identity. Only a few had begun to view the monarchy as the unifying symbol of a Thai nation-state composed of equal citizens.

Korean nationalism developed partly in response to Japanese colonial rule and partly from precolonial roots. As in Qing China, Korea's reactionary yangban ruling group blocked attempts by reformers to make the Choson monarchy a vehicle for change until it was too late to avert Japanese annexation in 1910. Reforms by the Seoul government were limited to halfhearted military self-strengthening, which failed to provide it with an effective Western-style army. Peasant unrest continued, combining anti-foreignism, resentment of tax burdens, and Taiping-style millenarian hopes for the inauguration of a paradise on earth. Nevertheless, the quarter-century prior to annexation saw important social and political changes, perhaps the most significant of which was the emergence of a new Western-educated elite. Western missionaries, especially American Protestants, played a major role in creating this elite by establishing schools and newspapers. Many of Korea's early nationalists such as Syngman Rhee (Yi Sung Man), who became the first president of the Republic of Korea in 1948, were products of this educational ferment and looked to the United States for encouragement and support.

Japanese colonizers aimed to transform Koreans into loyal but subordinate Japanese. This assimilationist goal did not differentiate them from other colonialists, but the vigor with which they pursued it was unusual, extending eventually to the banning of the Korean language and the requirement that Koreans assume Japanese names. Yet even mass indoctrination and police state controls failed to eradicate Koreans' belief that they formed a separate nation. Indeed, the more Japan tried to "Japanize" Koreans, the less inclined they were to accept it, at least inwardly. The dual legacy of Japanese colonialism in Korea was intense Japanophobia combined with an equally strong but unacknowledged tendency to regard Japanese as exemplars of modernity. This contrasts with the response of the Taiwanese. Japan had seized this island province of China in 1895, well before Chinese nationalism had begun to take hold. Taiwanese consequently put up little resistance to Japanization and, in fact, embraced it. Even today, many continue to see Japan in a favorable light, much to Beijing's annoyance.

5

The Rise of Imperial Japan

The most important geopolitical event in East Asia at the end of the nineteenth century and beginning of the twentieth was Japan's replacement of the collapsing Chinese Empire as the region's leading Asian power. Japan's rise was the result of the success of Meiji leaders in remaking their country on the model of the West. In the pursuit of this goal, they created virtually from scratch an industrial economy unparalleled elsewhere in East Asia and, indeed, the non-Western world. At the same time, they turned the improvised imperial government of the 1870s into a Western-style constitutional monarchy and nascent parliamentary democracy. In addition, they developed a powerful army and navy, which they employed to build a colonial empire in Northeast Asia through victorious wars against China in 1894–95 and Russia in 1904–5. Supported by most Japanese, the Meiji leadership gained admission to the Western imperialist club and "quit Asia" culturally and psychologically. By the end of the Meiji era in 1912, however, some Japanese were beginning to have misgivings about their identification with the West and the costs of Japan's headlong rush to modernity.

Meiji Modernization

Why did the Japanese, alone among East Asians, succeed in transforming themselves into a modern industrial and military power in the late 1800s? Some explanations favor cultural factors, such as their tradition of borrowing from more advanced countries, specifically China. However, this tradition does not differentiate them from the Koreans and Vietnamese, who also borrowed from China but were just as reluctant as the Chinese to emulate the Western model. Other interpretations emphasize contingencies such as Japan's good fortune in escaping colonization by the Western imperialists, and having unusually able and farsighted leadership at a critical juncture in its history. These contingencies are no doubt important, but they leave unanswered the larger question of why the Japanese as a people embraced Westernization. As suggested in previous chapters, the late-Tokugawa setting offers some clues. It is surely important, for example, that the samurai were predisposed to accept nationalism and jettison feudalism. Likewise, Meiji industrialization has its roots in the responsiveness of the late-Tokugawa economy to market incentives and the widespread diffusion of an "achievement ethic."

Notwithstanding such predisposing factors, the Meiji transformation was a revolution that involved wrenching and painful changes. It should not be supposed that the Japanese have any special propensity for such revolutions. For much of their history, they were content to remain secluded in their offshore islands, selectively adopting continental models and maintaining an evolutionary pace of change. Despite its internal contradictions, the Tokugawa system probably would have survived indefinitely had the West's sudden and forceful intrusion not created what the Japanese perceived to be a national crisis. The Meiji revolution was driven by this "crisis mentality" or sense of imminent external danger. Another psychological driver of radical change was shame. Many Meiji-era Japanese genuinely admired the West's civilization and considered it superior to their own. But their wholesale importation of Western institutions, customs, and ideas was prompted primarily by their desire to escape the taint of inferiority that they associated with the Unequal Treaties. Meiji modernization was ultimately about catching up with Westerners and beating them at their own game.

"Westernization" can be a misleading term to describe Meiji Japan's transformation insofar as it implies that the Japanese were passive and uncritical imitators of the West who brought nothing to the table. The reality was quite different. The Meiji government initiated and controlled the borrowing process, dispatching official "learning missions," carefully choosing Western "best practices," and rejecting models it deemed unsuitable or irrelevant. Moreover, it demonstrated considerable ingenuity in adapting traditional institutions and beliefs to modern purposes. Mention has already been made of the government's use of the samurai warrior code and loyalist ideology as the basis of mass nationalism. Another example is its refurbishing of Japan's ancient Shinto monarchy to serve as the unifying symbol of the modern Japanese nation-state. While this involved converting the emperor into a European-style king, Meiji leaders judged that a secular monarch like those of Europe would not elicit sufficient popular fervor. They therefore drew on Shinto folk religion to construct a new state religion aimed at endowing the emperor with the attributes of a transcendent "god-king."

The government's use of a traditional symbol, the monarchy, to sanction radical change gave Japan's march toward Western-defined modernity a "back to the future" character. Meiji leaders assiduously fostered the myth that the emperor's "restoration" represented a return to antiquity and recovery of Japan's indigenous roots. To this end, they revived ancient court titles and offices in the early 1870s. Although they soon dispensed with these expedients, their introduction of State Shinto lent credence to the notion that Japan was moving back in time to a prefeudal utopia in which a single, undifferentiated people had been united in reverence for their priest-king. This notion was a caricature of historical reality inasmuch as Japan's sixth-century monarch had been a primus inter pares among contending warrior-aristocrats who had their own tribal cults. But the restoration myth proved quite useful to Meiji modernizers. It sanctioned their abolition of feudalism as an alien system that had usurped the emperor's prerogatives and introduced disruptive class divisions. It also helped parry opposition to Westernization by portraying it as necessary to strengthen the foundations of imperial rule.

Not everyone in Meiji Japan bought into the government's restoration myth. Westernized intellectuals were put off by "primitive" Shinto superstitions that were invoked to sanctify the emperor, such as the idea that he was the divine descendent of the Sun Goddess. But these intellectuals were few in number and kept their views to themselves for fear of inviting ostracism or worse. The Education Minister was assassinated in 1889 for making light of the emperor's divinity. At the opposite end of the ideological spectrum were unreconciled nativists who believed that a pro-Western elite had hijacked the Meiji Restoration and misled the emperor into sanctioning a sellout to Westerners and their ways. Mostly embittered ex-samurai who were unwilling or unable to fit into the rapidly changing society around them, they called for another, "true" restoration to sweep away this elite and the corrupting Western influences. Although their call for an anti-Western restoration would later prove hugely appealing, it attracted little support during the Meiji era, and the government did not consider nativists a threat. Indeed, their patriotism and loyalism earned them toleration and even a measure of respect.

Constitutional Government

A more serious challenge to the Meiji government was the "Freedom and People's Rights Movement," which mounted nationwide demonstrations in the late 1870s and 1880s demanding the establishment of a constitution and parliament along the lines of those of Britain and France. This movement was inspired by European liberal thought as expounded by such figures as John Stuart Mill, which was imported into Japan in its rush to embrace Western "Civilization and Enlightenment" during the 1870s. Some People's Rights advocates called for popular sovereignty and cabinets responsible to an elected national assembly. Others envisioned power-sharing arrangements between the emperor and people. All, however, denounced Japan's existing political setup as "clique government" under which ex-samurai from several large former domains in the southwest monopolized power in the name of the emperor. The People's Rights movement was "modern" in its methods and organization, relying on the techniques of print journalism and mass rallies, and basing itself on Western-style political parties with dues-paying members, party platforms, and a national organization.

The two principal People's Rights parties, the Liberals and the Progressives, drew their membership from disaffected ex-samurai, an emerging Westernized elite in the cities, and rural landlords and entrepreneurs who considered themselves unfairly saddled with the burden of paying for Japan's modernization through high land taxes. The leaders of these parties were former members of the governing group who had broken with their colleagues over policy issues or personal rivalries. When offered suitable inducements to rejoin the government, they usually did so, creating the impression that the parties were little more than tools of the "outs" to pressure the "ins" for readmission to the ruling circle. But this is an oversimplification. The parties derived their élan and grass-roots appeal from the diffusion of the idea of citizenship, which was part and parcel of the nation-state ideal that Japan had imported from the West. Allied with peasant economic grievances, this idea had an explosive political potential, as was demonstrated by the 1884 Chichibu Rebellion near Tokyo, in which peasants shouting People's Rights slogans attacked government offices and had to be put down by army troops.

It would be a mistake to suppose that Japan was teetering on the edge of a political revolution from below in the 1880s. The Chichibu Rebellion was an isolated event. The parties were narrowly based and quarreled with each other as much as they did with the government. The latter used the police and "peace preservation" laws to limit their ability to organize and agitate. Moreover, the parties were ambivalent in their commitment to People's Rights. The imperial cult, propagated by mass indoctrination and State Shinto, was beginning to take hold of the popular imagination, inspiring increasing reverence for the emperor and the government he headed. Earlier calls for popular sovereignty were replaced by a growing consensus that the sacrosanct authority of Japan's god-king could not be limited. Advocates of People's Rights now had to justify constitutional and representative government on the grounds that it supposedly reflected the emperor's true wishes. The Western liberal idea that such government flowed from the will of the people and was essential to protect individual liberties against encroachments by the state was effectively abandoned.

The fading of Western liberalism was facilitated by the fact that virtually everyone in Meiji Japan was a fervent nationalist. Those who valued individual liberties over the claims of the nation were few and far between, being restricted mainly to a handful of Christians. Even "liberals" tended to be jingoists and often put themselves at the forefront of demands for a hard line against foreign slights and insults. Moreover, many favored constitutional government primarily as a means to unify the nation. In this, they were of one mind with the Meiji leaders who saw constitutional monarchy as an essential feature of the advanced Western countries that Japan aspired to join, and a device to help convince Westerners to dispense with the humiliating Unequal Treaties. The problem was selecting a form of constitutionalism that would satisfy the West without doing violence to Japan's unique emperor-centered polity. In the event, the Meiji leaders rejected the Anglo-French democratic model in favor of the more authoritarian constitution of Imperial Germany, which concentrated power in the hands of the emperor and his officials and severely limited the role of a popularly elected parliament.

The Meiji constitution of 1889 was not a liberal document, but it earned the approval of most Westerners, who considered it appropriate to Japan's stage of political development. At first glance, it appeared to establish a divine right absolute monarchy. Sovereignty lay with the emperor, whose authority was "sacred and inviolable." He chose the prime minister who, together with other state ministers, was solely responsible to him. He also approved all laws and treaties, decided on war and peace, and served as supreme commander of the armed forces. But the emperor was not a free agent, and in this respect the constitution continued Japan's tradition of figurehead rule. He was expected to act only on the recommendations of his cabinet ministers, service chiefs, and special advisory bodies such as the "privy council," which were composed of retired senior officials. The constitution also made it clear that the rule of law should prevail and it set up an independent judiciary outside the emperor's direct control. Furthermore, it granted an unprecedented array of rights and freedoms to Japanese citizens, even though these were qualified by the ambiguous phrase "within the limits of the law."

The constitution's main concession to democratic practice was its creation of a bicameral legislature, the diet, whose popularly elected lower house was given the power to approve legislation, including the government's budgets. The framers of the constitution hoped that this body would function as a safety valve, sounding board, and instrument for mobilizing public opinion behind the government's policies. In the event, however, the Liberal and Progressive parties exploited the power of the purse to steadily increase their influence over cabinets appointed by the emperor. In practice, the prime minister could govern only with the support of the majority party in the lower house. As a result, prime ministers became party heads and vice versa. By the end of the Meiji era in 1912, Japan was moving toward the Anglo-French model of responsible party government in which the head of the majority party automatically became prime minister. This development was neither expected nor welcomed by the Meiji leaders, but there was little they could do about it since the emperor could not govern by decree and amending the constitution to curtail party power was not politically feasible.

The principal virtue of the Meiji constitutional system was its flexibility, which permitted significant albeit unintended movement from authoritarianism toward democracy. But it bequeathed problems for "democratic consolidation," foremost among which was the legitimization of party rule. In political systems where sovereignty lies with the people, the right of their elected representatives to govern is rarely questioned. In the Meiji system, however, imperial sovereignty meant that politicians governed as "servants of the throne" and were viewed as legitimate only to the extent that they represented the emperor. This, by itself, might not have posed a serious problem were it not for the fact that politicians suffered in comparison with the emperor's other servants, soldiers and bureaucrats, inasmuch as the methods they employed to gain office seemed disreputable to many Japanese. Logrolling, pork-barrel tactics, and influence peddling are undesirable but inevitable and tolerable features of democratic party politics. In the Japanese context, however, they were seen as besmirching the imperial government and dishonoring the emperor. Politicians were, in a word, "corrupt."

Another shortcoming of the Meiji political system was its lack of a controlling center. In most polities, someone is ultimately in charge, be it a president, prime minister, or dictator. But there was a vacuum at the center of the Meiji state. Although the emperor held near absolute power, he was not a personal autocrat like the Russian tsar or German kaiser. His basic role was, rather, to ratify decisions made by his advisors. This posed no problem as long as his advisors formed a cohesive group that had sufficient clout to sell their decisions within the government. The Meiji leaders, as the founding fathers of the system, comprised such a group and made it work. But when they passed from the scene after 1912 through death and old age, the informal collective leadership they had provided broke down and was not replaced. The political parties, army and navy, and civilian bureaucracies emerged as contending power centers, each of which was intent on subduing the others and using Japan's figurehead emperor to advance its own agendas. After the Meiji era, there was, in effect, no one at the helm of the Japanese ship of state, only a jostling throng of would-be pilots proposing different courses.

Japan's Industrialization

The Meiji leadership early on decided that Japan would have to acquire a modern industrial base, since they realized that the West's power grew out of the smokestacks of its factories as well as the barrels of its guns. Under the slogan "Wealthy Country, Strong Military," they consequently attached a high priority to industrialization. But industrializing a backward and relatively poor country like early Meiji Japan was a daunting undertaking for which there was no non-Western precedent. Japan lacked the requisite capital, technology, entrepreneurs, and, except for some coal, natural resources. In contrast to today's world, moreover, there were no international aid programs. European and American banks might provide loans, but the interest rates were high and the penalties for default could include military intervention to enforce repayment, often through the seizure of customs or other tax revenues. Likewise, while Western firms were willing to set up railways, factories, and steamship lines, they typically monopolized the profits and resisted local interference. Shielded by the privileges and immunities of Unequal Treaties, they were well positioned to establish economic control.

Rather than risk falling under Western economic domination, the Meiji leaders agreed that Japan should industrialize by its own efforts as much as possible. This did not mean attempting to go it entirely alone. There was no alternative to buying the West's machinery and technology, and adopting its models of factory and business organization. By the 1870s, moreover, Japan was enmeshed in a global trading system controlled from Western financial capitals, and run by large European and American companies. The Meiji government could not prevent Treaty Port–based Western firms from gaining a commanding position in Japan's external trade as well as modern sectors such as banking, insurance, and shipping. The problem, in short, was finding a way to compete with Westerners before they economically overwhelmed Japan. The government responded by setting up modern enterprises of its own, including "import substitution" industries like glass, cement, and textiles. This was expensive, involving importing Western equipment and hiring Western advisors. Moreover, the government had to pay for it all out of its meager tax revenues.

The success of Japan's state-sponsored industrialization depended ultimately on the government's ability to extract wealth from agriculture and transfer it to industry. This, in turn, required an efficient tax system and expanding agricultural production. Peasants, after all, can hardly be expected to be a significant source of tax revenue if they are barely surviving at subsistence levels. In contrast to many developing countries today, both of these requirements were met in Meiji Japan. Indeed, its industrial revolution was based on an agricultural revolution much as had occurred more than a century earlier in Britain. Japanese farm output rose steadily through the early 1900s, generating surpluses sufficient to finance the government's industrialization and armaments programs, feed Japan's growing population, and even create a measure of rural prosperity. Agriculture supplied silk, Japan's leading export item and principal source of foreign exchange. The production and processing of silk, which were traditional peasant activities carried out mainly by women, boomed in response to surging demand in Europe and America for silk stockings and apparel coveted by their new middle classes.

As former samurai accustomed to trying to maximize the agricultural production of their domains, it was natural for the Meiji leaders to apply the same approach to the nation. To this end, they carried out sweeping reforms in the 1870s, including imposing a uniform land tax, legalizing private land ownership, and dismantling feudal barriers to the movement of goods and people. While not all peasants welcomed these innovations, many benefited from them. They now enjoyed secure tenure, predictable taxes, and unimpeded access to national and international markets. The chief winners were peasant entrepreneurs who had emerged in late Tokugawa times. They seized on these opportunities to boost their output of rice, tea, silk, and other profitable commodities. Their operations were small-scale and labor-intensive, since mechanization was not an option in the crowded Japanese countryside where farms were miniscule in size and labor cheap, skilled, and plentiful. Nevertheless, productivity rose through the introduction of better seeds, improved irrigation works, and greater use of commercial fertilizer. Japan's agricultural revolution was well under way in the 1880s and continued at full tilt during the 1890s.

The development of factory industry was slowed by the shortage of entrepreneurs willing to invest in what was seen as a novel and risky form of production. The government, no longer able to afford running the modern enterprises it had set up earlier, sold them off in the 1880s at bargain basement prices to a favored group of merchants and ex-samurai officials. The latter became known as zaibatsu or "financial cliques" and were the Meiji government's chosen instrument of industrialization. Showered with official contracts and subsidies, they mushroomed into large family-owned conglomerates with operations in manufacturing, mining, shipping, banking, insurance, and overseas trade. Zaibatsu combines like Mitsui and Mitsubishi dominated the modern sector of the economy, particularly shipbuilding and other "strategic industries," and worked hand in glove with the government, establishing a pattern of close government–business cooperation that persists to the present. The origin of this pattern lay in the late Tokugawa commercial ventures undertaken by feudal domains in partnership with merchants, which the Meiji leaders revived and adapted to modern purposes.

Government nurturing of a big business elite was a logical step for a "late developer" like Meiji Japan, which saw itself threatened by giant Western corporations with inexhaustible resources and global connections. But the concentration of economic power in the hands of a few privileged conglomerates did not, by itself, guarantee Japan's industrialization. It might well have led to what nowadays is called "crony capitalism," or the enrichment of a few without significant economic growth. This was the case, for example, in late-Qing China, where the factories, mines, and steamship lines established by Chinese self-strengtheners and their merchant collaborators fell victim to graft and corruption. The Japanese avoided this pitfall because they were motivated by the ideal of service to the nation, precluding the most blatant forms of peculation although not the accumulation of substantial private fortunes. Perhaps a more fundamental difference from Qing China, however, was the fact that Japan's industrialization was propelled less by zaibatsu than by the initiative of innumerable small-scale industrial entrepreneurs who owed little to government subsidies and coddling.

Japan's "take-off" into self-sustaining industrial growth began in the 1890s. Like Britain's earlier Industrial Revolution, it was driven by export-oriented textile manufacturing based on the mechanized spinning and weaving of imported raw cotton. This was a natural field of specialization for an aspiring industrial power. The technology was relatively simple and the capital requirements modest. Moreover, the "globalizing" trends of the day facilitated access to cheap raw materials and lucrative markets in China and elsewhere in Asia. In addition to its geographic proximity to these markets, Japan had another comparative advantage over Western competitors in its docile, low-wage work force composed of young peasant women seeking to earn dowries. While zaibatsu set up modern plants equipped with state-of-the-art machinery, the bulk of Japan's textile output came from small, independent producers who operated what were less "factories" than workshops run along the lines of extended families. Such workshops accounted for most of Japan's industrial employment and production well into the twentieth century, creating a "dual economy" of modern factories and traditional establishments.

The peasants, female and male, who comprised Japan's early industrial labor force were skilled, literate, trainable, and disciplined. They came out of patriarchal village communities in which deference to authority and service to the group were taken for granted and almost second nature. One social concomitant was the slow development of a self-conscious industrial proletariat. "Proletarians" were confined to zaibatsu-dominated heavy industries like shipbuilding, mining, and steel making, which employed a tiny proportion of the work force. As a result, trade unionism and socialism, the twin hallmarks of industrial capitalism in the West, made little headway. Another consequence was the unusual strength of peasant communitarian values and ideals. Japan, in effect, industrialized while holding its "pre-industrial" attitudes constant. This had important political ramifications. There was, for

Women workers in a Japanese silk-reeling plant, early 1900s.

example, a relatively low tolerance for behavior seen as selfish and disruptive of group harmony. There was also a tendency to idealize the nation-state as the village community writ large. Many saw their god-emperor as presiding over what they imagined to be a large extended family.

Japan's "family state" ideal was not unique; parallels can be found in Russia and other late developers where patriarchal and authoritarian values also reigned supreme. But it differentiated Japan from the advanced Western countries against which it measured itself, leading many Japanese to suppose that their national polity was indeed unique in its unity and harmony. They attributed this to the vitality of Japan's traditional values of loyalty and filial piety, which they contrasted with the West's selfish individualism and propensity for divisive infighting. By the end of the Meiji era, however, many Japanese were worried by signs that these "beautiful virtues" might be breaking down in the face of a new and unwelcome wave of Westernization. They were especially alarmed by the spread among intellectuals of liberalism, socialism, and anarchism, which seemed to threaten family state solidarity. The uncovering of an anarchist plot to assassinate the emperor in 1910 sent a shock wave through the country. Traditionalists were also disquieted by the unseemly wrangling of party politicians, strikes by trade unionists, and bribery scandals involving big business interests seeking to buy political influence.

Even as industrialization and Westernization opened up fissures in the facade of family state togetherness, they drew Japan into novel and unsettling dependence on the outside world. The shift of the country's economic center of gravity from agriculture to industry was accompanied by the transformation of its external trade. Imports, which had earlier been dominated by Western machinery and capital goods, now included a growing volume of Asian raw materials such as soybeans, cotton, and iron ore. Even rice, the national staple, had to be imported as demand outran domestic production. While silk remained an export mainstay and a key prop of rural livelihoods, cotton textiles and other light industrial goods bulked increasingly large in the export picture. These trends implanted among Japanese of all walks of life an acute sense of national vulnerability. They felt that their crowded and resource-poor island country was becoming dangerously dependent on foreigners for its survival. Most assumed that economic disaster would follow from any impairment of Japan's access to external sources of vital food and raw material imports, and foreign markets for its growing manufacturing sector.

Empire Building

Given Japanese economic insecurities, it might be supposed that their quest for overseas empire was driven by a search for captive markets and sources of raw materials. In fact, however, the Meiji leaders who planned and executed Japan's empire building were motivated primarily by political and strategic considerations. Coming out of a setting of rival feudal domains, they found it easy to understand the Western international system of competing nation-states. What struck them about this competition was its dog-eat-dog character. In the late nineteenth century, Western imperial expansion was in full swing and one non-Western state after another was crumpling before the European juggernaut. Viewed in light of then-fashionable social Darwinism, which Japanese quickly embraced, strong nations and peoples were subjugating weak and inferior ones just as occurred in the natural world. The leadership in Tokyo aimed to put Japan on the winning side of this lopsided "struggle for survival." In their view, this required not only building up Japan's national power and wealth to Western levels, but joining Westerners in carving out a colonial empire at the expense of "lesser breeds."

For the Meiji leaders, however, the 1870s and 1880s was a time for caution and restraint in foreign affairs. Japan had fortuitously escaped conquest and colonization by the European imperialist powers, but it was not yet out of the woods. It was militarily weak and preoccupied with domestic reform.

Overseas adventures would put an intolerable strain on the government's shaky finances and invite the attention of the Europeans who were completing their subjugation of Southeast Asia and alert for opportunities to extend their hegemony over the rest of East Asia. For these reasons, a proposal put forward in 1873 to use unemployed samurai to conquer Korea was summarily rejected. Nevertheless, the Meiji leadership was keenly interested in Korea, which it deemed vital to Japan's security by virtue of its geographical proximity. They projected a gradual expansion of Japan's influence in Choson Korea, leading to the ascendancy of pro-Japanese reformers who would carry out a Meiji-style revolution from above. As a first step toward the realization of this design, Tokyo employed gunboat diplomacy in 1876 to force Seoul to open the country under an Unequal Treaty favorable to Japan.

Japanese hopes for the emergence of a modernizing Korea aligned with Japan foundered on the conservatism, factionalism, and anti-Japanese sentiment of Korea's yangban elite. A few members of this elite looked upon Japan as a model and ally, but their attempt to seize power in an 1884 coup was crushed, leaving the anti-reform and anti-Japanese majority firmly in charge in Seoul. This majority looked to Qing China, Korea's traditional suzerain, for help in countering what they perceived as a Japanese threat. The Chinese were glad to oblige, seeing an opportunity to rebuild Beijing's prestige, which had been tarnished by its defeat in the Sino-French War. Although a conflict between Japan and China for predominance in Korea loomed, neither side wanted a war it was uncertain of winning. In 1885, Beijing and Tokyo concluded a nonintervention accord under which they agreed to refrain from unilaterally introducing troops into the peninsula and to avoid interfering in Korea's internal affairs. But China held the upper hand over the Choson court, and some Chinese officials aimed to convert Korea into a Western-style protectorate whose defense and foreign policy would be controlled by Beijing.

In the early 1890s, Tokyo concluded that the military balance had shifted decisively in its favor, making force an attractive option for expelling China from Korea and perhaps wringing other concessions from Beijing. An opportunity for a military showdown came in the form of a large-scale Korean peasant rebellion in 1894, which gave Japan an excuse to pour in troops, ostensibly to protect Japanese lives and property. Beijing rose to the bait. Condemning Japan's action as a violation of their 1885 accord, it sent in Chinese troops, and both sides declared war. The resulting conflict was an unmitigated disaster for the Chinese. Japan's army and navy, modeled respectively on German and British prototypes, quickly destroyed China's Yellow Sea fleet and drove Chinese forces from Korea. The Japanese army then advanced into southern Manchuria and northern Shandong (Shantung) Province, positioning itself for a march on Beijing. The Qing had no choice but to accept Tokyo's

Japanese fighting the Chinese in the Sino-Japanese War, 1894–95.

peace terms, which included the cession of Taiwan, the lease of the strategic Liaodong (Liaotung) Peninsula in southern Manchuria, and the granting of Unequal Treaty privileges to Japan in China.

As previously noted, the war was a shattering blow to China and the Qing, who were unable to defend their Manchurian homeland. For Japan, on the other hand, it was a "splendid little war" marked by low casualties and an unbroken string of easy victories on land and sea. The nationalistic Japanese public rejoiced, and many pressed for even more concessions from the help-less Chinese. Japanese who had earlier harbored doubts about the morality or feasibility of Western-style empire building were converted into ardent imperialists. It was all the more shocking and dismaying, therefore, when Japan was suddenly confronted in 1895 by a united demand by Germany, France, and Russia that it return the Liaodong Peninsula to China. Russia, coveting Liaodong for itself, had lined up German and French support for this "Triple Intervention" through diplomatic horse trading.

Faced by the veiled threat of force by three Great Powers, Tokyo backed down and "retroceded" Liaodong. The Qing leadership took comfort from this turn of events, which humiliated the Japanese. But Beijing would shortly have to reward the Russians, French, and Germans with territorial concessions.

Among the lessons drawn by the Japanese from the Triple Intervention fiasco was the fact that Japan was a weak and isolated player in the game of imperialist power politics, and that Russia now constituted the chief threat to its interests in Korea. To remedy its military weakness, Tokyo embarked on a crash naval and military buildup. It also broke out of its diplomatic isolation by concluding an alliance with Britain in 1902. Both Britain and Japan were alarmed by Russia's growing power and ambitions in Northeast Asia. The

Russian tsar, emboldened by the construction of the Trans-Siberian Railway, aimed to turn Manchuria into a Russian sphere of interest. To this end, he prevailed on the beleaguered Qing to give Russia a lease on Liaodong, along with its naval base of Port Arthur (Lushun), and permit it to construct railways in Manchuria. The Japanese suspected that these moves foreshadowed a Russian move into Korea, and their suspicions were confirmed by St. Petersburg's rebuff of a proposed modus vivendi in 1903 under which both sides would respect their spheres of influence in Manchuria and Korea. Tokyo concluded that war was the only way to stop the Russians.

Taking on Russia was a dangerous gamble for the Japanese inasmuch as its enormous army seemed likely to steamroller them. The Russians were confident of victory and contemptuous of the Japanese, whom they regarded as "mere Asians" incapable of standing up to European troops. But they got a nasty surprise. Japan's navy quickly bottled up the Russian Far Eastern fleet, while its army swept into southern Manchuria and besieged the Russian garrison in Port Arthur. Although the Russians turned out to be a more formidable opponent than the Chinese, they fell back under relentless Japanese attacks, surrendering Port Arthur and the southern Manchurian city of Shenyang (Mukden). The Russians also lost their Baltic fleet, which was intercepted and destroyed by the Japanese navy in the Tsushima Strait between Korea and Japan en route to Vladivostok. But the cost to Japan of these victories was high in both lives and treasure. It mobilized a million men of whom some 100,000 became casualties on Manchurian battlefields in horrific combat prefiguring that of World War I. The war bankrupted the government and severely strained the Japanese economy.

If the Sino-Japanese War heralded Japan's emergence as an imperialist power, the Russo-Japanese War marked its arrival as a Great Power. In Japan, the conflict aroused intense patriotic fervor and was even more of a "people's war" than its predecessor against China had been. The Japanese public, unaware of their country's exhaustion and elated by its victories on land and at sea, expected a large war indemnity and major territorial gains. In fact, Russian forces in Manchuria were still largely intact and capable of continuing the struggle. But the Trans-Siberian supply line had proved inadequate and the demands of the war had produced a revolutionary upheaval against the tsar. St. Petersburg desperately wanted peace and the only question was how much it was willing to give to get it. In the event, the Russians got off lightly. Under the terms of the 1905 Portsmouth Treaty, Russia paid no war indemnity, while ceding southern Sakhalin Island and transferring its southern Manchurian railway rights and Liaodong leasehold to Japan. This disappointing settlement provoked rioting in Tokyo. Nevertheless, Japan had avenged the Triple Intervention and humbled one of Europe's titans.

Russia's Baltic Fleet rushing the Tsushima Straits, 1905.

The Russo-Japanese War drove another nail into the coffin of the dying Qing monarchy, which watched helplessly as Russia and Japan fought over its Manchurian dependency and then acquiesced in its partition between them. But this partition did not resolve the question of who should control Manchuria. Chinese nationalists insisted that the Manchus' onetime homeland was now an integral part of the Chinese nation and should come under full Chinese sovereignty. They pointed to the fact that ethnic Chinese immigrants had flooded into the region, largely absorbing its original Manchu inhabitants. But Japan was unwilling to concede more than token Chinese sovereignty. It had fought hard and sacrificed much to gain its Manchurian foothold, and was intent on transforming it into a quasi-colony. Manchuria offered resources that Japan needed, including soybeans, wheat, and iron ore, and provided a buffer zone protecting Korea. Tokyo stationed a powerful army in its Liaodong leasehold and entrusted the exploitation of Manchuria's riches to the South Manchurian Railway Company, a giant semi-governmental corporation with interests in agriculture, mining, manufacturing, and transportation.

Japan's neutralization of the Russian challenge opened the way for its takeover of Korea, which now stood helpless and friendless. Tokyo still clung to the hope that it might be possible to induce the Choson monarchy and the yangban elite to accept Japanese tutelage. In 1905, it made Korea a protectorate supervised by a Japanese resident-general and corps of advisors backed by sizable military forces. But this arrangement proved unworkable. The Korean king balked and appealed unsuccessfully for Western help against Japan. His replacement with a more compliant figure did not bring order. Yangban and demobilized Korean soldiers combined to foment popular uprisings, and Korean patriots assassinated pro-Japanese collaborators. The killing in 1909 of the resident-general, one of founding fathers of the Meiji state, was the last straw for the Japanese. In 1910, they abolished the Choson monarchy and Seoul government, and formally annexed Korea. A Japanese-run colonial administration was established under army generals, which set about developing Korea as a source of raw materials, rice, and cheap labor for the Japanese "mother country."

By 1912, the surviving Meiji leaders could take pride in their handiwork. They had assembled a colonial empire and made Japan a full member of the Western imperialist club. The last Unequal Treaty privilege was revoked in 1911. Japan was a military ally of Britain, the leading imperial power of the day, and the "London-Tokyo axis" was the linchpin of East Asia's colonial order. After Japan's victory over Russia, moreover, no Western power even considered tangling with the Japanese. This included the United States, which had made itself an East Asian imperialist player by annexing the Philippines in 1899. As will be described in the next chapter, the Americans had reservations about Japan's encroachment on Chinese sovereignty in Manchuria, and Japanese-American relations were roiled by discrimination against Japanese immigrants in California. But the United States was not prepared to resist Japan. On the contrary, it was quite willing to accept Japan's colonization of Korea in return for Tokyo's assurances of its willingness to respect the American position in the Philippines, which Washington early on decided was a vulnerable and indefensible "Achilles' heel."

"Quitting Asia"

The colonial empire built by Meiji Japan between 1895 and 1910—Taiwan, Korea, southern Manchuria, and south Sakhalin—differed from those of the Western imperialist powers in East Asia insofar as it involved the subjugation of Chinese and Koreans who were racially and culturally akin to the Japanese themselves. There were both European and East Asian precedents for this situation. In Europe, one thinks of the colonization of Ireland by the English, and Poland by the Germans. Premodern East Asia offers many examples, including the conquest of Laotians by the Thai, Shans by the Burmese, and Cambodians by the Vietnamese. Nevertheless, the decision of the Japanese to join the West in seeking dominion over their fellow Asians raised potentially troubling questions that Europeans and Americans, as non-Asian interlopers, did not have to face. By siding with Western colonialists, had Japanese abandoned their Asian heritage and identity? Were they still "Asian" or had they become an exotic species of Westerner? If the former was the case, how could their acquisition of Asian colonies be justified? Should they not unite with their Asian brethren to resist the West?

As noted above, the Meiji leaders were untroubled by these questions. In their social Darwinist worldview, Westerners were winners and Asians were losers, and Japan had to be in the winner's circle. Most Meiji-era Japanese shared this view. What mattered to them was Japan's own quest for national autonomy and equality with the West. Few felt any solidarity with other East Asians or were much concerned by their fate at the hands of Western imperialists except as a warning and example of what might befall Japan. Moreover, "being Asian" was not an attractive identity for Meiji Japanese, since it connoted weakness and backwardness, and they were intent on becoming modern and strong. They sought to distance themselves from Asia lest they be tainted in Western eyes by the stigma of its cultural inferiority. The case for "quitting Asia" was made in the 1880s by Meiji Japan's leading educator. Writing in the context of the failure of pro-Japanese reformers to seize power in Korea, he argued that it was illusory to expect other Asians to follow Japan's lead in modernizing their societies and that Japan would, in effect, have to go it alone as a Westernized outpost "in" but not "of" Asia.

Quitting Asia culturally and psychologically did not mean retreating from it in other ways. Indeed, the late Meiji period was one in which the Japanese reengaged with their East Asian neighbors after almost three centuries of national isolation. Beginning in the 1890s, Japanese moved out into the region as soldiers, administrators, diplomats, travelers, businessmen, and even immigrants. In general, they were not favorably impressed by what they found there. China, idealized during Tokugawa times as a Confucian utopia, was particularly disappointing. In the Sino-Japanese war, for example, many Japanese troops derided their Chinese adversaries as effeminate cowards. Japanese immigrants in Korea were repelled by what they considered to be the squalor and indiscipline of Koreans. Southeast Asians fared no better. Japanese observers of European colonies were contemptuous of the slavish deference to Europeans and the happy-go-lucky ways of the "natives." Japanese, viewing other East Asians through the prism of their own modernizing and nationalistic society, found it hard to imagine that they had anything in common with them. But there were inescapable affinities.

In constructing a rationale for colonial rule over their fellow East Asians, Japanese empire builders appropriated the European concepts of a "civilizing mission" and cultural assimilation. However, they interpreted these concepts differently than Western colonialists. In Taiwan and Korea, they pushed assimilation—Japanization—with a determination unmatched in most European colonies. Behind this effort lay the assumption that Koreans and Chinese, although inferior to Japanese, were racially and culturally akin to them and hence capable of being turned into Japanese of a sort. Tokyo's goal was to transform them into "loyal imperial subjects," grateful for the benefits showered on them by the emperor and content with their second-class status in a larger imperial polity encompassing Japan and its overseas dependencies. Japanese considered their version of "the white man's burden" different from, and morally superior to, that of Europeans, whom they regarded as alien oppressors of nonwhites. They were unimpressed by the Western idea of "trusteeship" in which colonial wards were to be prepared for self-government and eventual independence in the distant future.

Despite their talk of kinship with Chinese and Koreans, few Japanese felt any closeness to them and did not treat them as equals. In the hierarchy of "imperial peoples," they were a notch above Ainu aborigines but inferior to Japanese and even Okinawans, who were viewed as a lesser breed of Japanese. Not all Japanese adopted such condescending attitudes. The counterparts of European "Orientalists" studied and admired classical Chinese and Korean culture, and lamented China's decline from its former greatness. But Japanese colonial administrators, businessmen, and soldiers took their own superiority as a given. Like their European and American equivalents, they enjoyed privileged lifestyles in enclaves shielded from "native quarters." Japanese colonial architecture, vestiges of which survive today in Korea, Taiwan, and

Manchuria, mirrored the monumental style favored by Europeans that was designed to project imperial grandeur. Japanese colonialists were no less paternalistic than Europeans in their dealings with the "natives," and equally single-minded in their determination to exploit the agricultural and mineral resources of their colonies for the benefit of their own country.

As much as Meiji Japanese emulated the West and sought equality with it, this goal proved elusive. While Westerners praised Japan's precocious modernization and accepted it as a political and diplomatic equal, they regarded the Japanese as an Asian people and, as such, inferior to themselves. The superiority of the "white race" over "coloreds," including Chinese and Japanese, was taken for granted in the West in the late nineteenth and early twentieth centuries. One manifestation of this racism was the prejudice meted out to Japanese immigrants in California, which Japanese resented and the Meiji government protested. Another was the notion of a "Yellow Peril," in vogue among European and American intellectuals and even some national leaders like the German kaiser. This notion, arising from fin de siècle handwringing over the future of Western civilization, posited a "barbarian" challenge by China's millions armed and led by a superficially Westernized Japan. For believers in the Yellow Peril, the nightmare was the combination of the West's technology with what they saw as the "fanaticism" of East Asians awakening from their age-old torpor.

Not surprisingly, some Japanese recoiled from West and turned to Asia, giving rise to the pan-Asianist movement touched upon in the Introduction. Although all late-Meiji pan-Asianists condemned Western imperialism, their priorities differed. Some called for cultural liberation from the West, involving the assertion of an Asian identity based on common aesthetic ideals and communitarian values. Westernized liberals dreamed of an Asia united by a commitment to individual liberty and political democracy. Nativists of the kind described earlier aimed to drive Westerners from Asia and extend the blessings of Japan's "imperial way." Since they bought into the official rationale of Japanese colonialism, nativists enjoyed a measure of favor and had the ear of some in the government. They were, moreover, organized in well-funded patriotic societies such as the "Black Dragon" or Amur River Society, which was set up in 1901 to help expel the Russians from Manchuria and speed Japan's takeover of Korea. Patriotic societies also aided Chinese, Vietnamese, and other Asian nationalists who flocked to Japan in the early 1900s, seeing it as a force for East Asia's liberation from Western colonialism.

It would be a mistake to exaggerate the political influence of late-Meiji pan-Asianism. It was out of step with the goals of the Meiji government and elite, which sought acceptance by the West, not confrontation with it. As Japan gained full membership in the Western imperialist club after the

Russo-Japanese War, the government found both Japanese pan-Asianists and their Asian nationalist friends an embarrassment and cracked down on them. Nevertheless, pan-Asianism did not die either in Japan or in East Asia. In Japan, it played to increasing doubts about Westernization, which seemed to be eroding the family-state ideal dear to most Japanese. Nativists' call for Japan to "return to Asia" as the leader of an anti-Western revolt gradually gained a broad following among Japanese. Meanwhile Koreans, subject to the full brunt of "imperial benevolence" after 1910, viewed Japan as an imperialist predator. So, increasingly, did Chinese. In Southeast Asia, however, Japan never entirely lost its attraction as a model and inspiration for anticolonial nationalists. As the latter became more numerous and militant during the 1920s and 1930s, it was perhaps inevitable that some of them should again look to the Japanese for help.

6

The Turbulent 1920s and 1930s

The interwar period witnessed the weakening of the Western-dominated colonial order in East Asia, paving the way for its eventual collapse. The immediate cause was World War I, which created new anti-imperialist forces and stimulated nationalism throughout the region. Chinese nationalists sought to reunify their country and cast off its semi-colonial constraints. This brought them into conflict with Japan, which was determined to maintain its prerogatives in China and foothold in Manchuria. The Washington Treaty System, a U.S.-inspired attempt to freeze the status quo, produced temporary stability in the 1920s. But this collapsed at the end of the decade under the impact of the Great Depression and Sino-Japanese rivalry over Manchuria. During the 1930s, the Japanese abandoned liberal democracy, broke with the Western powers, and embarked on a pan-Asianist crusade to liberate East Asia from Western colonialism. They seized Manchuria in 1931 and invaded China itself in 1937, hoping to forcibly enlist it in their crusade. The resulting Sino-Japanese War led to a confrontation between Japan and the United States, which by 1940 was committed to halting Japanese aggression.

Europe's "Great War"

In 1914, forty-three years of peace in Europe came to an abrupt end with the outbreak of the bloodiest and most destructive war in its history, far exceeding the ghastly toll of the Thirty Years' War of the early seventeenth century. Most Europeans did not expect this, anticipating a short and decisive conflict on the model of the Franco-Prussian War of 1870–71. They ignored the lessons of the 1861–65 American Civil War and the 1904–5 Russo-Japanese War, which suggested that warfare among industrialized nation-states would produce staggering casualties. Indeed, the harnessing of mass nationalism, science and technology, and industrialized economies to war efforts resulted in slaughter on an unprecedented scale. But the European citizen-soldiers who marched off to war in 1914 singing their national anthems and waving their national flags were oblivious to this. They were told that it would all be over by Christmas and they believed it. Four years later, after some 10 million had died in combat and millions more were injured, the survivors returned to their homes, many disillusioned with everything they had been taught to believe, including the superiority of European civilization.

The 1914–18 "Great War," as contemporaries called it, grew out of the breakdown of the European balance of power in the 1890s consequent to the rise of Imperial Germany and the determination of its leaders to assert its place in the sun. Feeling themselves threatened, Russia, France, and Britain formed a defensive alliance to contain Germany and its ally, Austria-Hungary. A military showdown between these rival alliances might have been averted if diplomacy had been up to the task and national leaders had grasped the implications of modern warfare. But most were captive to the notion that victory could be achieved by landing knockout blows. The Germans, in particular, planned on taking the French out with a quick offensive and then concentrating against the Russians before they could mobilize. The trigger that set this plan in motion was the assassination in August 1914 of the Austrian heir apparent by a Bosnian nationalist, which produced a confrontation between Austria and Serbia. When Russia intervened on the side of the Serbs, the Germans decided to strike while the iron was hot and invaded France, penetrating to within a few miles of Paris before they were checked.

The failure of Germany's opening gamble to defeat France led to a four-year war of attrition in northern France and Belgium in which both sides hurled themselves at each other in futile infantry assaults against heavily fortified positions. The fighting on the Eastern Front, mainly Russian Poland, was more mobile but casualties there were also high, especially among the Russians. No one, least of all the generals, had expected this or had any idea how to break the stalemate except by launching even larger offensives. But the widespread use of machine guns, barbed wire, and massed artillery made such offensives suicidal. As the war dragged on and its human and material costs mounted, morale among the combatants began to sag. The Russians broke first. In 1917, their army mutinied and deposed the tsar. A provisional government tried to continue the war, but it was overthrown in an October coup by Bolsheviks, a group of revolutionary Marxists. Lenin, the Bolshevik leader, negotiated a separate peace with the Germans in 1918 and denounced the war as a conflict among Europe's capitalist ruling classes, who had deluded the working masses into serving as cannon fodder.

Lenin's critique of the war was countered by U.S. president Woodrow Wilson, who led the United States into the conflict in 1917 on the side of the British and French in response to German submarine attacks on American shipping. Wilson, a fervent idealist and internationalist, defined the war as a struggle to "make the world safe for democracy" and realize the goal of national self-determination. He also envisioned a new postwar order in which national rivalries and alliances would be superseded by a League of Nations dedicated to cooperatively resolving international disputes and restraining aggressors. The British and French, who had less altruistic priorities, reluctantly signed on to Wilson's war aims as the price that had to be paid for securing American military help in defeating the Germans. Supported by American troops, they blunted Germany's last-ditch offensive on the western front in 1918. In the face of an Allied counteroffensive, the exhausted Germans lost heart. Their army began to disintegrate, the kaiser abdicated, and Berlin, joined by Vienna, requested an armistice. The Allies agreed, finally bringing the war to a close in November 1918.

The peace settlement worked out by the victorious Allies in Paris in 1919 fell short of the generous terms desired by Wilson. The British and French, economically prostrate and saddled with huge war debts to the United States, imposed unrealistically large reparation payments on the defeated Germans. In addition, Germany was forced to cede some of its territory and accept restrictions on its postwar military, including the demilitarization of the Rhineland region adjacent to France. Many Germans viewed these terms as punitive, sowing the seeds of German revanchism. The peacemakers' application of the principle of national self-determination created a host of new nation-states out of the debris of the Austro-Hungarian and Ottoman empires in central and southern Europe. But many of the newly drawn borders arbitrarily divided and combined national groups, bequeathing future problems. Wilson got what he most wanted, agreement to establish the League of Nations. However, he was unable to sell the League to the U.S. Senate, which saw membership in it as compromising U.S. sovereignty. As a result, the League was crippled from the outset of its existence by the refusal of the United States to join.

Lenin's Bolsheviks wanted no part of the League of Nations, which they regarded as a tool of capitalist and imperialist interests. Lenin's vision of the future was, in any case, quite different from Wilson's. His goal was nothing less than the overthrow of capitalism through worldwide revolutionary action inspired and directed by Russia, now reborn as the Union of Soviet Socialist Republics (USSR). In 1919, he set up the Communist International (Comintern), headquartered in Moscow, with the mission of recruiting, training, and advising foreign revolutionaries. War-ravaged Europe initially seemed to offer promising prospects for revolution. But while communist parties mushroomed in the war's aftermath, communist coups and insurrections in Germany and elsewhere fizzled and were easily suppressed. European proletarians, of whom communists considered themselves to be the vanguard, had little taste for revolutionary violence, and so the Comintern increasingly looked to East

Asia. Outside Japan, there were few industrial workers with whom to build proper communist movements. But there was no lack of willing recruits for the communist cause among anticolonial nationalists.

Effects in East Asia

The war in Europe stimulated an economic boom throughout East Asia, driven by the combatant countries' insatiable demand for food, raw materials, and manufactured goods. In Southeast Asia, mining and plantation agriculture grew apace, as did the transportation infrastructure necessary to support this growth. With the conversion of European factories to armament production, moreover, new opportunities opened up for East Asian manufacturers. Japan, having already established an industrial base, was in the best position to exploit these opportunities. Japanese industrialization accelerated during the war years as zaibatsu led a rapid expansion of heavy industries such as shipbuilding as well as a move into factory production of a wide variety of consumer goods.

Japan's wartime industrial surge was accompanied by stirrings of industrialization in a few colonial capitals and in China's treaty ports. Shanghai, the largest and most cosmopolitan treaty port, came into its own during the war as the center of China's modern manufacturing industry. Along with the British Crown Colony of Hong Kong, Shanghai was also the principal gateway of China's overseas trade.

East Asia's economic growth during World War I speeded social change, including the emergence of Western-oriented middle classes and, in some cases, self-conscious industrial proletariats. Again, Japan was in the vanguard of these developments. By the end of the war, a sizable urban bourgeoisie and industrial working class had appeared and were attuned to the same fashions, pastimes, and concerns as their counterparts in Europe and the United States. "Jazz Age Japan" seemed to be drawing closer culturally to the West, at least in Tokyo, Osaka, and other larger cities, where emancipated youth sported Harold Lloyd glasses and flapper outfits and frequented dance halls and movie theaters. Japanese trade unionists found audiences receptive to their appeals for worker solidarity against capitalist exploitation. Avant-garde professors and their students discussed the merits of cubist art and the fine points of Marxist doctrine. Liberals demanded universal manhood suffrage and responsible party government. Radicals called for more drastic reforms, ranging from the abolition of the emperor system to its renovation through a second, anti-Western restoration.

The same sort of intellectual ferment was evident among Westernized intelligentsias that arose elsewhere in East Asia, including Korea, Vietnam, Burma,

Jazz Age Japan.

Thailand, and Indonesia. Republican China offers a particularly interesting example. There, a new generation of Western-educated students came to the fore during the war, inspired by the goal of ridding China of what it saw as the triple evils of Confucianism, warlordism, and imperialism. Their enthusiasm for Western "science and democracy" and denigration of Confucian tradition alienated conservatives. But their high-minded zeal for saving the country appealed to the nationalist sentiments of emerging middle and working classes in the cities. In contrast to Japanese and Western colonies, China provided a relatively permissive setting for the development of student-led nationalism. Treaty ports like Shanghai were cosmopolitan, open cities under joint Western and Chinese administration that offered sanctuary to revolutionaries and refugees both foreign and Chinese. After the 1911 Revolution, moreover, there was no effective central government that might have sought to control and harness Chinese nationalism for its own purposes.

As noted in Chapter 4, students and intellectuals formed the nucleus of anticolonial nationalist movements that mushroomed in East Asia after World War I. None of these movements had deep roots among peasants, who everywhere comprised the vast majority of the population. Peasants had many reasons to be dissatisfied with colonial rule, but most still thought in terms of restoring the old order or religious revivalism, the two often being closely linked. Mention has already been made of the millenarian-tinged Saya San monarchist revolt in Burma in 1930. Another example is the syncretistic

Cao Dai sect, founded in Vietnam in 1925, which soon gained over a million adherents by promising a better life through religious faith and discipline. The sect also produced it own "pope" and ecclesiastical organization that implicitly challenged the French-run colonial administration. Some peasants absorbed Western ideas of patriotism through direct observation. More than a quarter of a million Chinese and Vietnamese served as laborers behind the lines in France during the war. Throughout the 1920s and 1930s, however, nationalism remained essentially an elite phenomenon.

For East Asia's new nationalists, both Wilson and Lenin offered compelling visions of the future, of which Wilson's was more attractive. After the collapse of tsarist Russia, the American president presided over a coalition of democracies that triumphed over old-fashioned German, Austro-Hungarian, and Ottoman autocracies. Western-style liberal democracy had proved itself superior and appeared to be the wave of the future. Even more appealing to East Asian nationalists was Wilson's call for national self-determination, which seemed to herald the postwar dissolution of European colonial empires and the liberation of subject peoples worldwide. This was not what Wilson had in mind. He limited self-determination chiefly to European nationalities formerly subject to the defunct Austro-Hungarian and Ottoman empires. Nevertheless, the perpetuation of European colonial rule over non-Westerners began to strike many as an embarrassing anomaly. Colonialists, now on the defensive, discarded older notions of civilizing missions and the white man's burden in favor of more up-to-date and seemingly liberal justifications for colonies based on the idea of temporary mandates.

The 1919 Paris Peace Conference first raised, and then dashed, the hopes of East Asian nationalists for decolonization. In March, more than a million Koreans staged nationwide rallies hoping to draw attention to their demand for independence from Japan. In May, Chinese cities exploded in violent demonstrations protesting the conferees' refusal to restore territory taken from China during the war by Japan. The March First and May Fourth movements, as these upheavals are respectively known, were ignored by the peacemakers in Paris, creating a backlash of bitterness and disillusionment that communists were quick to exploit. Lenin argued that capitalists would never voluntarily relinquish their colonies, and would have to be driven out by communist revolutionaries aided by the Comintern. Many Asian nationalists were attracted by this argument. Capitalism and colonialism appeared to be two sides of the same imperialist coin. Moreover, Lenin's theories had an aura of Western scientific certitude, and his prescription of revolutionary action pointed to a new world of proletarian brotherhood inasmuch as communists promised that the liberation of Asia would lead to the collapse of capitalism in Europe.

The Washington Treaty System

The postwar rise of nationalism and communism posed troublesome problems for East Asia's remaining imperialist powers. The Russian Empire, transformed into the Soviet Union, had quit the imperialist "club" and become a revolutionary state dedicated to overthrowing the colonial order. Indigenous nationalist movements had sprung up and were pursuing the same objective. For the United States, however, the most worrisome wartime development was Japan's apparent predilection for bare-knuckle imperial expansion. Tokyo, acting as Britain's ally, seized the opportunity offered by the outbreak of the European war to take over Germany's leasehold in Shandong Province and its western Pacific holdings. It followed this up in 1915 by confronting the weak Chinese government in Beijing with "Twenty-One Demands," including the transfer of the Shandong leasehold to Japan, the extension of its privileges in southern Manchuria, and China's acceptance of Japanese advisors. Although the Japanese considered these demands to be imperialist business as usual, the Chinese portrayed them to the alarmed Americans as an attempt to reduce China to the status of a Japanese protectorate.

President Wilson was appalled by Japan's behavior, which smacked of the old imperialism he sought to replace with the new internationalism embodied in his planned League of Nations. He also regarded Japan's encroachments on China as violating "Open Door" principles that had been the cornerstone of American policy toward China since 1899. As originally conceived, the Open Door assumed the continuation of the Unequal Treaty System and existing European spheres of influence, seeking only to maintain equality of commercial opportunity and China's administrative integrity. It was designed, in other words, to safeguard the U.S. economic stake in semi-colonial China by forestalling its partition into colonies. For idealists like Wilson, however, the Open Door also entailed a moral obligation on the part of the United States to act as China's mentor and protector as it struggled to transform itself into a modern nation-state. This self-appointed role appealed to American anti-imperialists, since it suggested that the United States acted from loftier motives. It was especially popular among American Protestant missionaries in China and their supporters in the United States, who had Wilson's ear.

The Shandong issue reemerged during the 1919 Paris Peace Conference, where the Japanese resisted U.S.-Chinese pressure to return the leasehold, arguing that they had succeeded to German rights with the wartime concurrence of their British ally. Their position disgusted Wilson and outraged Chinese nationalists, provoking the May Fourth demonstrations. Wilson was also irritated by Japan's refusal to fully apply Open Door principles to its southern Manchurian sphere of interest. Although the Japanese accepted nominal

Chinese sovereignty, they worked with the local Chinese warlord to exclude foreign competition and monopolize Manchuria's wealth for themselves. Some in the American government were willing to accept Japan's "special position" in Manchuria as the price that had to be paid for Tokyo's cooperation. In 1917, for example, Wilson's secretary of state concluded an agreement with his Japanese counterpart that seemed to recognize this position. But Wilson himself opposed any compromise of Open Door principles, even though he acquiesced in the Unequal Treaty System which Chinese nationalists regarded as a national humiliation.

U.S.-Japanese feuding over China seemed especially ominous because it took place against the background of a naval arms race. This race was triggered by the Americans, who launched a naval expansion program during the war aimed at giving them a fleet second to none. The Japanese responded by undertaking a buildup of their own, as did the British, who were reluctant to lose their traditional supremacy at sea. This rivalry dismayed the British inasmuch as their weakened postwar economy could not sustain it, and the Anglo-Japanese alliance confronted them with the unacceptable prospect of having to support Tokyo in the event of a U.S.-Japan clash. The Japanese shrank from such a clash. They were unwilling to confront the world's strongest industrial power and knew that the British would not back them. Under Wilson's successor, Warren G. Harding, who was less sympathetic to China and more inclined to cooperate with Japan, the United States also pulled back. Few Americans believed that their stake in China justified a collision with Japan. Moreover, their naval building program was expensive and they wanted a peace dividend and a return to what their new president called "normalcy."

The stage was therefore set for a political settlement and the Americans took the lead in shaping it. In 1921–22, they convened a conference in Washington of East Asian powers of whom the principal ones were Japan, Britain, China, and France. (The Soviet Union, viewed as a pariah state, was not invited.) There they proposed a set of treaties that together established a new framework for stability and cooperation in the region. The centerpiece was the Five Power Treaty, which ended the naval race and put in place a 5:5:3 ratio in capital ships among the United States, Britain, and Japan. The Japanese were compensated for their inferior ratio by a nonfortification agreement under which Britain and the United States undertook not to construct new bases east of Singapore and west of Hawaii. Japan thus secured naval supremacy in East Asia and the western Pacific. This, however, was less a concession than a confirmation of the existing balance of naval power. The American battleships that would have upset it were still under construction or planned, and Washington had no intention of completing them; indeed, it proved unwilling even to build up its naval strength to treaty limits.

Ending the naval race required dampening international rivalries and tensions in East Asia which, in the American view, meant devising a substitute for the Anglo-Japanese alliance and reviving the Open Door in China. The first objective was met by the Four Power Treaty, which replaced the alliance with an agreement among France, Britain, Japan, and the United States to consult and refrain from destabilizing unilateral actions. This was not a collective security pact, since it imposed no binding obligations and lacked enforcement provisions. Given the U.S. aversion to "entangling alliances," however, it was probably the most that could have been achieved. In regard to China, the Nine Power Treaty reaffirmed Open Door principles and committed the signatories to cooperate with the Chinese government in creating conditions conducive to the gradual elimination of the Unequal Treaty System. Although these undertakings disappointed Chinese nationalists, who wanted the immediate dismantlement of this system, they ruled out strong-arm tactics like the Twenty-One Demands and reflected the treaty powers' willingness to deal with China in a spirit of restraint and compromise.

The main defect of the Washington Treaty System was its assumption that rising Chinese nationalism could be reconciled with Japan's special position in Manchuria, which the Japanese regarded as lying outside the scope of the Open Door and were determined to defend at any cost. This contradiction was not, however, at first apparent. In the early 1920s, China lacked an effective central government and national unification was merely an aspiration without prospect of early realization. The Japanese, confident that southern Manchuria would remain securely under their control for the foreseeable future, proved willing to abide by the spirit of the Washington treaties. They returned the Shandong leasehold to China and joined Britain and the United States in entering into negotiations with Beijing aimed at revising the Unequal Treaties. In addition, Japan withdrew its troops from eastern Siberia in 1922, having accomplished nothing from its four-year anti-Bolshevik expedition there except to alienate the Soviets and arouse American suspicions of its imperialist ambitions. The army was blamed for this expensive fiasco and its standing among the Japanese public fell accordingly.

Japan's Democratic Interlude

Japan's embrace of naval arms limitation and diplomatic cooperation with China and the Western powers coincided with its shift toward liberal democracy. As described in the previous chapter, pro-Western party politicians moved in to fill the leadership vacuum at the apex of the Japanese state during the 1920s. Their ascendancy was built on the support of big business, the new urban middle class, and rural landlords. It was also underpinned by what Japanese elites perceived as the postwar "trend of the times." Democracy had triumphed over autocracy in the Great War and old-fashioned power politics seemed to be giving way to Wilsonian internationalism as embodied in the League of Nations. In line with these trends, party leaders eschewed territorial aggrandizement and put peaceful economic expansion at the top of Japan's foreign policy agenda. Domestically, they reined in the army and reduced its size, and opened the political system to greater popular participation. Their crowning achievement was the enactment of universal manhood suffrage in 1925, a move that appeared to herald Japan's entry into the ranks of Western parliamentary democracies.

"Taisho Democracy"—as the era of party rule between 1918 and 1932 is called, after the reign name of the Meiji emperor's son and successor—fell short of liberal democratic ideals. The parties were dominated by business-oriented conservatives suspicious of organized labor and hostile to leftists. In the same year that they adopted universal manhood suffrage, they passed a Peace Preservation Law arming the police with expanded powers to crack down on communists, anarchists, and others deemed to be subversives. As suggested by the 1919 Red Scare in the United States, however, Japanese party politicians had no monopoly on exaggerated fears of the Left. A more fundamental shortcoming of Taisho Democracy was the inability of its defenders to articulate a persuasive rationale for party government. Given virtually universal acceptance of family state togetherness under the sacrosanct authority of the emperor, the parties seemed to stand for discord and corruption. Their identification with zaibatsu and landlord interests, and their perceived propensity for squabbling and influence peddling undermined their legitimacy in the eyes of many Japanese.

The parties also had the misfortune to come to power at a time when the problems and conflicts generated by Japan's industrialization became acute. The postwar spread of labor strife, trade unions, and Marxism dismayed conservatives, who saw in these trends the breakdown of national unity and traditional values. Signs of increasing rural distress and inequality were equally alarming. By the 1920s, the growth and relative prosperity of agriculture during the Meiji period were a distant memory. Agricultural production and productivity had long since peaked, and the press of numbers had reduced many farmers to tenants who eked out a hardscrabble existence at the mercy of landlords. Japan's economic center of gravity was shifting from agriculture to industry, but the bulk of the population remained concentrated in the overcrowded and depressed farming sector. The response of the parties to these challenges was cautious and dilatory. They shied away from land reform, which might have ameliorated the plight of the rural poor, and pursued pro-business policies, attaching a lower priority to factory and other social legislation that addressed the needs of industrial workers.

Japanese Ultranationalism

Under these circumstances, it is hardly surprising that party rule came under attack from extremists on the Left and the Right. As different as they were in other respects, communists and right-wing ultranationalists agreed that Japan was threatened by the advance of capitalism, and both rejected Western-style liberal democracy. They parted company, however, on the issue of the emperor. Communists advocated abolishing the emperor system, which they regarded as a pernicious myth rationalizing capitalist exploitation of the masses. While utranationalists were no less hostile to capitalism, they agitated for the restoration of the emperor to his rightful place as the benevolent "father" of the national family, arguing that the conflicts besetting Japan would then spontaneously give way to harmony. Their restorationism struck a chord with many Japanese who were perplexed and troubled by the unsettling changes that engulfed the country in the 1920s. Despite its egalitarian and anti-elitist thrust, which implied a radical restructuring of Japan's society and polity, it meshed with the family state ideology and quasi-religious devotion to the emperor inculcated by the government since Meiji times.

Japanese ultranationalists resembled contemporary Italian and German fascists insofar as they combined an antipathy to communism and liberalism with a glorification of the nation imagined to possess organic unity and peerless virtues. They also shared with their European counterparts a determination to realize the nation's presumed will to greatness through military expansion. But they had special preoccupations that set them apart from European fascists. One of these was reviving the spiritual link between emperor and people that they felt had been broken by corrupt Westernized elites. Another was driving Westerners out of Asia. Japanese ultranationalists were militant pan-Asianists who believed that an imperial restoration should go hand in hand with a Japanese-led crusade to liberate Asia from Western economic, cultural, and political domination. Domestic support for their position grew during the 1920s, fed by widespread anger over the Anglo-American powers' exclusion of Japanese immigrants, which demonstrated the seeming futility of Japan's quest for equality with the "white race" and engendered feelings of solidarity with the West's Asian victims.

Most Japanese perceived no contradiction between opposing Western colonialism and upholding Japan's empire. As noted in the preceding chapter, they drew a distinction between Western colonies, which in their view involved the exploitation of Asians by racial and cultural aliens, and their own supposedly benevolent occupation of Korea and Taiwan, which offered kindred, albeit lesser peoples the benefits of imperial rule and cultural assimilation to superior Japanese ways. Ultranationalists carried this line of reasoning a step further, advocating Japan's forcible expulsion of Western colonialists from Asia and its transformation of their colonies and semi-colonies, including China, into a new family of nations that would look to Tokyo for inspiration and guidance. The Japanese Empire was, in other words, to become the champion of anti-colonial nationalism in Asia. As a precondition for undertaking this "sacred mission," ultranationalists insisted that Japan would have to free itself from its adulation of the West and recover its spiritual unity and Asian identity. This, in turn, required overthrowing its pro-Western party and business elite and restoring the emperor to the center of national life.

In contrast to European fascists, Japanese ultranationalists disdained mass organization and charismatic leadership. There was no counterpart of Hitler or Mussolini, and no fascist political party. Taking the antiforeign samurai zealots of the 1860s as their model, ultranationalists considered themselves "shock troops" whose task was to point the way to revolution through self-sacrificing individual heroics. Organized in small conspiratorial bands, they specialized in assassinating government and business leaders. The object of their restorationist fervor, Japan's imperial line, produced two unlikely "god-kings" after 1912. The Meiji emperor's successor proved to be mentally deranged and had to be removed from the throne in 1921. The latter's son took his place in 1926, assuming the reign name of Showa or "Brilliant Harmony." Better known in the West by his personal name, Hirohito, the Showa emperor was a diffident, bespectacled figure who was attracted to Western ways and whose chief interest was marine biology. While not entirely a cipher, he kept his opinions on politics to himself. He saw his role as a ratifier of decisions by his senior officials and rarely intervened in the policymaking process.

Military Discontent

Although Japan's ultranationalists operated more or less openly under the watchful but not unsympathetic eyes of the police, they had no prospect of gaining power or even posing a serious threat to the establishment. Their only hope of realizing their revolutionary goals lay in securing allies among the ruling groups, and the most promising candidate was the army. In the late 1920s, many army officers were attracted to the idea of a "Showa Restoration." They felt that the parties had sold out to the West and imperiled Japan's security by accepting naval inferiority, downsizing the army, and tying Japan's hands in China. They also held party government responsible for allowing fissures to develop in Japanese society between capital and labor, landlords and tenants, and city and countryside. As paragons of loyalty and duty to the emperor, moreover, professional soldiers were appalled by the spread of Western hedonism and selfishness as exemplified by dance halls and corruption scandals. A 1923 assassination attempt on then Crown Prince Hirohito by an anarchist underscored for them the growing danger posed by radical leftists despite police repression and roundups of communists.

The army was also drawn to ultranationalism by its reading of geopolitical trends and the changing nature of warfare. Army theorists envisioned a world dominated by competing blocs and a global struggle between capitalism and communism led, respectively, by the United States and the Soviet Union. In their view, Japan and its unique national polity would be overwhelmed unless it prepared for a military showdown with the Americans and Soviets. As adumbrated by the 1914–18 European war, this showdown would take the form of "total war" in which the economic, human, and spiritual resources of the nation would have to be mobilized for a fight to the finish. Faced by continental giants like the United States and the USSR, moreover, Japan would have to rally the Chinese and other Asian peoples behind it in a Japanese-led East Asian bloc. The calls of civilian ultranationalists for a Showa Restoration and a crusade to liberate Asia dovetailed with these priorities, providing a compelling ideological rationale for the mobilization of the Japanese people for total war behind the emperor, and the construction of an Asian bloc opposed to both Soviet communism and Western capitalism.

Although the army embraced the program of the radical nationalists, it was divided over how to implement it. The principal cleavage was between the "Imperial Way" and "Control" factions. In the early 1930s, Imperial Way zealots, mainly lower-ranking officers, joined civilian ultranationalists in assassinating traitors in high places and plotting an army coup aimed at establishing a military dictatorship that would nationalize industry, abolish the diet and parties, and strip elites of their wealth and privileges. In 1936, such a coup was attempted in Tokyo by a mutinous army division led by junior officers, but it was quickly suppressed and military discipline restored. Most army leaders supported the Control faction, which abhorred violence and coups, preferring a gradual takeover of the Japanese state through co-optation and compromise. Their approach left Japan's constitutional structure intact. After 1932, party heads were shunted aside as prime ministers in favor of figures who were responsive to the army's foreign and domestic priorities. But the parties continued to contest national elections, and the diet retained its power to approve budgets and legislation submitted by the government.

The End of Party Rule

The army might have been unable to gain power had the parties not been discredited by the Great Depression. The worldwide economic slump of 1929–32 hit Japan particularly hard, resulting in mass unemployment in the cities and near starvation in parts of the countryside as Western demand for silk, the mainstay of many farm households, collapsed. In Japan, as elsewhere, few had expected this calamity or knew how to cope with it. The economic orthodoxy of the day prescribed raising import barriers and slashing government spending in hopes of reviving business confidence and promoting exports. But these remedies proved counterproductive, leading to a further contraction of foreign trade and domestic demand. Faith in free-market capitalism and liberal democracy declined and support for fascism and communism increased. Germany, Japan's constitutional role model since Meiji times, abandoned Weimar democracy in favor of Hitler's version of fascism in 1933. The internationalism of the 1920s gave way to protectionism and beggar-thy-neighbor economic policies as governments struggled to extricate themselves from the crisis.

Japan recovered from the Depression fairly quickly through a combination of currency devaluation and government pump priming. But this recovery came too late to save party rule. In 1932, the emperor's inner circle of advisors decided that the politicians should hand over power to military figures who enjoyed greater public confidence and seemed better able to unify the country. Although there were earlier precedents for the selection of nonparty prime ministers, the situation in 1932 was different inasmuch as Japan was in the grip of an economic and political emergency. With unemployment soaring, civilian and military ultranationalists launched an assassination campaign against party prime ministers and others whom they held responsible for leading the country to ruin. Between 1930 and 1932, they gunned down two prime ministers and a number of senior officials in hopes of bringing about a Showa Restoration. Right-wing extremists were outraged by the nation's economic plight and by what they took to be renewed evidence of party leaders' willingness to compromise its security by agreeing to another round of cuts in Japan's fleet strength at the 1930 London Naval Conference.

The breakdown of party government was dramatized by its inability to restrain the army's Manchurian garrison from overthrowing the warlord regime there and setting up the Japanese-controlled puppet state of Manchukuo in 1931–32. This move had long been contemplated by the army; indeed, there was an abortive attempt to implement it in 1928 that was quashed by the high command in Tokyo. In 1931, however, army leaders approved the takeover and persuaded the civilian prime minister and his cabinet to go along. The army considered Japan's special position in Manchuria to be threatened by the buildup of Soviet forces in the Maritime Province, as well as moves by Chiang Kai-shek's recently established Nanjing government to bring Manchuria under its control. But the seizure of Manchuria was not merely defensive.

Army strategists also viewed it as the first step in the creation of the Asian bloc that Japan needed to wage total war against the Soviet Union and the Anglo-American powers. Manchuria offered mineral and agricultural riches, and provided a proving ground for the army's ideas about postcolonial Asian cooperation under Japan's aegis.

Japan versus China and the West

The Manchurian Incident, as the army's takeover of Manchuria is known, marked the end both of party rule and of Japan's adherence to the Washington Treaty System. The United States and Britain protested Japan's action as a violation of the Nine Power Treaty, and Washington expressed its disapproval by adopting a "nonrecognition" policy toward Manchukuo. The League of Nations undertook an investigation of the Manchurian Incident and issued a report critical of Japan. Tokyo reacted by walking out of the League in 1933. In the following year, it proclaimed a "Japanese Monroe Doctrine" over China, warning the Western powers not to interfere with its actions there. There was no effective Western response. The Americans and British were preoccupied with their domestic economic problems and hopeful that pro-Western moderates would regain control of Japanese foreign policy. In 1936, however, Japan refused to renew the naval arms limitation treaties of 1922 and 1930, and began a buildup of its fleet. Also in 1936, it signed an Anti-Comintern Pact with Nazi Germany, aligning itself with the ambitions of Hitler and Mussolini to overturn the 1919 Paris peace settlement.

Why did Japan renounce cooperation with the West, and why was there not greater domestic resistance to this course? Those who might have protested—the party and business elite, conservative elder statesmen, and the emperor himself—were cowed into silence or acquiescence. Overt dissent invited assassination by ultranationalists of the army's Imperial Way faction and their civilian allies. Moreover, Japan's seizure of Manchuria and its defiant stand toward the West were popular with the Japanese public. With little coaching by army propagandists, the mass media presented the establishment of Manchukuo as an act of self-defense necessary to secure Japan's "Manchurian lifeline." The media also celebrated the assertion of a Japanese Monroe Doctrine and endorsed pan-Asianist ideas of "Asia for the Asians" and Japan's "sacred mission" to lead an anti-Western crusade. Such ideas, held by a minority during the 1920s, became central to mainstream thinking about Japan's international role in the 1930s. Promoted by the military and sanctioned by the emperor, militant pan-Asianism replaced liberal internationalism as Japan's new foreign policy orthodoxy.

Japan's aggression put it on a collision course with Chinese national-

Chiang Kai-shek in 1945.

ism represented by Chiang Kai-shek. The takeover of Manchuria sparked anti-Japanese riots in Shanghai in 1932, which escalated into a major clash between Chinese and Japanese troops. But Chiang resisted being drawn into a war with Japan. He could expect no help from the League of Nations or the Western powers. His top priority, moreover, was annihilating his erstwhile communist allies who, as noted in Chapter 4, had established a peasant-based "Soviet republic" in the southeast. In 1933, Chiang accepted a truce with the Japanese and concentrated his German-trained army for a knockout blow against the communists. This almost succeeded. In 1934–35, his army overran their stronghold, forcing the survivors to undertake an epic 5,000-mile "Long March" to a new redoubt in the remote northwestern province of Shaanxi. There they prepared to make a final stand under the leadership of Mao Zedong, a veteran peasant organizer and specialist in guerrilla warfare who, unlike orthodox Marxist-Leninists, believed that China's communist revolution could be built on peasant discontent.

Mao might not have survived to test this theory had fate—and anti-Japanese Chinese nationalism—not given him and his embattled followers a new lease on life. In 1936, Chiang was kidnapped by one of his generals, who threatened to execute him unless he joined Mao's communists in resisting Japanese aggression. Chiang had no choice but to agree, especially since Chinese nationalist opinion strongly supported this course. Calling off a planned offensive against the communists, he formed a second united front with them and redeployed his army along the China–Manchukuo border with orders to stand firm against Japanese encroachments. Having earlier hoped to draw Chiang into a Sino-Japanese alliance, Japan's military leaders were dismayed by this turn of events. They deemed China's manpower and resources essential to the anti-Western and anticommunist Asian bloc they were intent on building. Chiang's apparent defection to the communists left them with no option except to attempt the conquest of China. Although this was a daunting prospect, military planners assured the high command that the Imperial Army would achieve a quick and decisive victory.

Japan's "New Order" in East Asia

Given the hard-line positions of Nanjing and Tokyo, a Sino-Japanese war was probably inevitable. The trigger was a 1937 skirmish at the Marco Polo Bridge a few miles north of Beijing. Both sides refused to back down and sent in reinforcements, leading to all-out but undeclared war. Japan's armies quickly seized Beijing and moved up the Yangzi to Chiang's capital of Nanjing which they captured and sacked, massacring several hundred thousand Chinese civilians. Despite these defeats, Chiang refused to surrender and withdrew with the remnant of his army to Chongqing (Chungking) in the west. The Japanese now found themselves entangled in an unwinnable war of attrition. Although they held China's eastern cities, they lacked sufficient strength to pursue Chiang or control the countryside. Rural areas were soon teeming with anti-Japanese guerrillas organized by Mao's communists, who were past masters at this type of warfare. Japan's forces were tied down in garrison duties and pacification campaigns. These campaigns produced mounting Japanese casualties and inflicted heavy damage and loss of life on the peasantry, but failed to break Chinese resistance or induce Chiang to come to terms.

For Japanese military leaders, a silver lining in the China quagmire was the opportunity it afforded to accelerate Japan's mobilization for total war. In 1938, the government announced the creation of a "national defense state." Its bureaucrats and planners took over direction of the economy and harnessed it to armament production. Big business, rewarded with lucrative defense contracts, fell into line. So did labor unions, which gave up their agitation for worker rights and reorganized themselves as patriotic associations. The media, academia, and other previously autonomous sectors followed suit. In 1940, the

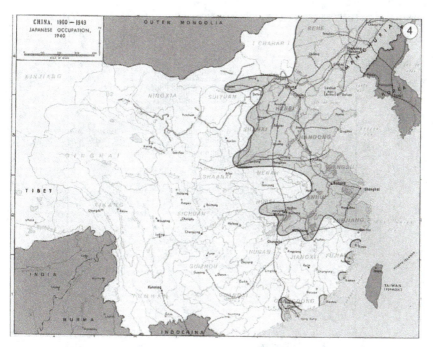

Japanese-occupied China in 1940.

political parties voluntarily dissolved and amalgamated themselves into the "Imperial Rule Assistance Association." Economic and political mobilization went hand in hand with spiritual mobilization. Aided by the patriotic fervor engendered by the war, the government brought emperor worship and belief in the superiority of Japan's unique polity to a fever pitch. It also attempted, with less success, to discourage Western pastimes such as golf and baseball. Resisters, of whom there were few, were branded as unpatriotic and hounded by the Interior Ministry's thought police.

The "China Incident," the Japanese euphemism for the war, also provided the impetus for the clarification of Japan's foreign policy goals. In 1938, the government proclaimed these to be the rollback of Soviet communism and Western colonialism, and the establishment of a "New Order" in East Asia built around a China–Manchukuo–Japan bloc. As presented by Tokyo, the New Order promised East Asians national liberation, economic development, and recovery of their cultural identity under Japan's benign tutelage. Manchukuo was the showcase and laboratory of what the Japanese had in mind for China and Western colonies. Behind the facade of an independent Manchuria presided over by China's last Manchu emperor, Pu Yi, the Japanese army developed a heavy industrial base; constructed modern, well-laid-out

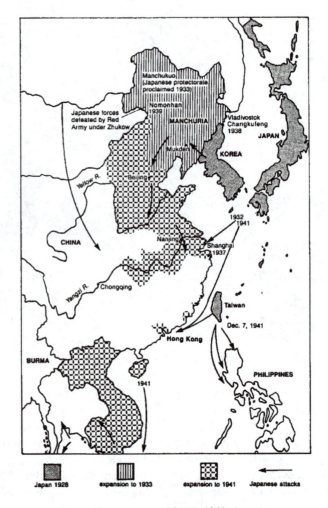

Japanese expansion to 1941.

cities; and provided public services and an efficient rail system, including the ultramodern Asia Express. The army touted Manchukuo as a model of racial harmony among Manchus, Chinese, Japanese, Mongols, and Koreans, and an exemplar of the "Kingly Way," or the traditional Confucian ideal of humane government by sage-kings.

Japan's offer of Manchukuo-style nominal independence under Japanese supervision did not apply to Koreans and Taiwanese. In Tokyo's view, these peoples were part of the Japanese nation, not separate nations fallen victim to colonial oppression like the Chinese, Burmese, and others. Redefining themselves as anticolonial liberators in the late 1930s, the Japanese sought to rid themselves of the residual taint of colonialism by accelerating their assimilation of Koreans and Taiwanese. For both groups, the New Order consequently meant intensified "Japanization." This involved a determined effort to blot out their separate cultural and national identity by requiring them to take Japanese names, speak Japanese, and worship at Shinto shrines. Their assimilation of Koreans and Taiwanese did not mean that Japanese thought better of them or were more inclined to treat them—or other Asians—as equals. Japan's New Order rhetoric of Asian brotherhood and equality was accompanied by a strident assertion of Japanese superiority that made brutality and atrocities against their fellow East Asians, such as the 1937 "Rape of Nanjing," almost a matter of course.

Tokyo's declaration of a New East Asian Order threw down the gauntlet to the Soviet Union and the Anglo-American powers, but it was unclear how or even whether Japan would move against them. With most of its army tied down in China, it seemed unlikely to take on powerful new adversaries. Stalin, however, took no chances, funneling aid to Chiang's beleaguered army and beefing up the Soviet Union's Far Eastern forces. In 1938–39, he put down a marker by ordering his troops to stand firm in two major clashes with the Japanese along Manchukuo's border with Mongolia and the Soviet Far East. Japan came off second best in both of these encounters. The larger, 1939 conflict in the disputed Nomonhan area between Manchukuo and Mongolia, a Soviet client state, amounted to an undeclared war in which both sides committed substantial forces. Soviet mechanized units decisively defeated the Imperial Army, inflicting some 20,000 casualties and forcing it to pull back. This defeat had a sobering effect on the high command in Tokyo. Although it did not abandon the idea of a strike against the Soviet Union, it acquired greater respect for Soviet military capabilities.

Japan's invasion of China and proclamation of a New Order in East Asia at first elicited little more than diplomatic protests from the Western powers. Britain and France were preoccupied with Hitler's aggression in Europe, and the United States was immobilized by isolationist sentiment. Besides, Japan respected Western treaty rights in China, and offered apologies and compensation for sinking several American and British gunboats. Tokyo hoped that the West would acquiescence in its New Order and help bring Chiang to heel. But this did not happen. U.S. president Franklin Roosevelt was appalled by Japanese aggression against China, which he likened to "international gangsterism," and was determined to resist. The U.S. Congress and public balked at taking a strong stand against Japan. By 1939, however, Roosevelt had won congressional approval for undertaking a naval buildup and applying economic pressure on Japan by restricting the flow of American oil, scrap iron, and other strategic materials essential to its war effort. A U.S.–Japan confrontation was thus taking shape, but whether it would lead to war was still an open question as the 1940s began.

7

The Pacific War

The war launched by Japan against the United States in 1941 was a gamble that disastrously failed. Having hoped to force Washington to recognize their dominance over East Asia, the Japanese were instead confronted by an unstoppable American counteroffensive across the Pacific that culminated in their surrender 1945. But Japan's failed bid for regional hegemony under the pan-Asianist banner of "Asia for the Asians" decisively reshaped East Asia. It shattered the European colonial order and set in motion powerful nationalist forces that led to a new era of independent nation-states. It also tilted the Communist-Guomindang power balance in China in favor of Mao Zedong, laying the foundations for his triumph over Chiang Kai-shek when the Chinese civil war resumed after the war. The American victory over Japan enabled the United States to replace the Japanese and Europeans as East Asia's leader and the chief arbiter of its affairs. But the Americans did not have the field to themselves. The Soviet Union exploited the Pacific War's endgame in 1945 to make itself a major regional player and position itself to challenge U.S. preeminence during the subsequent Cold War.

An Unwanted War

During 1940–41, the United States and Japan drifted into a war they neither wanted nor expected. Each miscalculated the will and intentions of the other, leading to an action–reaction cycle that culminated in the Pearl Harbor attack. Japan set this fateful process in motion in 1940 by concluding a military alliance with Nazi Germany and fascist Italy—the Tripartite or Axis Pact—and announcing that its New Order now encompassed "Greater East Asia," including Southeast Asia. By Tokyo's lights, these moves seemed eminently reasonable. Hitler's blitzkrieg victories in Europe in early 1940 weakened the British, French, and Dutch, making their resource-rich Southeast Asian colonies vulnerable to Japanese diplomatic pressure and possible military action. Control over Southeast Asia would speed victory in the China war by cutting

Chiang's supply lines and providing the strategic materials, particularly oil, that Japan needed to prosecute the war without having to rely on American imports. The Japanese calculated that the Tripartite Pact would cause the United States to stand aside by confronting it with the possibility of German intervention if it tried to impede Japan's move into Southeast Asia.

The Axis alliance confirmed President Franklin Roosevelt's worst fears about Japan. Having earlier regarded it as a regional "rogue state," he now viewed it as part of a global fascist conspiracy that threatened both the United States and the hard-pressed British whom he was committed to supporting. Fighting with its back to the wall in Europe against Hitler, Britain faced losing its access to Southeast Asia's vital rubber, tin, and bauxite if the Japanese moved into the area. Any doubt about their intention to do just that was erased by their military occupation of northern Indochina in 1940 with the acquiescence of the pro-Axis Vichy French colonial authorities. The Roosevelt administration therefore concluded that the Japanese advance into Southeast Asia would have to be stopped. Despite the unpreparedness of the U.S. military for a possible conflict with Japan, Washington policymakers were confident that Japan would never dare attack the United States. They also assumed that its reliance on American-supplied oil and other strategic materials gave them the whip hand. Washington's first turn of the economic screw was cutting the flow of aviation gasoline and scrap metal to Japan.

Contrary to American expectations, these sanctions made the Japanese more aggressive. Faced by the prospect of a total American embargo, they resolved in 1941 to accelerate their seizure of Southeast Asian resources, using military force as necessary. The prelude was Tokyo's conclusion of a nonaggression pact with the Soviet Union, which reduced the danger of a war with the Soviets. The next step was the deployment of Japanese forces into southern Indochina, positioning them for strikes against British Malaya and the Dutch East Indies. Although detailed planning for a war with the United States got under way, Tokyo wanted to avoid such a conflict. It expected that a show of force in Indochina would induce Washington to back away from further sanctions and adopt a more accommodating position toward Japanese aims in Southeast Asia. This expectation was not groundless. At the time, Roosevelt was preoccupied with coping with the larger menace posed by Nazi Germany, and helping Britain survive Hitler's U-boat campaign to sever its Atlantic lifeline. It was thus reasonable to suppose that he would seek to avoid a dangerous confrontation with Japan.

Roosevelt instead countered by freezing Japanese assets in the United States, which had the effect of halting all American exports to Japan, including oil shipments critical to its economy. He was convinced that the Japanese would back down in the face of this crippling embargo, and discounted

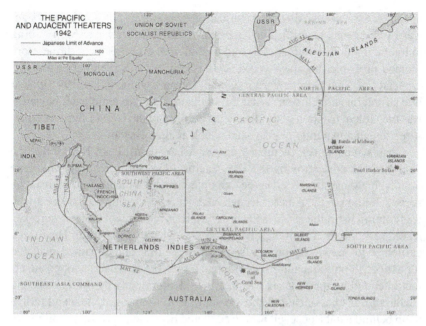

Fullest extent of Japanese conquests in 1942.

warnings from some of his advisors that Japan might respond by invading Southeast Asia. It seemed inconceivable to him that Japan, with an economy only one-tenth the size, would risk war with the United States. Roosevelt was so sure that he was dealing from a position of strength that he raised the ante for a settlement, informing Tokyo that the United States would lift the embargo only if Japan withdrew from both Indochina and China. The Japanese seriously considered a pullback from Indochina, but China was a different matter. Too many lives had been expended in what the Japanese people had been told was a "holy war" to free China from Western exploitation and the threat of communism to make a retreat there politically feasible. In late 1941, negotiations between Washington and Tokyo consequently deadlocked, and the Japanese prepared to invade Southeast Asia.

Japanese planners assumed that an attack on British Malaya and the Dutch East Indies would require a simultaneous strike against the American Pacific Fleet based at Pearl Harbor in Hawaii, which they considered certain to intervene. They did not seriously examine the possibility that Roosevelt might be unable to persuade his isolationist congress to approve U.S. military intervention in the absence of a direct attack on American soil. Although the Japanese realized that taking on the United States was a dangerous gamble, they believed that they could induce Washington to accept their dominance over East Asia by knocking out American naval power in the Pacific. This belief was by no means fanciful. The Americans, after all, had never been willing to fight a major war in East Asia and had no vital interests there. It therefore seemed probable that they would acquiesce in Japan's regional hegemony, especially if Nazi Germany triumphed in Europe, which in late 1941 looked like a foregone conclusion. What the Japanese failed to anticipate, however, was the violent reaction of the American public and the U.S. Congress to their surprise and apparently unprovoked attack against Hawaii.

Japan's audacious December 7 carrier strike against Pearl Harbor had the dual purpose of destroying the U.S. Pacific Fleet and shattering American morale. It almost succeeded in the first objective, but failed disastrously in the second. Although the Americans had advance warning that a Japanese attack was coming in Southeast Asia, the Pearl Harbor raid caught them by surprise, resulting in the sinking of their battleships with heavy loss of life. The Fleet's carriers were, however, fortuitously away at the time and remained available for action. In political and psychological terms, the raid had the opposite effect intended by the Japanese. Rather than demoralizing the Americans and encouraging isolationist and antiwar sentiment, it outraged them and rallied them behind what Roosevelt promised would be a relentless counteroffensive across the Pacific that would end only with Japan's total defeat and unconditional surrender. Americans were particularly incensed by what they regarded as Japan's "sneak attack," since a declaration of war came only after the raid had begun. Tokyo's initial hopes of forcing the United States to accept its domination of East Asia consequently died at Pearl Harbor.

The War in the Pacific

The raid on Pearl Harbor coincided with a carefully planned Japanese offensive in Southeast Asia that cleared the area of American, British, and Dutch forces in early 1942. Malaya was the first to fall, along with the supposedly impregnable bastion of Singapore whose British garrison surrendered to an attacking Japanese force half its size. The fall of Singapore and the sinking of two British battleships sent to defend it were among Britain's worst-ever defeats. In the face of the advancing Japanese, who enjoyed air and naval superiority, the Dutch then surrendered in Java and the British retreated from Burma to India. A U.S.-Filipino army under General Douglas MacArthur held out in the strongholds of Bataan and Corregidor until May 1942, when it, too, capitulated. In Indochina, the Japanese left the Vichy French colonial government in place under their control. But they had, in a matter of months, ended a century of Western colonial rule and destroyed its mystique of white supremacy. Eager to humiliate Europeans and Americans in the eyes of their

British General Arthur Percival surrenders at Singapore, February 15, 1942.

erstwhile colonial subjects, the Japanese treated prisoners with a brutality exceeded only by the Nazi invaders of the Soviet Union.

Japan's victories gave it an expanded empire that stretched from Burma in the west to the Marshall Islands in the central Pacific, and from Manchuria in the north to New Guinea in the south. Chiang Kai-shek still held out in western China, sustained by a trickle of supplies flown from India over the Himalayan "hump." But Japan's control of Southeast Asia positioned it to realize the militarists' vision of an East Asian bloc. The British, forced back into India, posed no immediate threat. Nor did the Soviets, who were fighting for survival against Nazi Germany. But the Americans were more troublesome. One of their aircraft carriers carried out a surprise raid on Tokyo which did little damage but shocked the Japanese. Others checked a seaborne Japanese advance against Australian-held southeastern New Guinea. Japan therefore concentrated its fleet in a thrust toward Hawaii, hoping to annihilate the American carriers around Midway Atoll. However, the Japanese plan misfired. In the June 1942 Battle of Midway, Japan sustained a major defeat, sinking only one American carrier while losing four of its own. It thereby lost the capacity for further offensive naval operations and was forced on the defensive.

Japan's Pacific defenses were strong, being built around heavily fortified island bases supported by the still powerful Japanese navy. Thanks to Hitler's declaration of war on the United States after Pearl Harbor, moreover, the U.S. adopted a Europe First strategy that made the war against Japan a secondary priority. Much of the output of American industry in 1942–43 was devoted to winning the Battle of the Atlantic, supplying the Soviet struggle against Germany, and supporting Allied landings in North Africa and Italy. In the southwestern Pacific, the Americans, backed by Australians and New Zealanders, fought holding operations in New Guinea and the Solomon Islands. By late 1943, however, they had sufficient resources to mount a large-scale offensive against the Japanese. This came from two directions. In the central Pacific, the U.S. Navy conducted amphibious assaults on Japanese-held islands beginning with Tarawa Atoll in the Gilbert Islands. In the southwestern Pacific, the U.S. Army moved against Japanese bases along the northern coast of New Guinea. Both of these thrusts relied on growing American naval and air superiority, and novel leapfrog tactics that entailed bypassing and isolating Japanese strongholds, allowing them to wither on the vine.

Pacific land battles were marked by unparalleled ferocity. Neither side took prisoners, and the Japanese invariably fought to the last man, preferring to immolate themselves in suicide charges rather than surrender. Americans were horrified and mystified by this behavior, but it testified to the efficacy of Japan's imperial cult, which made dying for the emperor a duty and virtue. Despite fierce resistance, however, the Japanese were unable to stem the American advance. Their problem, in essence, was that they had taken on a superpower that far outclassed them industrially and technologically. The Americans developed superior weapons and produced them in numbers unimaginable by Japanese standards. They also learned to employ their weapons to telling effect, a case in point being the submarine. Initially used against warships, American submarines were redeployed in 1943 against merchant ships, which the Japanese navy proved incapable of protecting. Over the next two years, U.S. submarines played a key role in sinking 95 percent of the Japanese merchant marine fleet, cutting Japan's supply line to Southeast Asia and starving its industry of raw materials.

In 1944, the war went from bad to worse for the Japanese. The U.S. central Pacific offensive penetrated to the Mariana Islands which were within bomber range of Japan. In bloody fighting, American marines stormed Saipan and other islands from which the United States commenced the aerial bombardment of Japan using the B-29, its newly developed long-range heavy bomber. The Battle for the Marianas also witnessed the destruction of Japan's carrier aviation in what victorious American pilots described as a "turkey shoot." Further south, the U.S. Army began the liberation of the Philippines with a landing on Leyte Island in the center of the archipelago. The Japanese responded by throwing their remaining battleships against the U.S. invasion fleet, coming close to crippling it before they were annihilated in the war's only major engagement of capital ships. In a harbinger of things to come, Japanese defenders of the Philippines resorted to the use of suicide planes—bomb-laden aircraft piloted by zealots willing to sacrifice themselves for emperor and country by crashing into American warships. But such attacks failed to prevent the American conquest of Leyte.

In China, Japanese forces undertook an offensive in 1944 aimed at capturing air bases in the west from which American B-29s had begun bombing Japan. Although they were largely successful in this, the significance of the offensive was negated by the Americans' acquisition of better B-29 bases in the Marianas. Also in 1944, the Japanese army showed that it was far from finished by launching an invasion of India from Burma across the mountainous Indo-Burmese frontier. Advancing Japanese troops nearly won a major victory in Assam before they were repulsed by British forces. Their retreat turned into a rout, laying Burma open to Allied counteroffensives from India and China. At the beginning of 1945, however, Burma, China, and the Philippines were sideshows. Japan's fate turned on its ability to defend its home islands, against which powerful American naval and air armadas were converging. The outlook for the Japanese was bleak. Their cities were under air attack and their industry was strangled by raw material shortages. Their navy had been destroyed along with most of their conventional air power. Moreover, the defeat of Nazi Germany, their only ally, now loomed in Europe.

The Last Battles

Given these circumstances, one might expect Japan's leadership to have considered suing for peace. But this did not happen, at least not right away. Allied terms were unconditional surrender, and surrender was not in Japan's political vocabulary. Moreover, the Japanese high command had a plan for salvaging an honorable peace from impending defeat. This plan rested on the hope that the Americans might be forced to negotiate if sufficiently horrific human and material losses could be inflicted on them in a series of decisive "last battles" for the Japanese homeland. The military claimed that it had the means to implement this strategy, including interior lines of communication, thousands of suicide planes, and millions of loyal soldiers ready and willing to die for the emperor. Tactically, the plan called for luring the Americans into attacks against underground bunker complexes immune to U.S. firepower. While American troops were chewed up in hand-to-hand fighting, waves of suicide planes would devastate their invasion fleets standing offshore. If all else failed, Japanese civilians, armed with bamboo spears and other improvised weapons, were to hurl themselves against the invaders.

The proving ground of Japan's strategy was the volcanic islet of Iwo Jima located midway between Tokyo and U.S. B-29 bases in the Marianas. The Americans needed Iwo Jima as an emergency landing and refueling point for their aerial assault against Japan. Expecting an amphibious landing, the Japanese constructed elaborate underground defenses and manned them with elite troops ordered to fight to the last. The American marines who stormed ashore in February 1945 consequently entered a carefully prepared killing field. Although they took Iwo Jima and wiped out the defenders, their casualties were the highest yet in the war. The April–June Battle for Okinawa, Japan's southernmost prefecture, involved carnage on an even larger scale. Over 100,000 dug-in Japanese soldiers perished, most preferring suicide to surrender, along with perhaps one-third of the island's civilian population. But they inflicted a fearful toll on U.S. ground troops, and mass attacks by Japanese suicide planes resulted in heavy losses of American ships and sailors. The United States lost 38 ships and sustained 50,000 casualties, including 12,000 dead.

The Americans meanwhile brought total war to Japanese civilians. In early 1945, B-29s began incendiary attacks on Japan's cities, which, being constructed of wood, were highly combustible. One firebomb raid on Tokyo in March killed 120,000 people and reduced the center of the city to ashes. At the same time, American warships, cruising off the coast, bombarded cities and rail lines, and paralyzed coastal shipping. Despite the bombing and mounting shortages of food and other necessities, civilian morale showed little sign of breaking, and the military began preparations for an Okinawa-style defense of Kyushu and Honshu against anticipated American landings. With Germany's surrender in May and the loss of Okinawa in the following month, however, some of the emperor's advisors tilted toward peace. Unlike the military, they were unwilling to go down fighting in a national "Götterdämmerung" that might end in the destruction of the imperial institution. They pinned their hopes on the Soviet Union, which had maintained neutrality during the Pacific War and might be willing to mediate a conditional surrender to the Allies that would leave Japan with a semblance of peace with honor.

Japanese hopes for Soviet-mediated peace proved illusory. Stalin had already committed the Soviet Union to enter the war against Japan as soon as Germany was defeated, and was positioning his forces in the Soviet Far East for an attack on Manchuria and Korea. Moreover, the United States had secretly produced several atomic bombs which President Harry Truman, Roosevelt's successor, decided to drop on Japanese cities with the aim of inducing the Tokyo leadership to give up. In early August, the Japanese were stunned by the simultaneous Soviet attack and American atomic bombing of Hiroshima and Nagasaki. The emperor's inner circle was divided between those who urged a fight to the finish

B-29s on bombing run over Japan in 1945.

and those who recommended unconditional surrender, trusting the Americans to preserve the monarchy. Called upon to break the deadlock, Hirohito made one of his rare personal decisions by opting for surrender. Army diehards attempted a coup, but it was quashed by loyal troops. On August 15, the emperor broadcast his surrender decision in his first ever radio address to the incredulous Japanese people, asking them to "endure the unendurable" for the sake of peace.

Greater East Asia

The United States and Japan had different terms for the 1941–45 conflict and attached different meanings to it. The Americans called it the Pacific War and viewed it as a U.S.-led struggle to roll back Japanese aggression and uphold the universal principles of freedom and democracy. For the Japanese, however, it was the Greater East Asia War, a crusade by Japan to liberate eastern Asia from Western colonialism in the name of national self-determination and cultural autonomy. In the aftermath of surrender in 1945, many Japanese, particularly those on the resurgent Left, denounced this pan-Asianist crusade as a fraud concocted by militarists to justify Japan's imperialist expansion. Others, however, took comfort from the fact that they had given their all in a noble cause. In their view, the problem was not with the goals of the Greater East Asia War, but rather with the faulty assumption of the militarists that Japan could prevail against the overwhelming might of the United States. The postwar triumph of anticolonial nationalism and the retreat of Western colonialists from Asia suggested to defeated Japanese that, unlike their German allies, they had been on the right side of history after all.

The Japanese defined Greater East Asia in terms of a series of concentric zones or circles. The core was East Asia proper, the Sinic culture area of Northeast Asia comprising China, Korea, Mongolia, and Japan on which they constructed their Japan–Manchukuo–China bloc. They saw Southeast Asians as constituting a second, closely related zone possessing racial and some cultural affinities with Northeast Asia, such as Buddhism. The peoples of British India comprised a third and more peripheral zone. In the Japanese view, Indians were culturally and racially distinct from both Northeast and Southeast Asians. But they were still Asians and victims of Western colonialism and, as such, deserving of liberation. Pacific islanders, regarded by the Japanese as non-Asians, fell outside this scheme, although they were incorporated into it for purposes of building a Pacific shield against the United States. The European inhabitants of Australia and New Zealand had an uncertain but probably grim future in Greater East Asia. The Japanese intended to isolate them with their navy and deal with them later.

In the event, the progress of Japanese arms limited Greater East Asia to Northeast and Southeast Asia, or what is today thought of as East Asia. Here the Japanese set about establishing what they called a "Greater East Asian Co-Prosperity Sphere," or autarkic economic bloc with Japan as its industrial hub. They also promised national independence, and to some extent delivered. By the end of the war, they had created nominally independent, pro-Japanese governments in the Philippines, Burma, China, Laos, Cambodia, and Vietnam, and were moving to do the same in Indonesia. A third element of the Japanese program was cultural liberation and self-realization. In part, this involved the rejection of Western languages and ways, and encouragement of respect for Japan as the cultural "Light of Asia." The Japanese demanded universal reverence for their emperor and observance of their customs such as ceremonial bowing. As in Manchukuo, however, they also acted as patrons of indigenous arts and letters, and promoted the revival of precolonial traditions. Greater East Asia was, in other words, intended by the Japanese to be a multicultural as well as multinational regional entity.

East Asian Reactions

How did East Asians react to Japan's calls for national liberation, co-prosperity, and cultural autonomy? This question has little relevance for Koreans and Taiwanese, who were not part of the intended audience. Defined by Tokyo as second-class Japanese, they were expected to give unconditional loyalty to the emperor and unquestioningly obey directives handed down by the government. For them, as for the Japanese themselves, the Greater East Asia War was a time of intensified regimentation, heightened indoctrination, and increased demands for patriotic self-sacrifice. Over 600,000 Koreans and Taiwanese were conscripted for labor service in Japan and other parts of Greater East Asia. Many volunteered for the Japanese army, and some were accepted, including a future president of South Korea. In contrast to Taiwan, where there was no nationalist movement, wartime mobilization created deep fissures among Korean nationalists. Those in Korea were forced to collaborate with the Japanese along with virtually the entire Korean elite, leading exiles to regard them as traitors. The seeds of Korea's postwar political turbulence and divisions were thus sown during the war.

In China, the Japanese failed to make much headway in selling their idea of Asian unity and cooperation against the West. This is hardly surprising. As alien and ruthless invaders, they had outraged most Chinese nationalists, who rallied behind the patriotic resistance led by Chiang Kai-shek and Mao Zedong. What the Japanese needed was a nationalist leader of comparable stature who would collaborate with them. They thought they had found such a figure in Wang Jingwei, Chiang's second in command in the Guomindang, who defected in 1940 and agreed to form a pro-Japanese republic based in Nanjing. But Wang's government proved unable to attract the loyalty or respect of the Chinese. It was transparently under the thumb of the Japanese army, which insisted on freedom of action to conduct pacification campaigns and interfere in local administration. Moreover, Wang's realm, Japanese-occupied eastern China, swarmed with Japanese carpetbaggers who engaged in everything from drug trafficking and labor contracting to mining and manufacturing enterprises. Although Tokyo tried to prop up his regime by renouncing its Unequal Treaty privileges in 1943, this was too little, too late.

The Japanese had more success in Southeast Asia. Except for Filipinos, the colonial peoples there felt no loyalty toward their Western masters and were glad to see them go. They were, moreover, deeply impressed by Japan's string of military victories in 1941–42. The spectacle of Europeans and Americans surrendering en masse convinced them that the era of Western colonial rule was over, and that a new age was dawning in which their hopes for national independence might be realized. The Japanese, for their part, fanned these hopes, and their slogan "Asia for the Asians" enjoyed broad appeal. Several other factors worked in their favor. Unlike the Chinese and Koreans, Southeast Asians knew little about the Japanese and were unfamiliar with their ruthless methods. Japan was thus an unknown quantity, and many were inclined to take its idealistic slogans at face value. For some, an equally compelling reason to cooperate with Tokyo was that it at first looked like a winner. Until the Americans launched their Pacific counteroffensive in 1943–44, it was reasonable to suppose that Japan would be able to fight the Anglo-American powers to a draw, and dominate East Asia indefinitely.

Thailand, as Siam renamed itself in 1939 to emphasize its Thai identity, was attracted to Japan by a combination of ideological and political factors. Marshal Phibun Songkhram, the head of its military-dominated government, admired the discipline, patriotism, and martial spirit of the Japanese, and attempted to instill these qualities in the Thai people, albeit with only limited success. An ardent nationalist, he was also fired by the ambition of restoring Thailand's past greatness by recovering the territories ceded under duress to Britain and France in the 1890s and early 1900s. An alliance with a powerful anticolonialist Japan offered a means to achieve this end. The Thai-Japanese alliance took shape in 1940–41 as Tokyo forced the Vichy French to hand over parts of Laos and Cambodia to Thailand in return for permission to use Thai territory to attack Malaya and Burma, and Bangkok's declaration of war against Britain and the United States. In 1942–43, the Japanese sweetened the deal for Phibun by allowing him to reclaim former Thai territories in northern Malaya and eastern Burma. In exchange, Thailand contributed food and raw materials to Japan's war effort, but no troops.

The Japanese correctly anticipated strong support from Burmese nationalists, who were vehemently anti-British. The retreating British were sped on their way in 1942 by the Burmese Independence Army, a small Japanese-trained force led by Aung San, an ex–student activist who looked upon the Japanese as liberators. Tokyo rewarded him and his comrades with key positions in the pro-Japanese regime it set up in Rangoon 1942 and granted nominal independence in 1943. But Aung San's nationalists were ideologically fragmented. While united in opposing British rule and the foreign-run capitalist system to which it had given rise, they ranged from communists to liberal democrats and Buddhist visionaries. Moreover, they spoke primarily for the ethnic Burman majority. Minorities such as Kachins, Shans, and Karens, who constituted one-third of Burma's population, did not favor an independent Burma in which they would be dominated by Burmans. Some remained loyal to the British and saw themselves as forming separate nations that deserved independence in their own right.

Tokyo did not at first consider either British Malaya or the Dutch East

Indies to be potential nation-states. In the Japanese view, these colonies were a hodgepodge of semiautonomous sultanates and rival ethnic groups whose only unity derived from the presence of their British and Dutch overlords. This assessment was largely accurate in the case of Malaya, where there was no nationalist movement and little sense of nationhood. For the Japanese, as for the British, governing Malaya meant maintaining a balance among the majority Malays and ethnic Chinese and Indian minorities. In the event, however, the Japanese severely disrupted this balance. Regarding the Chinese community as a hotbed of sympathizers of Chiang and Mao, they imposed a reign of terror, including arbitrary arrests, executions, and property confiscations. At the same time, they cultivated Malays by deferring to their sultans, enrolling Malays in their administration, and patronizing Islam. The long-term effect of these policies was to exacerbate hostility between Malays and Chinese. In the short term, they radicalized Chinese, giving rise to an anti-Japanese resistance movement dominated by communists.

In the Dutch East Indies, the Japanese initially solicited the cooperation of sultans and Islamic religious leaders. But most sultans were powerless figureheads, and Islamic leaders were alienated by Japan's emperor cult. The Japanese consequently turned to the Indonesian nationalist movement led by Sukarno, and sought to use it to mobilize support for their war effort. Sukarno proved to be a willing and valuable ally, using his oratorical skills to encourage large numbers of Javanese to volunteer as laborers for the Japanese army. In return, the Japanese rewarded him with control over youth and other organizations, and allowed him to form a paramilitary force that became the nucleus of the later Indonesian army. But they held off endorsing Indonesian independence or permitting Sukarno to form a national government. Unimpeded access to Indonesian oil and other resources was too important to the Japanese to risk local interference. Tokyo did not formally promise to grant Indonesia independence until 1944, and even then dragged its heels in implementing this pledge until the last days of the war. In the end, Sukarno himself proclaimed Indonesian independence as Japan surrendered.

The Philippines was Japan's most improbable ally in Southeast Asia. Filipinos were pro-American; they had fought with the Americans against the Japanese in 1942; and the United States was committed to recognizing their independence in 1946. Nevertheless, the Filipino elite proved willing to collaborate with the Japanese for reasons of self-preservation or in hopes of mitigating the rigors of the occupation. Some also saw Japan's Co-Prosperity Sphere as the wave of the future. The Japanese welcomed their cooperation as a means of pacifying the country, and in 1943 declared the Philippines an independent republic under a collaborationist government headed by Jose Laurel, a prominent prewar politician. The Laurel regime, dominated by the

Japanese army, never won legitimacy in the eyes of Filipinos. Nor did it stem anti-Japanese guerrilla resistance, which escalated after 1943 as the advance of American forces made liberation imminent. This resistance was intertwined with long-standing peasant grievances against landlords, who were often collaborators, giving it a social revolutionary dimension that Filipino leftists and Communists eagerly exploited.

Southeast Asian communists were nowhere more successful in using the war to position themselves for a bid for power than in Vietnam. The Vietnamese Communist Party barely survived French repression in the 1930s. But its prospects brightened in 1941 when Ho Chi Minh formed the Vietminh, or "Vietnam Independence League." Although communist-controlled, it catered to nationalists of all ideological persuasions, enabling Ho to broaden his political base. Instead of frittering away Vietminh forces in hopeless attacks on the Japanese-backed Vichy French, Ho bided his time, building up their strength with weapons supplied by China and the United States. His chance came in early 1945. The Japanese suddenly turned on the French and imprisoned them, creating a power vacuum. They then persuaded the last Nguyen king, Bao Dai, to proclaim Vietnam's independence. But Bao Dai was powerless. A longtime French puppet, he had no administration or army and little popular support. As the Japanese surrendered, Ho's Vietminh occupied Hanoi, coaxed Bao Dai to abdicate, and proclaimed the establishment of the Democratic Republic of Vietnam.

By 1944–45, the Japanese had long since overstayed their welcome in Southeast Asia and resistance to them was everywhere mounting. From the beginning, the arrogant behavior of Japanese officers and troops, ranging from face slapping to the desecration of holy places, belied their claim to represent Asian brotherhood. Moreover, the promised benefits of their Co-Prosperity Sphere not only failed to materialize but turned into a nightmare of inflation, unemployment, shortages, and black marketing. Japan's war economy, devoted to munitions production, was never in a position to supply consumer goods to Southeast Asia or absorb its agricultural exports. In addition, American submarine and air attacks brought maritime trade to a standstill, resulting in near-famine conditions in Vietnam, Malaya, and other areas where local crop failures could not be alleviated by food imports. To make matters worse, the Japanese army, its supply lines impaired, lived off the land. It requisitioned what it needed, paying with worthless occupation currency, and sat on military stockpiles of food, raw materials, and consumer goods while Southeast Asians did without and in some cases starved.

As Japan's defeat loomed, many of its erstwhile friends and allies switched sides. In Thailand, for example, Marshal Phibun stepped down in 1944 in favor of a pro-American civilian who encouraged the establishment of a "Free

Thai" movement. As the war ended, Free Thai forces were preparing to attack the Japanese in hopes of ingratiating Bangkok with Washington and London. In Burma, Aung San set up the Anti-Fascist People's Freedom League, and deployed his Japanese-trained army in support of the advancing British with the same objective in mind. But not everyone turned on the Japanese or forgot their contributions. Indonesia's Sukarno stuck with them until the end and was dismayed by their surrender. For him, as for other Southeast Asian nationalists, the Japanese had smashed the European colonial order and paved the way for the emergence of powerful nationalist movements. Whatever the shortcomings and inequities of Japan's short-lived Greater East Asia Co-Prosperity Sphere, moreover, it had reconnected East Asia economically, culturally, and politically for the first time since the collapse of the Chinese tributary system in the mid-nineteenth century.

The War in China

The war against Japan turned into a curse for Chiang Kai-shek but a boon for Mao Zedong. Chiang's problems stemmed ultimately from the situation in which he found himself in his wartime capital of Chongqing. This city was the center of Sichuan Province, a relatively backward agricultural area. It was much poorer than his original power base in the lower Yangzi valley around Nanjing, which had fallen under Japanese occupation. In order to rebuild his shattered army after the setbacks of 1937–38, Chiang imposed heavy taxes and manpower levies on Sichuanese peasants, provoking rural unrest and resistance. The only alternative to agricultural taxation was printing money. But this fueled inflation, which adversely affected Chiang's urban middle-class supporters, resulting in disenchantment with his government among them as well. Chiang was, in short, impaled on the horns of a fiscal and political dilemma that worsened as the war dragged on and its economic demands increased. Widespread discontent in "Free China," as Chongqing-ruled western China was called, gave rise to demoralization, which, in turn, fed official corruption, tax evasion, profiteering, and smuggling.

Mao's Shaanxi stronghold in the northwest was even more impoverished and backward than Chiang's Sichuan base. But Mao's guerrilla army was self-sufficient and did not depend on taxes and forced requisitions on the rural population to keep itself in the field. Indeed, Mao insisted that his guerrillas win over the peasants by refraining from depredations and addressing their grievances. This "mass line," as he termed it, also involved avoiding the persecution of capitalist landlords and rallying entire village communities against the larger national enemy represented by the Japanese invaders. Mao's strategy proved to be quite successful, not least because the

Mao Zedong in 1938.

Japanese played into his hands by striking back with "kill all, burn all, loot all" pacification campaigns that radicalized peasants and drove them into the arms of his guerrillas. American observers as well as the Chinese themselves were understandably puzzled as to exactly what Mao stood for. Impressed by his downplaying of social revolutionary rhetoric, many supposed that he was fundamentally a nationalist with an agrarian reform agenda that did not conflict with capitalism, democracy, and cooperation with the West.

Mao was in fact both a fervent nationalist and a dedicated communist for whom national liberation, the overthrow of capitalism, and the establishment of a communist dictatorship were inseparably linked. Like Ho Chi Minh, he was prepared to set aside the latter two objectives temporarily in order to broaden the Communist Party's support and position it for a run for power. Mao's anti-Japanese united front with Chiang was another short-term expedient directed to the same ends. Chiang, for his part, also viewed this arrangement as a marriage of convenience and was determined to dissolve it at the first opportunity. As long as the war against Japan continued, neither could formally renounce their united front without calling into question his own patriotism. By 1942, however, it was a matter of form only and both sides, anticipating Japan's defeat by the United States, began to square off for a postwar showdown. For

Chiang, this meant conserving his army by avoiding set-piece battles with the Japanese and deploying it in blocking operations against Mao's guerrillas. Mao, meanwhile, sought to bring as much as possible of the countryside of northern and central China under communist control.

The Americans stepped into the middle of this gathering conflict with what turned out to be a set of unrealistic hopes and goals. President Roosevelt conceived of Chiang's China as an important partner in the wartime Grand Alliance of Great Britain, the Soviet Union, and the United States, which he assumed would continue to cooperate after the defeat of the Axis powers to order the affairs of the postwar world. Although both Churchill and Stalin had doubts about Chiang's qualifications for this role, Roosevelt did not. He was heir to Wilson's romantic notions of a special relationship between China and the United States based on supposed Chinese affinities for American ways. There was, moreover, a domestic political angle to his championing of China's Great Power status. Chiang, a Christian, and his American-educated wife were immensely popular in wartime America where they were seen as personifying China's spirit of resistance to Japanese aggression and its readiness to act as America's key Asian ally. For some Americans, it became almost unpatriotic to point out serious internal problems in Chiang's Free China or suggest that he might not be able or willing to fulfill U.S. expectations.

In the early stages of the Pacific War, American military strategists hoped to induce Chiang to launch a major ground offensive against the Japanese in China to complement the U.S. naval drive across the Pacific. But this was not to be. Chiang argued that his forces were not up to the task without more training and equipment, and complained that the United States was not allocating enough war material to the China front. There was some substance to this complaint, although Japan's severing of the overland route from India to China through northern Burma precluded a large-scale American supply effort. In any case, Chiang had no intention of allowing his army to be chewed up in frontal assaults on the Japanese while Mao's guerrillas continued to grow in numbers and strength. The Japanese showed that they were still militarily superior by pummeling Chinese forces in their 1944 offensive aimed at eliminating U.S. air bases. In the event, the American seizure of the Marianas reduced China to a strategic backwater by opening the way for a direct U.S. assault on Japan. Except for participating in the British reconquest of Burma in 1944–45, Chiang's army played little part in the last battles of the war.

Well before Japan's surrender, it had become apparent to American observers on the ground that the political advantage in China was shifting in Mao's favor. The good order and patriotic élan in communist base areas contrasted with the discontent and demoralization in Chongqing-controlled Free China. Unlike Chiang's army, moreover, Mao's guerrillas carried the war to the

Japanese by launching frequent small-scale attacks on their supply lines and outposts. Although these attacks could not defeat the Japanese army and were intended to goad it into reprisals, they created the impression that Mao, rather than Chiang, was leading China's national resistance against Japan. Chiang's weakening domestic political position led Washington to try to bolster him. It urged him, with little effect, to regain popular support by carrying out economic and political reforms. It also tried to broker the creation of a Communist-Guomindang coalition government. Mao and Chiang professed interest in such a government, since the united front ideal still appealed to Chinese nationalist opinion. In fact, however, both were intent on renewing their suspended civil war as soon as Japan was out of the picture.

Enter the Soviets

In 1944–45, Stalin watched Japan's impending defeat and developments in China from the standpoint of a neutral but not disinterested bystander. For the Soviet dictator, a surprise attack on the reeling Japanese offered an irresistible opportunity to avenge Russia's humiliation in the 1904–5 Russo-Japanese War, reclaim its lost rights in Manchuria, and reestablish its influence in the Korean Peninsula. It would also position the Soviet Union to participate in an Allied occupation of Japan. The rise of Mao presented a more perplexing problem. As a fellow communist, it might be assumed that Stalin would bend every effort to help him achieve power in China. But this was not the case. Stalin had doubts about Mao's loyalty as well as his bona fides as a Marxist-Leninist, describing him as a "margarine communist" or one who only appears to be a communist. In Stalin's estimation, moreover, Chiang was in a relatively strong domestic political and military position, and was likely to remain China's ruler for the foreseeable future. It therefore seemed preferable to ignore Mao and deal with Chiang, extracting from him Chinese recognition of Soviet rights and prerogatives in Northeast Asia.

Working in Stalin's favor was the fact that Roosevelt was eager for Soviet military assistance in winning the war against Japan and bringing Mao and Chiang together in China, and was prepared to cut the Soviet leader considerable slack in setting his terms. At the February 1945 Yalta Conference, Roosevelt, Stalin, and Churchill concluded an agreement defining these terms. Stalin undertook to attack Japan within three months of the surrender of Nazi Germany, and help persuade Mao to join a coalition government with Chiang. In return, he was to receive tsarist holdings in Manchuria plus southern Sakhalin and the Kurile Islands, which Russia had ceded to Japan in 1875. Stalin also got assurances that China would recognize Soviet-backed Mongolia. In the interests of secrecy, Roosevelt accepted these terms without consulting Chiang. The latter subsequently acquiesced, and was rewarded with a Soviet Treaty of Friendship in which Stalin acknowledged him as the head of China's legitimate government. But Yalta left a bitter aftertaste among Chinese nationalists, including Mao, who was stuck with implementing its humiliating Manchurian provisions when he took power four years later.

Yalta also left a contentious legacy in Soviet-Japanese relations. Having carefully honored their 1941 nonaggression pact with Moscow, the Japanese had no reason to expect a Soviet attack and, indeed, looked to Stalin for help in ending the war. He strung them along by dangling the hope of Soviet mediation even as he moved his army into position. When the Soviets struck in early August 1945, Japanese forces in Manchuria and Korea were consequently unprepared to put up their customary diehard resistance and surrendered en masse. Tens of thousands of captured Japanese soldiers were marched off to a grim fate in Soviet labor camps in Siberia, while fleeing Japanese civilians were left to the mercy of vengeful Koreans and Chinese. Many Japanese did not forgive or forget what they perceived to be an unprovoked "stab in the back." For them, Soviet duplicity and rapacity were symbolized by Stalin's gratuitous seizure of the Kuriles. All postwar Japanese governments have demanded that Moscow return the four southernmost islands, arguing that these are historically and geologically an extension of Japan's national territory rather than part of the Kurile chain.

Yalta did not specifically deal with Korea, which the Allied powers had already decided should become independent after a period of international trusteeship. It did, however, set the stage for the peninsula's postwar division by giving a green light to a Soviet invasion and occupation of northern Korea which Washington and Moscow agreed should be the Soviet occupation zone. Stalin's troops brought with them a large number of well-armed Korean communist guerrillas who had formerly operated in the Soviet-Manchurian-Korean border area. These soldiers quickly took control in the north and suppressed anti-communist dissidents. In contrast, American forces had no political blueprint or body of collaborators at hand in their occupation zone south of the thirty-eighth parallel. Infighting among rival political groups led to the ascendancy of returned anticommunist émigrés, who refused to cooperate with the communists. The political and ideological polarization of southern and northern Korea ensued as perhaps an inevitable, albeit unplanned, result of this situation, frustrating subsequent American, Soviet, and United Nations efforts to work out a formula for the peninsula's peaceful unification.

Stalin had succeeded in positioning the Soviet Union to play a major role in postwar East Asia, but in 1945 it was difficult to foresee what this role would be. Although Allied unity was beginning to break down in Germany and Eastern Europe, it was by no means obvious that a Soviet-American collision was in the offing. What was clear was that the Pacific War had fundamentally transformed East Asia's political and geopolitical landscape. The United States had become the region's preeminent power by virtue of its triumph over Japan and the projection of its military forces into the Japanese and Philippine archipelagos. The victorious Americans faced at least three critical challenges in East Asia in addition to dealing with the rising influence of the Soviet Union. One was deciding how to treat defeated and war-ravaged Japan which passed under U.S. military occupation in 1945. A second was fashioning a coherent response to the collapse of the European-run colonial order and the emergence of strong nationalist movements in Southeast Asia. A third challenge was finding a way to head off the resumption of the Chinese civil war and keep China united under Chiang Kai-shek.

8

From Postwar to Cold War

In the aftermath of its victory over Japan in the Pacific War, the United States aspired to create a new, postcolonial order in East Asia in partnership with Chiang Kai-shek's China, which was to be based on Western-oriented liberal democracies and free market economies. By 1950, however, this vision had foundered on the messy realities of decolonization, the fall of China to Mao Zedong's communists, and the extension of the U.S.-Soviet Cold War from Europe to East Asia. The 1950–53 Korean War polarized the region into competing Soviet and U.S. blocs that were anchored, respectively, on China and Japan. The Soviet bloc proved less cohesive in part because Moscow had to deal with obstreperous "national communists" such as Mao. In the 1960s, the Sino-Soviet alliance collapsed and Moscow and Beijing became bitter ideological and political foes. The U.S. alliance system, founded less on ideology than concrete economic benefits, turned out to be more durable and unified. Its Achilles' heel was American hubris and misperception of the nature of the Sino-Soviet threat in Southeast Asia, which led the United States and its allies into a disastrous war in Vietnam in 1965.

America's New Order

For a few years after the end of the Pacific War, it seemed possible that the United States might succeed in replacing Japan's defunct New Order in East Asia with one of its own. The "American New Order " was an outgrowth of President Franklin Roosevelt's larger vision for the postwar world, which was based on Wilsonian principles of collective security, liberal democracy, and national self-determination. Like Wilson, Roosevelt championed the creation of a world body, the United Nations, to promote collective security. But he was enough of a realist to realize that the United Nations would suffer the same fate as the League of Nations unless it was underpinned by new cooperative arrangements to restrain rogue states and economic nationalism. He consequently supported the establishment of the Bretton Woods System, a set of rules and institutions such as the World Bank and International Monetary Fund that were designed to provide a framework for orderly growth and stable trade. Roosevelt also embraced the idea that the United States, Britain, China, and the Soviet Union should cooperate as global "policemen" to enforce order and prevent the reemergence of "gangsters" like Hitler.

As applied to East Asia, Roosevelt's vision called for the transformation of the region into a community of liberal democracies and free market economies that would harmoniously interact under the benevolent leadership of the United States. Chiang's China would be America's chief ally and partner, while Britain and the Soviet Union would play subsidiary roles. Japan was to be admitted to this community, but only after being rehabilitated by the United States to rid it of its antidemocratic and militarist tendencies. Washington made it clear that fascist and communist dictatorships would not be welcome, nor would European colonies. Roosevelt regarded the British, Dutch, and French colonial empires in Southeast Asia as anachronisms that should be dismantled and replaced by independent nation-states as soon as possible. In the American view, decolonization should occur peacefully and by mutual agreement, resulting in the establishment of sturdy liberal democracies. The Philippines was the model. There the United States had set up a self-governing commonwealth in 1935 endowed with American-style political institutions; the Philippines was duly granted independence in 1946.

Reinventing Japan

The American New Order in East Asia came closest to realization in Japan which the United States succeeded in converting into a democratic "peace state." President Harry Truman entrusted this mission to General Douglas MacArthur, the hero of the 1942 defense of Bataan and Corregidor. A political conservative at home, MacArthur was a liberal idealist as far as Asians were concerned, and saw his task as remaking Japan on the model of Roosevelt's New Deal America. Armed with proconsular powers, he had a free hand to implement this program, and staffed his occupation government with New Dealers. In 1945–47, they carried out a flurry of reforms aimed at democratizing and demilitarizing Japan, including abolishing the military and purging militarists; breaking up zaibatsu; encouraging labor unions; eliminating farm tenancy; and rooting out "feudalistic" holdouts in education. Their crowning achievement was revising Japan's constitution in 1947 to enshrine the principle of popular sovereignty and confer a panoply of democratic rights and freedoms. Article Nine also committed Japan to abjure the use of force in settling international disputes and refrain from maintaining an army, navy, or air force.

Japanese conservatives were appalled by some of MacArthur's reforms,

General MacArthur receives Emperor Hirohito, September 27, 1945.

particularly Article Nine, which, in their view, deprived Japan of the means to defend itself and made it a plaything of stronger powers. However, a large majority of the Japanese people enthusiastically endorsed MacArthur's "Peace Constitution" and his other reforms. They did so, in part, because they blamed the military for having led them into a calamitous war and a humiliating defeat. But more was involved than simply an antimilitarist reaction. MacArthur offered a fresh start and the promise of a New Japan, which would again be the "light of Asia," this time as a beacon of democracy and pacifism. Moreover, many of his reforms, such as the promotion of worker rights and the extension of democratic freedoms, were consistent with trends in the "liberal twenties" that the militarists had aborted or reversed in the 1930s. Finally, as drastic as MacArthur's reforms were, they occurred within a framework of stability and continuity. The diet continued to function, the economic bureaucracy was largely unscathed, and Emperor Hirohito remained on the throne, albeit stripped of his divinity and political power.

Despite such continuities, the "MacArthur revolution" marked as sharp a break with the past as had the Meiji revolution seventy years earlier. Except for a handful of diehards on the extreme right, there was broad agreement that the pre-1945 system of emperor worship, ultranationalism, and militarism could not and should not be revived. Japan was now irrevocably committed to liberal democracy at home and pacifist internationalism abroad, and there was no going back. The question, rather, was how its new ideals were to be implemented. Party politicians, whom MacArthur put firmly and unambiguously in charge of the Japanese state, were divided on this issue. Well before the end of the U.S. occupation in 1952, they began to separate into two camps. Self-styled "progressives," mainly socialists and communists, wanted complete disarmament, reliance on a United Nations security guarantee, and economic democratization. Conservatives favored rebuilding a self-defense capability, maintaining close security and political ties with the United States, and reconstructing Japan's industrial base with the long-term goal of restoring Japan as a major economic power.

Decolonization Problems

Although the Americans succeeded in Japan, their decolonization hopes in East Asia were largely disappointed. Korea offers a prime example. As noted in the last chapter, the U.S. and Soviet military occupations resulted in the entrenchment in power of rival communist and anticommunist groups in the north and south. Since they refused to cooperate, unification through United Nations–supervised national elections became impossible. In 1948, the peninsula was partitioned into separate republics each of which was dedicated to overthrowing the other by conquest or subversion. The communist north, which called itself the Democratic People's Republic of Korea (DPRK), was headed by Kim Il Sung, an ex-guerrilla fighter and Soviet protégé. He imposed a communist dictatorship that brooked no opposition. The anticommunist Republic of Korea (ROK) in the south was led by Syngman Rhee, a veteran nationalist who had presided over a Korean government-in-exile in the United States. Although Rhee's regime was democratic in form, his reliance on strong-arm methods and indifference to land reform created widespread discontent, which communists exploited.

In Burma, the problem was less establishing a nation-state than making it work. Having resolved to quit India, the British had little reason to try to hold on to Burma and granted it independence in 1948. However, independent Burma nearly died aborning as ethnic minorities rose in revolt against what they perceived to be ethnic Burman tyranny. Aung San, an astute politician who had acquired the status of a national hero, might have held the country together, but he was assassinated by a political rival in 1947 and his successors were not up to the task. Their formula for unity, a federal government with local autonomy, proved unworkable. Mutual suspicion ran too deep and was inflamed by the spread of nationalism among disaffected minorities. Large parts of upland Burma became a political no-man's-land in which the Burmese army and ethnic rebels battled for control. Fleeing Guomindang troops from China and Burmese Communist Party insurgents joined the fray. Warlords emerged to exploit the anarchy in the northeastern Shan states where they soon took over the lucrative opium trade, turning themselves into the heads of criminal syndicates that masqueraded as national liberation movements.

British plans to move Malaya toward independence foundered on communal rivalry between ethnic Malays and Chinese, and Malay resistance to any diminution of the autonomy of its sultanates. London's attempt in 1946 to form a centralized "Malayan Union" in which Chinese would enjoy equal citizenship rights had to be abandoned in the face of opposition by politicized Malays who established the United Malays National Organization (UMNO) to defend their privileges. UMNO reflected the emergence of a new Malay nationalist movement, but this movement excluded Chinese and did not demand immediate independence, viewing the British presence as a check on the restive Chinese. Anticolonial nationalism arose, rather, among aggrieved members of the Chinese minority who perceived the British as oppressors of a multiethnic Malayan nation. The Malayan communist Party, which was built around wartime anti-Japanese guerrilla fighters, soon captured the leadership of this movement. In 1948, the communists dusted off their rifles and returned to their jungle hideouts where they launched a guerrilla war against the British in the name of Malayan nationalism.

By 1948, anticolonial nationalist rebellions were also in full swing in Vietnam and Indonesia. Both of these rebellions grew out of recolonization attempts by the French and the Dutch who, unlike the British, were loathe to abandon their imperial holdings in Southeast Asia. They had been humiliated by the Germans during the war; now, a revival of empire would be just the thing to salve their wounded national pride. But this course brought them into a collision with emerging mass nationalism in Vietnam and Indonesia, led, respectively, by Ho Chi Minh and Sukarno. After independence negotiations broke down in 1946, the Dutch and French poured in troops backed by tanks, artillery, and aircraft, expecting that the old combination of superior firepower and divide-and-rule tactics would again prevail. It did not. They

Indonesian President Sukarno

found themselves fighting a new kind of war in which virtually the entire population resisted them and their forces were subject to incessant attacks by elusive partisan bands. Like the Japanese in China a few years earlier, the Dutch and French easily occupied the cities but were sitting ducks in the countryside where their detachments and outposts were decimated by ambushes and hit-and-run raids.

Although the United States was unsympathetic to the neocolonial ambitions of the French and Dutch, it suspected that Sukarno and Ho Chi Minh were communists and did not want Vietnam and Indonesia falling under their control. In 1948, however, Sukarno demonstrated his anticommunist credentials by quashing a coup attempt by the revived Indonesian Communist Party. This led the Truman administration to, in effect, lower the boom on The Hague by threatening to withdraw American aid unless it came to terms with Sukarno. The Dutch had no choice but go along, and reluctantly recognized Indonesia's independence in 1949. Vietnam was a different story. Even though Ho proclaimed his attachment to American

Vietnam's Ho Chi Minh.

democratic ideals and his Vietminh included many noncommunists, the Americans regarded him as a dyed-in-the-wool communist and, as such, unworthy of U.S. support. Prior to 1950, however, Washington did not actively back the French colonial war in Vietnam. Rather, it stood on the sidelines, extending lukewarm support to a French attempt to use the restored Nguyen monarchy headed by Bao Dai as a rallying point for noncommunist Vietnamese nationalists.

Even the Philippines, touted by the United States as a model of decolonization and democratization, was soon beset by severe problems. In 1948, former anti-Japanese guerrilla fighters rose in revolt. Known as the Hukbalahap (People's Anti-Japanese Army) or Huks, they drew their support from disaffected peasants in central Luzon and were inspired by communist ideology. The Huk rebellion was a symptom rather than a cause of the Philippines' difficulties. The Americans had nurtured and transferred power to a landowning oligarchy descended from the nineteenth-century *ilustrados*, and this elite was intent on maintaining its political, economic, and social privileges. American-style liberal democracy did not work as advertised in this setting, serving instead to legitimize elite competition for the spoils of office with little regard for the welfare of Filipino peasants. The Manila government, for example, refused to carry out land reform even though peasant land hunger and resentment against landlord oppression lay at the heart of the Huk insurgency. These weaknesses have haunted the Philippines ever since, creating endemic rural unrest that has invited communist exploitation.

Showdown in China

From the American perspective, East Asia's decolonization problems paled in importance compared to Mao's victory in the 1946–49 Chinese civil war, which dashed Washington's hopes for the continuation of the wartime U.S.–China alliance as the linchpin of regional stability. As suggested in the last chapter, a military showdown between Mao and Chiang was all but inevitable insofar as both were spoiling for a fight and thought they could win. American mediation efforts in 1945–46, which Stalin halfheartedly supported, were therefore unlikely to succeed. Indeed, American and Soviet actions helped push Chiang and Mao into civil war. A U.S. airlift of Chiang's troops into the cities of eastern China and Manchuria gave the lie in Mao's eyes to Washington's claim to be an honest broker, and contributed to Chiang's overconfidence. The Soviets, for their part, added fuel to the fire by turning over to Mao's guerrillas large stocks of weapons and ammunition captured from the Japanese in Manchuria. Although this infusion of arms did not greatly reduce the lopsided material advantage enjoyed by Chiang's American-equipped army, it evened the odds enough to give Mao's communists a fighting chance.

At the beginning of the renewed civil war in 1946, Chiang's troops outnumbered the communists by a three-to-one margin and were well supplied with tanks, artillery, trucks, and aircraft, which Mao's forces lacked. To observers like Stalin, it seemed inconceivable that Chiang could lose, but this is what happened. Disregarding the counsel of some of his advisors, who urged that he concentrate on regaining full control of his Yangzi Valley base area, he dispersed his army in an attempt to reassert Guomindang authority in provincial capitals throughout the country. This repeated the mistake of the Japanese, enabling Mao's guerrillas to dominate the countryside. Disaster ensued in Manchuria, where the cream of Chiang's army, bottled up the cities and cut off from supplies, surrendered en masse in 1948. The communists then shifted to positional warfare and closed in for the kill against Chiang's demoralized forces in northern and central China. In the last battles, these gave up and switched sides by the hundreds of thousands, often without offering serious resistance. In 1949, Chiang fled

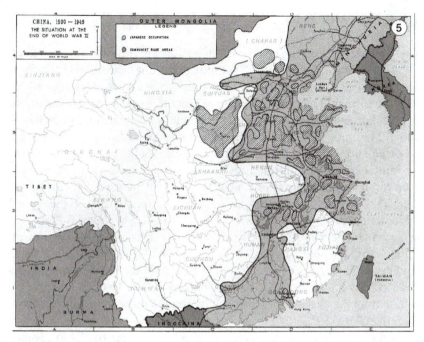

China in 1945.

with the remnant of his government and army to Taiwan, where he prepared to make a last stand.

The causes of Chiang's defeat were as much political and economic as military. By 1948, few Chinese supported his restored Nanjing regime or were willing to fight for it. The problem, in essence, was that the weaknesses of his wartime Chongqing government carried over and became more acute during the civil war. Inflation, for example, skyrocketed in 1946–48, rendering the currency virtually worthless and wiping out the savings of the Chinese middle class on which Chiang depended. Official corruption, onerous exactions on the peasantry, and profiteering also worsened, aggravated by the tendency of Chiang's returning troops and officials to look upon the population of the former Japanese occupation zones as collaborators. This attitude was especially pronounced in Manchuria and Taiwan, where Chiang's vengeful Guomindang governor massacred much of the Taiwanese elite in 1947. For most Chinese, Mao offered an attractive alternative to Chiang's corruption and economic mismanagement. The Chinese communists promised unity and reconciliation, economic reform, and good government. Moreover, they largely delivered on these promises in the areas of China where they gained control.

The Cold War Intrudes

The United States disengaged from Chiang during the civil war, providing some economic and military aid, but ruling out American military intervention to try to save him. Truman administration officials were appalled by his inept performance and inclined to write him off. Some were also interested in reaching an understanding with the People's Republic of China (PRC), which Mao proclaimed in Beijing in October 1949. However, there were no conciliatory signals from Mao, who feared that the United States was planning to prevent him from finishing off Chiang in Taiwan, and perhaps even roll back his takeover of China. Mao's suspicions were not unreasonable. The "loss of China" became a domestic political issue in the United States in 1949, helping to inspire a congressional witch-hunt for communist sympathizers in the government, particularly the State Department. Truman resisted political pressure to rescue Chiang and confront the PRC, but he was unwilling to follow the British lead in recognizing Beijing. As described by his secretary of state, his policy in late 1949 and early 1950 was "letting the dust settle" in hopes that something positive might emerge from the China debacle.

Stalin saw in Mao's unexpected victory a historic opportunity to advance Soviet interests and communism in East Asia, the two being one and the same in his mind. With Mao and the limitless manpower of China behind him, the Soviet leader believed that it would be possible to exploit pro-communist sentiment and insurgencies in South Korea, Vietnam, Burma, Malaya, Indonesia, and the Philippines to isolate and weaken the United States in the region. At a minimum, the Americans would have to devote more attention and resources to East Asia, hopefully leading them to drop their guard in Western Europe, which remained the primary focus of Soviet ambitions. For the ever cautious Stalin, a political-military offensive in East Asia presented few risks. Having declined to oppose Mao's conquest of China, the region's strategic prize, the United States seemed unlikely to resist communist takeovers of minor players like Taiwan, South Korea, and Vietnam. If it did, Mao's Chinese, Kim Il Sung's Koreans, and Ho Chi Minh's Vietnamese would have to do the fighting and dying. The Soviet Union would furnish economic and military assistance, but Stalin had no intention of embroiling it in a direct confrontation with the United States that could result in a third world war.

Stalin had another reason for wishing to open an East Asian front in his Cold War rivalry with the United States. The initial round of this contest in Europe in the late 1940s had not gone well for Moscow, and the Soviet dictator was looking for easy triumphs to burnish his tarnished prestige. Although the

Soviet Union had secured control over Eastern Europe, it had been rebuffed in Western Europe by Truman's 1947 Marshall Plan, which offered generous American economic reconstruction assistance. Worse yet, Stalin miscalculated U.S. resolve to defend its rights in Germany by imposing a Soviet blockade on Allied-occupied West Berlin in 1948. He supposed that this move would demonstrate Soviet power and force Washington to abandon its plans to create a unified West Germany. But Truman countered with an airlift to Berlin, which he dared the Soviets to try to stop. Confronted by the prospect of war, Stalin backed down, and the formation of West Germany went ahead. The Berlin Crisis also catalyzed Western European fears of a Soviet threat, enabling the United States to put together an anti-Soviet military alliance in 1949, the North Atlantic Treaty Organization (NATO).

The first step in Stalin's design to roll back American influence in East Asia was concluding an alliance with Mao. This was no easy task, since the two disliked and distrusted each other. Mao was not beholden to Stalin for his rise to power either in the Chinese Communist Party or in China itself. Indeed, Stalin had favored Mao's rivals in the party and had been quite willing to accept Chiang as China's legitimate ruler. Precisely for these reasons, Stalin was inclined to see Mao as potentially another Tito, the Yugoslav communist leader who broke with Moscow in 1948 to pursue "national communism." But mutual need trumped mutual suspicion. Mao wanted Soviet economic assistance and a security guarantee against what he imagined to be imminent American military intervention to block his "liberation" of Taiwan. Stalin needed Mao as his point man in a communist advance in East Asia. Both sides got what they wanted in the February 1950 Sino-Soviet military alliance. Mao received a security guarantee and Soviet aid, albeit less than he expected and at the price of accepting humiliating Soviet privileges in Manchuria. Stalin secured what he hoped would be a loyal and subordinate Chinese ally.

The Korean War

The significance of the Sino-Soviet alliance for East Asia quickly became apparent in Vietnam and Korea. Beijing and Moscow recognized Ho Chi Minh's Democratic Republic of Vietnam, and China began providing his Vietminh with weapons and advisors. Ho's anticolonial struggle against the French was thus transformed into a proxy war that pointed to a coordinated Sino-Soviet offensive in Southeast Asia. A similar transformation occurred in the Korean Peninsula but in an even more dramatic way. There intermittent skirmishing between the feuding regimes of Kim Il Sung and Syngman Rhee, which had been under way for more than a year, suddenly escalated in June 1950 when Kim launched a blitzkrieg attack on the south using Soviet-supplied tanks, trucks, and artillery. To the surprised Americans, it seemed obvious that this attack was authorized by Moscow and Beijing, and that it had less to do with the ongoing inter-Korean conflict than Stalin's ambition to expand his satellite empire and undermine the U.S. position in Northeast Asia. Control of South Korea would give him a forward base from which to intimidate American-occupied Japan only 120 miles away across the Tsushima Strait.

The American assessment of the origins of the Korean War was essentially accurate. Stalin and Mao had given Kim a green light to invade the south, and Korean unification was incidental to their purposes. Stalin perceived the weak and unpopular South Korean regime to be easy pickings, the conquest of which would alter the balance of power in Northeast Asia in favor of the Soviet Union. The ROK lay outside the publicly announced U.S. "defense perimeter" in eastern Asia, and Washington had made no moves to build up its army or treat it as an ally. It therefore seemed defenseless. Moreover, Kim was confident that he would be able to overrun the south before the Americans could react if, indeed, they did react, which Kim doubted. After all, they had stood aside while China fell to Mao only a few months earlier. Stalin was nevertheless concerned about U.S. military intervention and the possibility of an eventual North Korean defeat. He told Kim not to expect a Soviet bailout if he got into trouble, since the Soviet Union was not prepared to risk war with the United States over Korea. It would be up to Mao to pull Kim's chestnuts out of the fire if the need arose.

In the event, the forcefulness of the U.S. response took Kim, Mao, and Stalin by surprise. Declaring the North Korean invasion to be a flagrant act of aggression reminiscent of Hitler's behavior in the 1930s, Washington secured United Nations approval for a "police action" to halt it. The Americans simultaneously committed ground troops, backed by overwhelming air and naval power, which soon routed Kim's army and sent it reeling back across the thirty-eighth parallel. Truman then, in effect, took a leaf from Stalin's book and resolved to unify the peninsula by force. As American and South Korean forces swept north in late 1950, Stalin implemented his backup plan, calling on Mao to intervene to stop them and assuring him of Soviet logistical support. Mao agreed, partly to safeguard his Manchurian industrial base, and partly because he calculated that his battle-hardened army could achieve victory. A surprise winter attack by Chinese "volunteers" caught the Americans off guard and drove them back into the south in early 1951. But U.S. firepower and air superiority again came into play, forcing the Chinese to give ground until the front line stabilized around the thirty-eighth parallel.

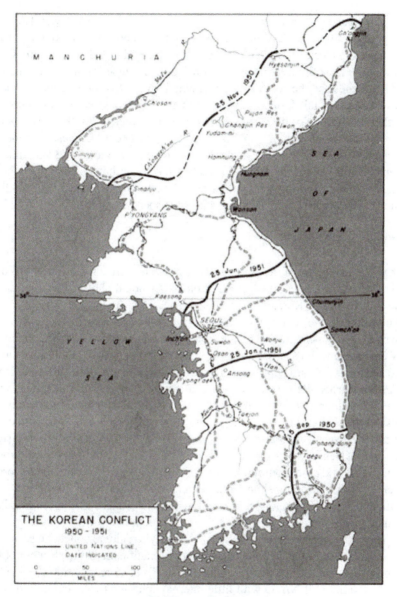

The Korean Conflict.

The Korean conflict, officially a United Nations "police action," dragged on for two more years, becoming a war of attrition in which neither side could gain a decisive advantage. Truman considered, but rejected, using nuclear weapons and attacking China. Unlike his field commander, General MacArthur, he did not regard the stakes in Korea as worth the risks of a wider war. He also suspected a Soviet feint intended to weaken the American position in Europe. He therefore elected to fight a limited war with the aim of demonstrating U.S. resolve to check Sino-Soviet aggression. But this course was unpopular in the United States and the cost was high, claiming over 140,000 American casualties—dead, wounded, or missing. (Estimates of Chinese casualties reach as high as 900,000; North Koreans 520,000; South Koreans 300,000.) Truman's successor, President Dwight D. Eisenhower, persuaded the Chinese to come to terms with a veiled threat of nuclear escalation. A 1953 armistice agreement, signed by the Americans, Chinese, and North Koreans but not the South Koreans, ended the fighting. There was, however, no follow-up peace treaty and the inter-Korean conflict remained in a state of suspended animation.

American Alliances

The principal effect of the Korean War was to accelerate the division of East Asia into rival Soviet and American blocs. As noted above, the Americans viewed the North Korean attack as evidence of a Soviet-led conspiracy to "communize" the region by conquest or subversion. As in Europe several years earlier, Washington concluded that this threat would have to be contained by erecting a wall of anticommunist states allied with the United States and backed by its forward deployed forces. But East Asia was quite different from Western Europe. Parts of it, such as Malaya, Singapore, and Indochina, still lay under colonial rule. Moreover, there was no unanimity on the seriousness of the Soviet threat. Indonesia and Burma, for example, were attracted to the Afro-Asian Solidarity movement promoted by Indian prime minister Jawaharlal Nehru, which called for peaceful coexistence and friendly relations with China and other communist states. Even among anticommunist governments, mutual suspicions ran high, particularly toward Japan. South Korea's Syngman Rhee, for example, was as much anti-Japanese as anticommunist, and refused to consider any kind of security cooperation with Tokyo.

There was, in short, no basis for a NATO-style regional collective security organization in East Asia. The closest approximation the United States could cobble together was the 1954 Southeast Asia Treaty Organization (SEATO), a pale imitation of NATO with little internal cohesion that eventually disintegrated. Only two of SEATO's eight members were Southeast Asia nations, Thailand and the Philippines, the others being the United States, Britain, France, Australia, New Zealand, and Pakistan. By default, therefore, Washington had to rely primarily on bilateral alliances with anticommunist states that were willing to partner with it. Japan, South Korea, Chiang's Republic of China on Taiwan, the Philippines, Thailand, and Australia and New Zealand were amenable, and in the early 1950s the United States concluded military alliances with them. Specific arrangements varied. Australia and New Zealand joined with the United States to form the trilateral ANZUS pact, and the Thai-U.S. alliance was based on SEATO commitments rather than a bilateral treaty. Britain, meanwhile, looked after the security of Malaya, Singapore, and northern Borneo, which remained temporarily under British rule.

Japan, having regained its sovereignty in 1952 with the end of the occupation, became the foundation of the American alliance system. It provided the principal bases for forward deployed American air, naval, and ground units in East Asia, including the home port of the U.S. Seventh Fleet and the staging area for marine expeditionary forces. Japan's reviving industrial economy increasingly functioned as the "workshop" of noncommunist East Asia, buying its raw materials and supplying its manufactured goods. By the 1960s, Japanese investment and aid, initially linked to war reparations, were also making a significant contribution to regional economic growth. Tokyo loyally supported U.S. Cold War policies. In particular, it backed Washington's efforts to isolate the PRC and uphold Chiang's rump Republic of China on Taiwan as the legitimate government of mainland China and the rightful holder of its seat on the United Nations Security Council. In return, the United States opened its domestic market to Japanese imports and sponsored Japan's admission to international economic institutions. The 1964 Tokyo Olympics marked the international "coming out party" of the New Japan.

The 1951 U.S.–Japan Mutual Security Treaty committed the United States to defend Japan, but required the Japanese to do little in their own defense and nothing to support U.S. forces in regional military conflicts. Washington was disappointed by Japan's military passivity, and some Japanese deplored Japan's lopsided dependence on the United States, which, in their view, made it an American protectorate. However, mainstream conservatives argued that popular support for the pacifist ideals embodied in Article Nine of the 1947 Constitution precluded anything more than the creation of a modest Self-Defense Force (SDF) whose only mission was the defense of the Japanese home islands in the unlikely event of a direct attack. Even this was too much for left-wing progressives who, rallying under the slogan of unarmed neutrality, vehemently opposed both the American alliance and the SDF as unconstitutional. Massive demonstrations in 1960 against the renewal of the U.S.–Japan Security Treaty underscored the depth of pacifist and neutralist sentiment. To some observers, the demonstrations also reflected the fragility of Japan's new liberal democratic political order.

In any event, the moderate conservative leaders of the ruling Liberal Democratic Party (LDP) succeeded in winning public acceptance of the American alliance during the 1960s. They did so, in part, by co-opting the pacifist agenda of the Left represented by the Japan Socialist Party. Under the LDP, Japan banned arms exports, prohibited nuclear weapons, capped defense spending at 1 percent of GNP, and abstained from all forms of collective security, including even United Nations peacekeeping operations. Equally important, the LDP diverted the attention of the Japanese people from divisive defense and foreign policy issues to economic priorities. Capitalizing on Japan's unique advantages, such as its highly skilled, disciplined, and frugal labor force, the conservatives presided over a surge of sustained double-digit growth, enabling Japan to surpass West Germany in 1968 as the world's third largest economy. Moreover, the LDP ensured that the fruits of this growth were equitably distributed, resulting in undreamed-of material prosperity for almost all Japanese. By 1970, the Left was fading as a political force and permanent LDP hegemony was taking shape.

Japan was not the only economic beneficiary of the American alliance system. South Korea, Taiwan, Thailand, and, to a lesser extent, the Philippines laid the foundations of their future economic growth in the early Cold War period, aided by heavy inputs of U.S. development assistance. By the 1960s, military-dominated governments ruled South Korea and Thailand, while Chiang's Guomindang ran Taiwan as an authoritarian one-party state. However, these regimes allowed technocrats considerable leeway in managing their economies to maximize growth. In the ROK, for example, General Park Chung Hee, who took power in a 1961 coup, launched an ambitious economic modernization program modeled on Japan. A onetime Japanese army officer, he was not pro-Japanese, but he admired their discipline, organization, and efficiency, and sought to instill these qualities into South Koreans. Park also reorganized South Korea's economy along Japanese lines, reproducing Japan's system of close government–business collaboration, reliance on large conglomerates to lead industrialization, and centralized bureaucratic guidance over what remained a free enterprise economy.

Soviet Alliances

The Soviet Union was unable to replicate in East Asia the obedient satellite states that Stalin created in Eastern Europe between 1944 and 1948 with the aid of the Soviet army. Except for Mongolia, which had been a Russian protectorate since 1912, there were no East Asian equivalents of these satellites. Mao Zedong, Kim Il Sung, and Ho Chi Minh were "national communists" who had independent power bases and were unwilling to take orders from Stalin and his successors. To be sure, as Marxist-Leninist true believers they were inclined to defer to Moscow as the center of the world communist movement. They also looked to the Soviets for military and technological assistance, as well as models of political organization and economic modernization. Stalin had turned the Soviet Union into a superpower in the 1930s through the imposition of a ruthless communist dictatorship, the liquidation of class enemies, the embrace of state planning, the collectivization of agriculture, and the buildup of heavy industry. His East Asian admirers were impressed by this achievement and sought to emulate it. But they had their own priorities and preoccupations, and were in no sense Soviet puppets.

Kim Il Sung offers an example. In the 1950s and 1960s, he built a Stalinist state in North Korea that by most economic measures was more successful than its southern rival. Kim benefited both from Soviet aid and from the substantial industrial base left behind by the Japanese colonialists. But his regime had several peculiarities that raised eyebrows in Moscow and other communist capitals. Kim elevated himself to the status of a living god in the eyes of North Koreans and preached a gospel of "Juche," or national self-reliance, which glorified the virtues and genius of the Korean people. Perhaps the closest parallel to this quasi-religious personality cult was pre-1945 Japan's system of emperor worship. Even more alarming to Moscow was Kim's proclivity for risky provocations against South Korea, including a 1968 attempt by his commandos to assassinate President Park Chung Hee in his Seoul residence. By Kim's lights, such actions were quite reasonable. Viewing himself as Korea's national savior and the ROK as a house of cards presided over by American puppets detested by South Koreans, he adopted shock tactics designed to trigger a pro-DPRK uprising in the south.

Mao proved to be even more unmanageable than Kim, becoming in the 1960s a rival and implacable enemy of the Soviet Union. The breakdown of the Sino-Soviet alliance in the late 1950s is at first glance surprising. Beijing and Moscow faced a common adversary in the United States, China needed Soviet economic and technical assistance, and the Chinese and Soviets were ideological comrades in the march to a future communist utopia. But a falling out was probably inevitable. Mao was inspired by a sense of his own and China's greatness, which made subordination to foreigners unacceptable. Moreover, he regarded Khrushchev, Stalin's successor, as a backslider from communist revolutionary ideals, and saw himself as Stalin's true heir. Mao supposed that his twenty-year struggle against the Guomindang, Japanese, and Americans offered lessons that were relevant to communist revolutionaries in what was by the 1950s widely known as the Third World. In particular, he believed that he had hit upon a formula for unleashing the creative energies of peasant masses in China and other Third World countries that could overcome all obstacles, political, military, or economic.

Dissatisfied with the slow pace of Soviet-style industrialization through agricultural collectivization, Mao applied his "peasant power" formula in the

1958–60 Great Leap Forward in which he sought to accelerate China's industrialization and hasten the arrival of the communist millennium. This involved concentrating peasants into giant communes reminiscent of those established by the Taipings a century earlier. There, party cadres exhorted them to set up backyard blast furnaces to manufacture iron and steel, and meet impossibly high agricultural production quotas. The results were economic chaos and mass starvation, exacerbated by crop failures. Reaction within the Chinese Communist Party against his extremism in the early 1960s led Mao to incite yet another mass upheaval in the 1966–68 Great Proletarian Cultural Revolution. This time his objectives were to purge those he considered "rightists" from positions of power in Chinese society, and to rekindle the revolutionary fervor of the Long March and Yanan period, which he saw dying out. His chosen instruments were the Red Guards, fanatical Chinese youth who were given free rein to persecute Mao's real or imagined opponents.

While Mao convulsed China in the Great Leap Forward and Cultural Revolution, he moved it into a confrontation with the Soviet Union. In the early 1960s, he began a public feud with the Soviets, labeling them "revisionists," which in the communist lexicon was the equivalent of heretics or apostates. In Mao's view, their sins included dismissing his pretensions to be a world communist leader, scoffing at his revolutionary utopianism, and treating China as a subservient Soviet satellite. Mao was particularly incensed over Khrushchev's reneging on his promise to provide China with nuclear weapons technology, and his unwillingness to back the PRC's saber rattling against Taiwan in 1958 and a 1962 border war with India. The Soviets regarded Mao as a loose cannon and renegade. Despite his efforts to compete in winning over Third World states, they might have ignored him had it not been for the fact that he acquired nuclear weapons in 1964 and seemed intent on challenging their position in Mongolia and the Soviet Far East. Border clashes escalated in the late 1960s, leading Moscow to seriously contemplate a preemptive strike against Chinese nuclear facilities in Xinjiang.

The United States and Vietnam

The Sino-Soviet feud presented the United States with an opportunity to play off Moscow and Beijing and perhaps come to terms with the latter as the weaker of the two. Until the end of the 1960s, however, Mao showed no interest in reconciling with Washington. Indeed, he regarded "American imperialism" and "Soviet hegemonism" as equally menacing and opposed both. The Americans consequently had no reason to lower their guard toward China. On the contrary, Mao's talk of promoting "people's wars" modeled on his own guerrilla struggle against the Japanese made him seem particularly dangerous. But the extent to which he practiced what he preached was open to different interpretations. In the mid-1950s, Beijing championed peaceful coexistence and courted Burma and other neutral states in Southeast Asia, notably at the 1955 Bandung Afro-Asian conference. On the other hand, the PRC extended moral and material support to communist insurgents in Southeast Asia, and cultivated ethnic Chinese minorities in the region. After 1958, moreover, China adopted a harder line against the United States and put greater rhetorical emphasis on people's wars.

Although Mao may have been willing to tolerate friendly neutralist states elsewhere in Southeast Asia, he was committed to helping Ho Chi Minh prevail in Vietnam. More than communist solidarity was involved here. Vietnam and Korea had been key tributaries of Imperial China, which fought wars with France and Japan in the late nineteenth century to defend its suzerain rights over them. Just as Stalin had sought to reassert the prerogatives of the tsars, so Mao aimed to reclaim the lost dependencies of the Qing, and Vietnam and Korea were at the top of his list. The Americans, too, attached great importance to Vietnam, but for a different reason. They were beguiled by the notion that it was the bellwether of Southeast Asia or, in their analogy, the lead "domino" in a row of dominos that were ready to topple into communism at the slightest push. Similar thinking underlay the U.S. effort to prop up Western Europe in the late 1940s and its intervention in Korea in 1950, but the American fixation on Vietnam was extraordinary. They regarded it as highly vulnerable to communist subversion and, on analogy with its role as the staging area for Japan's 1940–41 advance into the region, the gateway for China's push into Southeast Asia.

Washington's attempt to hold the containment line in Vietnam met a major setback in 1954 when the French finally threw in the towel, having been outmaneuvered and decisively defeated by the Vietminh in the battle of Dienbienphu. Under the terms of a settlement worked out in Geneva by Britain, France, the PRC, and the Soviet Union, Cambodia and Laos became independent neutralist states, and Vietnam was temporarily partitioned at the seventeenth parallel between Ho's Democratic Republic of Vietnam (DRV) and a noncommunist state in the south headed by Bao Dai. The settlement further specified that Vietnam was to be reunified through internationally supervised elections in the north and south in 1956. These arrangements displeased both the Vietnamese communists and the Americans. Ho thought he had been cheated out the fruits of victory, but he acquiesced because his Soviet and Chinese patrons pressured him to do so, and because he was confident of winning the scheduled nationwide elections. The Eisenhower administration viewed the Geneva settlement as an exercise in Munich-style appeasement and, not being a signatory, considered itself under no obligation to honor it.

Beginning in 1955, the United States underwrote the transformation of South Vietnam into an anticommunist frontline state. Its ally in this undertaking was Ngo Dinh Diem, a conservative nationalist who pushed aside Bao Dai, proclaimed himself the president of a new Republic of Vietnam (RVN), and ignored the elections required by the Geneva accord. Although the RVN was modeled on South Korea, the Korean and Vietnamese situations were different. In contrast to Kim Il Sung, Ho Chi Minh was a national hero who had many admirers in the south. Moreover, Diem, a Catholic, proved to be an unpopular and inept leader, alienating the Buddhist majority and avoiding land reform that might have rallied peasants behind his regime. Nevertheless, the RVN stood a good chance of survival. Diem benefited from massive American economic and military assistance. The Vietminh had always been relatively weak in the south, which was soon filled with refugees who wanted no part of Ho's oppressive communist dictatorship in the north. Furthermore, Ho was preoccupied in the late 1950s with consolidating this dictatorship and quashing rural resistance to agricultural collectivization.

In 1959–60, Ho felt strong enough to launch a full-scale guerrilla insurgency in the south using Vietminh cadres who formed the core of the Vietcong, or National Liberation Front. Disaster followed for Diem and the RVN. Counterinsurgency techniques that had worked in the early 1950s against Malayan and Filipino communists failed in South Vietnam. Vietcong supply lines through Laos and Cambodia could not be cut, and attempts to concentrate peasants in fortified "strategic hamlets" foundered on administrative incompetence. By 1963, most of the countryside had passed under Vietcong control. Diem was overthrown in a military coup, but the generals who succeeded him had no better success in reasserting the government's authority. Washington thus faced the prospect of a humiliating defeat in what it regarded as Southeast Asia's key domino. From the U.S. perspective, the stakes were too high to permit withdrawal and a neutralization formula like the one applied in Laos in 1961 to dampen a growing civil war between communist and anticommunist Laotians. Moreover, memories were still fresh of the loss of China in 1949 and the domestic political recriminations that had followed.

In 1965, President Lyndon B. Johnson made the fateful decision to commit U.S. troops in another land war in East Asia, and within three years over 540,000 were fighting in South Vietnam, largely displacing the faltering RVN army. The Vietnam and Korean conflicts were similar in that both were undeclared limited wars waged to roll back what the United States saw as Sino-Soviet aggression. But Korea was a conventional war in which civilians did not participate. Vietnam, in contrast, was essentially a guerrilla war even though North Vietnamese regulars played an increasingly prominent role. Two consequences followed. Like the French before them, the Americans found their superior firepower to be ineffective and counterproductive insofar as it inflicted heavy collateral damage on South Vietnamese peasants, driving them into the arms of the Vietcong. Second, Johnson's argument that he was countering external communist aggression was undermined by the Vietcong claim that they represented the aspiration of the South Vietnamese people for national unification. Many Americans were troubled by the possibility that they were trying to crush an authentic nationalist revolution.

The moment of truth in Vietnam came in early 1968 with a surprise Lunar New Year (Tet) offensive by the Vietcong, which turned out to be America's Dienbienphu. Having been assured by Johnson and his generals that the Vietcong were all but defeated, American television viewers were astonished and dismayed to see communist fighters swarming into South Vietnamese cities, including the capital Saigon, where they even laid siege to the American embassy. U.S. public and congressional support for the war evaporated virtually overnight. Those who saw it as unjustified and immoral joined with others who viewed it as unwinnable in demanding a U.S. pullout. It did not matter that the Vietcong were thrown back with heavy losses that crippled them as an effective fighting force. Ho Chi Minh had correctly concluded that the American "center of gravity" or point of vulnerability was political rather than military, and that in that respect the real battlefield was American public opinion, not South Vietnam. Although the Vietnam War dragged on for seven more years, engulfing Laos and Cambodia, 1968 marked the beginning of a U.S. disengagement from Indochina and Southeast Asia.

9

The Late Cold War

The U.S.–PRC rapprochement of 1971–72 dramatically altered the character of the Cold War in East Asia. The product of Washington's need to extricate itself from Vietnam and Beijing's fear of the Soviets, it aligned the United States, Japan, and the PRC against the Soviet Union. Although the Cold War continued in Korea and Indochina, China reconciled with its neighbors and, under Deng Xiaoping, embraced economic modernization on the capitalist model. The resulting relaxation of tensions facilitated the rise of the Association of Southeast Asian Nations (ASEAN) as a major diplomatic player in Southeast Asia. Japan, now an economic superpower, moved away from its previously deferential posture toward the United States and began using its economic clout to cultivate special relationships with China and Southeast Asia. By the 1980s, East Asia was coming together as a coherent economic region that was centered on Japan and based on widespread emulation of that country's system of export-oriented, state-guided capitalism. At the same time, tensions in the U.S.–Japan alliance escalated into acrimonious trade disputes exacerbated by a revival of Japanese nationalism.

The Indochina Endgame

The top priority of Lyndon Johnson's successor, President Richard Nixon, was extricating the United States from the Vietnam quagmire. Cutting and running was unacceptable. As in the case of the Japanese in China twenty years earlier, too much American blood had been spilled and too much American prestige had been invested to make this option politically salable to Nixon's supporters in the United States. He did not want to be the first American president to lose a war, and he was concerned that a precipitous French-style withdrawal might destroy U.S. credibility and unravel U.S. alliances in East Asia. On the other hand, Nixon judged that the Vietnam War was unwinnable and that the days of the RVN, now under a weak military government headed by General Nguyen Van Thieu, were numbered. He was also acutely aware that the war was bankrupting the United States and tearing it apart politically by feeding a vocal antiwar movement and a growing congressional challenge to executive branch leadership. Nixon, in short, needed an exit strategy from Vietnam that would placate domestic antiwar critics yet preserve U.S. leadership in East Asia and satisfy his constituents' demand for "peace with honor."

Nixon's strategy called for gradually withdrawing American troops while giving the Saigon-based Thieu regime a chance for survival. A key element of this strategy was "Vietnamization," or building up the RVN army so that it could hold its own against Vietcong guerrillas and the North Vietnamese army, which after 1968 was its main adversary. Another equally critical element of Nixon's strategy was inducing Hanoi to accept a cease-fire and Vietcong participation in a coalition government with Thieu. However, North Vietnam's leaders were not interested in these terms, believing that victory was within their grasp. Aided by weapons from China and the Soviet Union, Hanoi matched the U.S.-supplied buildup of the South Vietnamese army. Moreover, DRV forces enjoyed a decisive edge in morale, training, and leadership. U.S. air power reduced the North Vietnamese advantage, pounding them with both precision and saturation bombing. However, the communists proved adept at using camouflage and tunnel complexes to limit damage from this air assault. In addition, they enjoyed sanctuaries in Cambodia and Laos, which also served as their main supply routes, the so-called Ho Chi Minh Trail.

Nixon considered the elimination of these sanctuaries essential to the success of Vietnamization, and this, in turn, required the cooperation of Cambodian and Laotian anticommunists. In 1970, the Cambodian army obliged by overthrowing the neutralist monarchy of Prince Norodom Sihanouk and launching an unsuccessful offensive against the North Vietnamese intruders. The main effect of this coup was to provoke a guerrilla insurgency against the new military regime in Phnom Penh by Cambodian communists, the Khmer Rouge, who were as much anti-Vietnamese as they were anti-American. A different pattern developed in Laos. There the monarchy survived, nominally governing under neutralist Prince Souvanna Phouma, who had been restored to power in Vientiane under the 1961 neutralization agreement. Laotian rightists, backed by Thailand and the United States, tried but failed to drive pro-DRV Pathet Lao communists from their strongholds in northern and eastern Laos. While enduring a pummeling by American B-52 long-range bombers, the Pathet Lao bided their time and cooperated with Vientiane, waiting for orders from Hanoi to take over the country.

Vietnamization was a failure. Thieu's bloated but dispirited and incompetent army was incapable of resisting the North Vietnamese without U.S. air support, and this came to an end in 1973 when Hanoi agreed to Nixon's peace terms. It did so under pressure from Mao, who made it clear to his Vietnamese

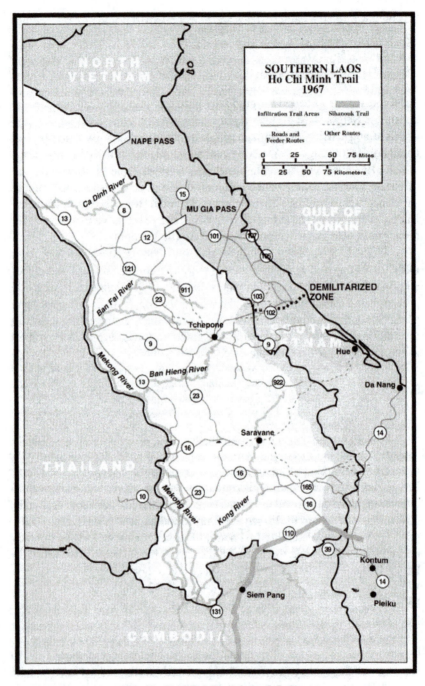

The Ho Chi Minh Trail through Laos.

comrades that China had bigger fish to fry than Vietnam's unification and expected them to knuckle under to the Americans. Although the successors of Ho Chi Minh, who died in 1969, deeply resented this perceived betrayal, they had no choice but to go along. In the event, the 1973 Paris Peace Accord merely postponed the fall of South Vietnam. Neither Saigon nor Hanoi had any intention of honoring it, and Nixon, who faced an uncooperative Congress and was driven from office in 1974 by the Watergate scandal, was unable to enforce it. In 1975, with the Americans out of the picture, the Indochinese dominos fell. The Thieu regime, deprived of expected American military and economic aid, collapsed in the face of a North Vietnamese assault. Simultaneously, the Khmer Rouge ousted the pro-American government in Phnom Penh and the Pathet Lao "liberated" Vientiane.

The U.S.–PRC Rapprochement

Under the American domino theory of the 1950s and 1960s, one might expect that the fall of Indochina to the communists would have emboldened China to redouble its efforts to foment people's wars in neighboring countries. In fact, however, exactly the opposite occurred. In the wake of U.S. disengagement from Vietnam in 1969–73, Beijing scaled back its rhetorical and material support for communist insurgencies in Southeast Asia and reached out to anticommunist governments in the region. Even more surprisingly, the United States and China, in effect, buried the hatchet, ending twenty years of bitter enmity. What lay behind this extraordinary reversal? The catalyst was the dissipation of mutual threat perceptions among the handful of decision makers who directed U.S. and PRC policy, Mao, Nixon, and their advisors. Each became in the view of the other less dangerous and more amenable to cooperation. But this attitudinal shift, by itself, would not have sufficed to bring about the reversal. The other necessary element was the discovery by Mao and Nixon of common interests important enough to justify setting aside their differences and overriding domestic opposition.

At the end of the 1960s and beginning of the 1970s, Mao had reason to regard the United States as less threatening than it had previously seemed. Nixon's pursuit of Vietnamization and an honorable peace in Vietnam did not conceal the fact that the Americans had been defeated there and were intent on withdrawing from Indochina. In his 1969 Guam Doctrine, moreover, Nixon indicated that there would be no more Vietnams and that Washington expected its East Asian allies to do more in their own defense. Underscoring the message of strategic retrenchment, he withdrew an American infantry division from South Korea in the following year. To Mao, a chastened but still powerful United States presented an ideal counterweight to the Soviet Union which was, in his view, becoming more menacing. The danger was high-lighted by the Soviet invasion of Czechoslovakia in 1968 and the subsequent announcement of the Brezhnev Doctrine, under which Moscow reserved the right to use military force to quash heretics in the communist world. Against the background of 1969 Sino-Soviet border clashes, Mao feared that he might be next on the Soviets' hit list.

Detaching the PRC from the Soviet Union and drawing it into a cooperative relationship had been constant U.S. objectives since 1949. The first objective was achieved in 1960, and Nixon perceived in 1969 that the second was within reach. Despite Mao's bellicose anti-American rhetoric and talk of people's war, he had made no move to intervene in the Vietnam War or exploit it by undertaking military provocations against Taiwan. By 1969, moreover, the radicalism of the Cultural Revolution was receding and moderates were begin-ning to make a comeback in Beijing. Having been informed by Moscow that it was considering a preemptive strike against the PRC, Nixon understood the seriousness of the Sino-Soviet confrontation and China's need for external assistance. Waving an olive branch by suspending U.S. naval patrols in the Taiwan Strait, he signaled his receptivity to a rapprochement. In subsequent diplomatic exchanges with the Chinese, Nixon set forth his conditions for a deal. The United States would cooperate with the PRC in restraining the Soviet Union in return for Beijing's help in ending the Vietnam War and moderating its behavior in East Asia.

Taiwan was the potential stumbling block. Mao wanted Washington to recognize PRC sovereignty over the island, sever its diplomatic ties with Taipei, and abrogate the 1954 ROC–U.S. defense treaty. This Nixon refused to do. He had built his early political career on his strong support of Chiang Kai-shek and he was not prepared overtly to sacrifice Taiwan on the altar of political expediency. An obvious sellout carried the potential to unravel American alliances in East Asia and provoke pro-ROC American conserva-tives into trying to sabotage his 1972 reelection bid. Nixon preferred to set the Taiwan issue aside, calculating that Mao's interest in securing U.S. help against the Soviets would lead him to go along. This calculation proved largely accurate, but there was another factor in play. In 1971, Mao scored a major diplomatic victory over Chiang when the United Nations, with Washington's acquiescence, ousted the ROC from the Security Council and invited the PRC to replace it. Mao thus achieved one of his primary goals—international rec-ognition as the legitimate ruler of China. His triumph was made even more complete by Chiang's withdrawal from the United Nations in protest.

Mao's United Nations success paved the way for Nixon's 1972 visit to Chi-na, which sealed the U.S.–PRC rapprochement. To Chinese, this visit evoked historical images of a barbarian king paying homage to the Son of Heaven.

President Nixon meets Mao Zedong in 1972.

But Nixon gave nothing away on Taiwan. In an artfully worded communiqué issued in Shanghai on the eve of his departure, he seemed to back Mao's "One China" position without in fact doing so. Nor did he unambiguously commit the United States to derecognizing Taipei and abrogating the 1954 defense pact. It fell to Nixon's and Mao's successors, Deng Xiaoping and Jimmy Carter, to work out a compromise that permitted U.S.–PRC normalization in 1978–79. Under this compromise, Washington endorsed Taiwan's eventual reunification with the mainland as long as it was accomplished peacefully, a condition Beijing refused to accept. The United States also cut its formal diplomatic and military ties with Taipei. To Deng's chagrin, however, the U.S. Congress passed a Taiwan Relations Act in 1978 that provided for continued American arms sales to Taiwan. Basic differences were thus merely papered over and Taiwan remained a de facto American protectorate.

China's Economic Modernization

Although the Sino-American rapprochement left Taiwan's status unresolved, it transformed the nature of the Cold War in East Asia. During the 1970s, the United States, the PRC, and Japan entered into an entente or quasi-alliance aimed at containing Soviet expansion, which resulted in China's diplomatic and economic integration with its anticommunist neighbors. The Japanese, who had been unhappy with earlier U.S. efforts to isolate Beijing, enthusiastically supported this realignment. In 1972, their prime minister followed Nixon's lead in journeying to Beijing to present his obeisance to Mao and offer war reparations. Mao disdained reparations as beneath China's dignity. What he wanted was Tokyo's backing of an anti-Soviet front and the severance of its official relations with Chiang's ROC. Japan paid Mao's price, going so far as to explicitly state its opposition to Soviet hegemonism in the 1978 Sino-Japanese peace treaty. The Japanese envisioned the establishment of a special relationship with China in which they would provide heavy inputs of official development assistance (ODA) and Beijing would look upon Japan as its principal economic partner and mentor.

In the years around Mao's death in 1976, it was unclear where the PRC was headed. Mao had committed China to cooperation with the West, but this course was controversial within the Chinese Communist Party. Rivalry between radicals and moderates again flared up, sharpened by a succession struggle. The radicals, centered around Mao's wife and others who had played prominent roles in the Cultural Revolution, insisted that there should be no retreat from the party's revolutionary ideals at home and abroad. Moderates, on the other hand, favored jettisoning the utopianism of the Great Leap and Cultural Revolution, and moving ahead with building up China's national wealth and power. They were led by Deng Xiaoping, one of Mao's longtime lieutenants who had been purged in the Cultural Revolution for his "rightist" views. Deng perceived that the Soviet Union was falling behind the West economically, suggesting fundamental weaknesses in its command economy. Impressed by the growth of neighboring East Asian countries, he concluded that China should abandon the Soviet economic model and embrace market incentives within the framework of continued Communist Party rule.

In 1977–78, Deng emerged as China's leader, having outmaneuvered both party radicals and Mao's designated successor. He then set about implementing his new economic program, which he dubbed "market socialism." One aspect of this program was replacing communes with family farms and allowing peasants to sell their produce on the open market. These moves proved highly popular in rural areas, where they stimulated a surge in agricultural production during the 1980s. Other innovations included opening China to Western aid, trade, and investment, and promoting the rise of a new class of Chinese capitalists. Deng welcomed Japanese ODA, consisting mainly of soft loans, which he used to improve China's relatively backward infrastructure. He also dismantled state monopolies on foreign and domestic trade, creating opportunities for private entrepreneurs to enter these fields. In addition, he established Special Economic Zones on the southeastern coast near Hong

Kong and Taiwan. There, Japanese, American, and overseas Chinese investors set up export-oriented light manufacturing operations, lured by tax incentives and an abundant supply of skilled, low-wage labor.

Deng discontinued Mao's early Cold War flirtation with Third World people's wars in favor of an exclusive reliance on formal state-to-state relations. This shift had begun in the 1970s, facilitated by the PRC's retreat from the extremism of the Cultural Revolution and its acquisition of Great Power status as a permanent member of the United Nations Security Council. But Deng accelerated the trend. In noncommunist Southeast Asia, he severed all but the most tenuous links with communist insurgents and revived the peaceful coexistence policy of the mid-1950s as the centerpiece of China's approach to the region. In the 1950s, this policy had been aimed at blocking U.S. efforts to put together anti-PRC alliances. In the 1980s, however, Deng promoted peaceful coexistence primarily as a means of attracting trade and investment to support China's economic modernization. Although many Southeast Asians remained suspicious of the PRC and did not forget its earlier sponsorship of communist insurgencies, Deng made some progress in building friendly relations with previously hostile states, particularly Thailand, which carried out its own rapprochement with China beginning in the 1970s.

Deng's peaceful coexistence line and economic outreach activities extended to the early Cold War anticommunist bastions of South Korea and Taiwan. By the 1980s, both were conducting rapidly growing indirect trade with the PRC through Hong Kong. Deng hoped that these ties would pave the way for Taiwan's reunification with the mainland under a "one country, two systems" formula. In addition, he was impressed by the successful industrialization of Taiwan and South Korea, and looked upon them as potentially valuable economic partners and models for China. The Guomindang regime in Taipei, headed by Chiang's son after his death in 1975, was initially unresponsive to Deng's feelers, continuing to proclaim itself the sole legitimate government of China despite its increasing diplomatic isolation. But the ROK's military rulers were intrigued by China's shift to a more conciliatory stance under Deng. They saw in this shift an opportunity to drive a wedge between the PRC and DPRK, which might force Kim Il Sung to moderate his hostility toward the ROK. Seoul consequently courted Beijing and began reducing its previously close ties with Taiwan as a signal of its desire for a rapprochement.

The most striking continuity between the foreign policies of Mao and Deng was the latter's continuation of Mao's opposition to Soviet hegemonism. Deng's maintenance of the anti-Soviet position of his predecessor is at first glance surprising. The rift between Moscow and Beijing grew out of Mao's ideological challenge to Moscow's dominance of the world communist movement and their rivalry for the allegiance of anti-Western Third World countries.

Deng Xiaoping in Texas, 1979.

But Deng made no pretense of being an authority on the interpretation of Marxist-Leninist dogma. Indeed, he had little interest in communist ideology except as a convenient, albeit increasingly unpersuasive, rationale for perpetuating Communist Party rule in China. Nor was Deng much concerned with asserting Chinese leadership in the Third World. Irrespective of its origins, however, the Sino-Soviet feud had acquired a life of its own, and mutual threat perceptions remained high. From the late 1960s to the mid-1980s, Moscow deployed large military forces along the Chinese-Soviet border. Like Mao, therefore, Deng had reason to regard the Soviet Union as the principal external threat facing China and its main rival in East Asia.

The Cold War Continues

The chief beneficiary of the continuation of the Sino-Soviet conflict was North Korea's Kim Il Sung who exploited the opportunity it offered to extract support from both Moscow and Beijing. Kim had need of such support. During the 1970s, his command economy faltered and increasingly fell behind the more dynamic capitalist economy of South Korea. Kim's problems mirrored in microcosm those of his Soviet patrons. He was committed to an expansion of the DPRK's army and military-industrial complex that exceeded the carrying capacity of its relatively small and inefficient economy. As in the Soviet Union, central planning, mass regimentation, and ideological exhortation worked well enough in the early stages of industrialization when the main task was harnessing agriculture to the rapid development of heavy industry. Once this task was accomplished, however, Soviet central planning and bureaucratic controls proved counterproductive insofar as they stifled individual initiative and innovation that were essential to sustaining growth. Neither the Soviets nor their emulators like Kim found a way to overcome the Soviet system's inherent tendency toward economic stagnation.

Given Kim's economic difficulties, one might expect that he would have backed away from his expensive military confrontation with South Korea, especially since the United States seemed inclined to withdraw. In the mid-1970s, the Carter administration announced plans for a phased pullout of U.S. forces from the ROK in hopes of ending the South-North standoff, which Carter regarded as an early Cold War anachronism. Kim wanted the Americans out of the South, but he rejected Carter's linkage of U.S. withdrawal to a buildup of ROK military capabilities and Pyongyang's participation in three-party talks with Seoul and Washington. Kim never wavered in his belief that South Korea was teetering on the brink of civil war and that the Seoul "puppets" survived only with American backing. He therefore refused to accept any arrangement that enhanced their power and legitimacy. His preferred method of dealing with the ROK was another invasion and he was confident that this time the Americans would not intervene in light of their humiliating ejection from South Vietnam in 1975. However, neither Moscow nor Beijing would support such a risky gambit and Kim could not act without them.

The inter-Korean confrontation thus continued unabated into the 1980s. North Korea's economic stagnation deepened, and it became increasingly dependent on Soviet and Chinese aid. Kim nonetheless avoided meaningful reform and disdained the PRC's experiment with market socialism, believing that his Juche-based system would ultimately prevail in his contest with the South. He also remained convinced that the ROK was on the verge of political collapse, a view seemingly substantiated in 1979–80 by President Park Chung Hee's murder by his own intelligence chief and the bloody suppression of a popular antigovernment uprising by Park's successor, General Chun Doo Hwan. Kim's strategy for toppling the ROK called for using both carrots and sticks. The sticks involved blows such as the 1983 Rangoon bombing in which DPRK commandos almost succeeded in assassinating Chun and part of his cabinet. The carrots entailed offers of dialogue and reconciliation aimed at disarming South Korean suspicions of Pyongyang. Kim employed such peace initiatives when he judged political conditions in the South suitable for a soft-line approach, first in 1972–73 and then in 1984–85.

Although Sino-Soviet rivalry sustained the standoff between the two Koreas, it did not lead to a second Korean war. In Southeast Asia, however, it contributed to the outbreak of a third Indochina war in 1978 when the Vietnamese invaded Cambodia , triggering an eleven-year guerrilla struggle against them. The origins of this conflict lay in Cambodian hostility toward Vietnam and Vietnamese ambitions to dominate Cambodia, both of which had deep historical roots that trumped their shared communist ideology. The Khmer Rouge followed up their victory in 1975 by imposing a reign of terror over Cambodia. Led by Pol Pot, a fanatical communist visionary who was influenced by Mao's Great Leap Forward and Cultural Revolution, they drove the urban population into the countryside where they set them to work tilling the soil in improvised communes. Mass starvation ensued, accompanied by Pol Pot's ruthless persecution of ethnic Vietnamese and Cambodians suspected of collaborating with Hanoi. These provocations, together with border clashes initiated by the Khmer Rouge, outraged Vietnam's leaders, who resolved to eliminate Pol Pot's regime by military force.

The Vietnam–Cambodia conflict might have played itself out in isolation had not the PRC and Soviet Union intervened on opposite sides. Beijing aligned itself with the Khmer Rouge, even going so far as to launch a punitive strike into northern Vietnam in 1979. The Chinese were angered by Hanoi's hegemonic pretensions in Indochina, its mistreatment of ethnic Chinese in Vietnam, and its intransigent stand on Sino-Vietnamese territorial disputes. Worse still, the Vietnamese had in Chinese eyes betrayed China's twenty-year support of Vietnam's struggle against the French and the Americans by tilting toward Moscow in the Sino-Soviet feud. Behind Chinese indignation lay the tacit assumption that Vietnam owed China deference as a onetime tributary and, since the 1940s, a pupil of Mao's people's war strategy. The Vietnamese, on their part, considered themselves in no way beholden to China. They were proud of their victories over France and the United States, which they felt had been achieved by dint of their own efforts and sacrifices. They also resented what they remembered as China's willingness to sell them out in 1954 and 1973, and its long history of bullying them in premodern times.

The Soviet Union lined up behind Vietnam, funneling military and economic aid to Hanoi, which enabled it to sustain protracted counterinsurgency operations against the PRC-backed Khmer Rouge and other anti-Vietnamese guerrillas. For Moscow, the war over Cambodia was a target of opportunity in its late–Cold War push to expand its influence in the Third World by aggressively exploiting civil wars and political conflicts. In the East Asian context, their alliance with Vietnam offered the Soviets a means to outflank China in Southeast Asia and secure access to Vietnam's Cam Ranh Bay naval base to support the expansion of their Far Eastern Fleet into the South China Sea. But the Cambodian conflict proved costly to both the Soviets and the Vietnamese. The latter had no difficulty occupying Phnom Penh and installing a compliant pro-Vietnamese regime, but their army could not crush the rebels, who retreated to jungle sanctuaries along the Thai-Cambodian border that were supplied from Thailand. Bangkok regarded the Vietnamese invasion as posing a threat to itself, and concluded a quasi-alliance with China to back the Cambodian insurgents and rally regional opposition to Hanoi.

The Rise of ASEAN

The Cambodian civil war provided the backdrop for the emergence of the Association of Southeast Asian Nations (ASEAN) as a major diplomatic player. Established in 1967 by Thailand, Singapore, Malaysia, Indonesia, and the Philippines, ASEAN was dismissed by the Soviets and Chinese as an anticommunist alliance similar to SEATO. But this assessment was off the mark. Although ASEAN's members were pro-Western, they were not interested in setting up a military alliance or joining the U.S. containment system. Their objective, rather, was to create an "entente cordiale" or informal coalition of like-minded states that would cooperate to minimize Great Power interference in their affairs and maximize their leverage vis-à-vis these powers by speaking with one voice. This was an important objective for the newly independent states of Southeast Asia. During the 1950s and 1960s, their instability and conflicts made them prime targets of Cold War rivalry in which they figured as prizes and pawns of the contending Chinese, Soviets, and Americans. They formed ASEAN in hopes of ending this situation and making Southeast Asia an autonomous political and diplomatic actor.

As noted in the introduction, Southeast Asia was an unpromising venue for regional cooperation, since it had little cultural unity or experience of working together. But the 1942–45 Japanese-imposed Greater East Asia Co-Prosperity Sphere acted as a seedbed of Southeast Asian regionalism insofar as it implanted ideas of Asian unity and cooperation. The postwar pan-Asianist and Afro-Asian movements revived these ideas, adding to them the principles of noninterference, nonaggression, and nonalignment. Southeast Asian intellectuals and politicians were prominently involved in these movements, and absorbed their rhetoric and ideals. However, translating the "New Asianism" into regional cooperation proved difficult. Neutralist Burma, Laos, Indonesia, and Cambodia refused to join any organization that included U.S.-allied Thailand and the Philippines. The Federation of Malaya, which became independent in 1957 under British protection, was on poor terms with Sukarno's Indonesia, which viewed it as a base for Western interference in its politics. In addition, Sukarno had little interest in regionalism, seeing himself an actor on the world stage.

The prospects for Southeast Asian regionalism further dimmed in the early

1960s. Burma retreated into isolation under the xenophobic military regime of General Ne Win who overthrew the civilian government in 1962. In the following year, Sukarno led Indonesia into a military confrontation with Malaya over the latter's plans to incorporate Singapore and British territories in northern Borneo into the new state of Malaysia. He denounced this move as a neocolonialist plot by the British and Americans, which he claimed ignored the desire of Bornean peoples to join Indonesia. The Philippines entered the squabble by advancing its own claim to British North Borneo. With British military support, Malaya's prime minister, Tunku Abdul Rahman, went ahead with the establishment of Malaysia. However, tensions between Kuala Lumpur and Jakarta continued, and in 1965 Malaysia ejected Singapore, which became independent under its British-educated prime minister, Lee Kuan Yew. This split grew out of Tunku Abdul Rahman's fears that Singapore's largely ethnic Chinese population might disrupt the Malay-Chinese balance on which Malaysian political stability depended.

In 1965, there was little reason to suppose that Indonesia, Malaysia, Singapore, and the Philippines could cooperate. Yet two years later they set aside their differences and joined with Thailand to form ASEAN. The catalyst for this about-face was Sukarno's fall from power in a 1965–66 army coup involving the massacre of tens of thousands of Indonesian communists and ethnic Chinese. His successor, General Suharto, was a Southeast Asian regionalist, paving the way for a rapprochement between Jakarta and Kuala Lumpur. ASEAN's founding fathers—Suharto, Tunku Abdul Rahman, Lee Kuan Yew, Philippines president Ferdinand Marcos, and Thai military strongman Thanon Kittikachorn—were pro-Western and staunchly anticommunist. But they were uncomfortable with their dependence on British and American security guarantees, which they suspected might not be entirely reliable. Britain's 1967 announcement of its intention to withdraw militarily "east of Suez" heightened their concerns, as did the beginning of American disengagement from South Vietnam in 1968. Marcos and Thanon also had to contend with domestic nationalist criticism of their excessive deference to Washington.

For ASEAN's founders, the creation of an anticommunist alliance along the lines of SEATO was a nonstarter. Indonesia and Malaysia were attracted to the Non-Aligned Movement and subscribed to its call for peaceful coexistence and neutrality in the Cold War. Moreover, a military alliance seemed both unnecessary and provocative. In the view of the leaders of the ASEAN states, moreover, the principal threat facing them was communist subversion. A conventional military alliance would not address this threat and was likely to arouse the suspicion of outside powers. Their preferred alternative was informal cooperation aimed at devising "regional solutions to regional problems." In practice, this meant consultation, compromise, and consensus, which they dubbed the "ASEAN Way" and claimed was rooted in distinctive Southeast Asian cultural values. They employed this approach to declare Southeast Asia a Zone of Peace, Freedom and Neutrality in 1971, and to sign a Treaty of Amity and Cooperation in 1976 that enshrined the principles of nonaggression, noninterference, and respect for national sovereignty as the basis of Southeast Asia's international relations.

Vietnam's invasion of Cambodia in 1978 challenged ASEAN's vision of Southeast Asia's future and dashed its hopes of inducting Hanoi as a member. The ASEAN states did not see eye-to-eye on the nature of the challenge. Indonesia and Malaysia were suspicious of China's long-term intentions in the region, and favored a conciliatory stance toward Vietnam which they viewed as a buffer state. But they closed ranks behind Thailand's insistence that ASEAN counter Vietnamese aggression by exerting diplomatic pressure on Hanoi and assisting Cambodian resistance. Having been derided earlier by some Western observers as a mere talk shop capable only of issuing high-sounding declarations, ASEAN demonstrated an unexpected capacity for effective collective action during the late 1970s and 1980s. It held Vietnam's feet to the fire in United Nations resolutions, blocked its efforts to legitimize its Cambodian client state, and provided diplomatic and material support for the Khmer Rouge and other anti-Vietnamese guerrillas. ASEAN's activism on Cambodia led the major powers in East Asia to sit up and take notice, none more so than Japan.

"Asia's New Giant"

In the 1970s, it was reasonable to expect that Japan would soon cast off its dependence on the United States and reassert itself as an autonomous political and perhaps even military actor in East Asia. It had become "Asia's new giant," possessing a dynamic economy which dwarfed those of its neighbors, and which some predicted might eventually surpass that of the United States itself. Historical experience suggested that states usually tried to translate their economic prowess into political and military power. Moreover, the U.S.–Japan alliance was fraying. Bilateral trade friction, initially centered on Japanese textile exports, was on the rise, and many Japanese were angered by Nixon's cavalier treatment of them in 1971 by unilaterally forcing an upward revaluation of the yen and keeping Tokyo in the dark about his opening to the PRC until he publicly announced it. In subsequent years, the Americans were consumed by internal wrangling over the Vietnam debacle and the Watergate scandal, and beset by stagflation arising from the 1973 oil crisis. The United States seemed to be fading as East Asia's leading power, leaving a vacuum that a resurgent Japan would fill.

Japan, however, remained content with its role as a junior partner of the United States and mounted no serious bid for regional hegemony. The reasons for this lie in Japanese domestic politics. The settlement engineered by the Liberal Democratic Party (LDP) in the 1960s required nonparticipation in international power politics and a concentration on economic priorities. In political-military terms, Japan retreated into isolationism, a move rationalized by the LDP's co-option of the Left's pacifist agenda. Japanese defined themselves as conscientious objectors committed to realizing the ideals of their "no war" constitution and abstaining from military conflicts like the Vietnam War. They embraced the American alliance because it insulated them from such conflicts, enabled them to indulge their pacifist idealism, and underwrote their new national prosperity. The Left continued to advocate unarmed neutrality and the Right remained committed to resuming "normal" international political-military responsibilities. But neither had much support. The LDP mainstream and the majority of Japanese became wedded to the status quo, which meant upholding the alliance and accepting a subordinate role in it.

Tokyo nevertheless enjoyed leeway within the American alliance to stake out independent policy positions and diversify its overseas partnerships, and its concerns over U.S. unilateralism and unpredictability led it to move in these directions. The result was a shift in the 1970s to what the Japanese called "omnidirectional diplomacy" and "comprehensive security." These catchphrases reflected the determination of LDP leaders to reduce what they considered to be Japan's excessive deference to Washington and overreliance on the American security guarantee. Japan's security, in their view, should also be based on the deployment of its economic power through aid, trade, and investment to "win friends and influence people" in accordance with its national interests, which might, or might not, coincide with those of the United States. An early and pointed expression of omnidirectional diplomacy was Tokyo's tilt toward the Arab side in the 1973 Arab-Israeli war despite Washington's disapproval. Japan thereby signaled that it had its own interests in the Middle East, chiefly assuring its oil supplies, which it was intent on protecting irrespective of U.S. wishes.

The principal focus of Japan's more independent foreign policy was China, Korea, and Southeast Asia. As noted above, Tokyo quickly moved in behind Nixon's opening to China, normalizing diplomatic relations in 1972 with the aim of establishing a Sino-Japanese partnership in which Japan would play the role of the PRC's main economic benefactor and mentor. Deng's embrace of economic modernization on the capitalist model after 1979 solidified this partnership. But there were tensions in the relationship. China lacked the capital and expertise to handle the technologically advanced industrial plants offered by Japan, resulting in the cancellation of a number of high-profile projects in the early 1980s with heavy financial losses for Japanese investors.

In 1982, moreover, allegations by the Japanese press that the government had ordered the "whitewashing" of school textbooks to play down World War II atrocities provoked an uproar in China as well as Korea and other East Asian countries. Mao may have been willing to overlook Japan's past aggression, but many ordinary Chinese and Communist Party members were not, adding a new and disruptive element to Sino-Japanese relations.

The ROK–Japan relationship was burdened by a colonial hangover unparalleled elsewhere in East Asia. In contrast to Taiwanese, many of whom looked back on Japanese rule with nostalgia, Koreans neither forgot nor forgave what they remembered as their national humiliation at the hands of Japanese colonizers. Their animosity was inflamed by the perceived mistreatment of the Korean minority in postwar Japan and by territorial and fishing disputes. Seoul and Tokyo did not establish diplomatic relations until 1965 and then only under U.S. pressure. Nevertheless, economic ties burgeoned beginning in the late 1960s, facilitated by Park Chung Hee's encouragement of Japanese investment and his adoption of the Japanese economic model. This model proved relatively easy to transplant in South Korea. As much as Koreans resented the Japanese, they were so drawn to them that the ROK government found it necessary to ban films, magazines, and other Japanese "cultural imports." Taiwanese were equally inclined to emulate the Japanese and did not share Koreans' animus toward them. It is no accident that Taiwan and South Korea became Japan's star economic pupils.

Although the Japanese began eyeing Southeast Asia in the 1960s, the Vietnam War and Malaysian-Indonesian confrontation kept them on the sidelines. They were bit players compared to the Americans, British, Chinese, and Soviets, who dominated the scene in the early Cold War period. Japan's opportunity to play a larger role came with the stabilization of the region consequent to the emergence of ASEAN, the U.S.–PRC rapprochement, and the restriction of Cold War rivalry to the Sino-Soviet conflict over Indochina. In the 1970s, the Japanese moved in behind the retreating Americans and British with offers of development assistance, lucrative trade deals, and manufacturing investments. As was underscored by anti-Japanese riots in Bangkok and Jakarta in 1974, however, their growing economic presence in Southeast Asia was unpopular. Their clannish ways, cultural insensitivity, and focus on extracting oil and other natural resources evoked unpleasant memories of their World War II Co-Prosperity Sphere. Their image was further tarnished in the eyes of some Southeast Asians by the perception that they acted in collusion with corrupt authoritarian regimes.

Under the 1977 Fukuda Doctrine, so named after the Japanese prime minister who enunciated it, Japan launched a concerted effort to allay Southeast Asian suspicions and engage ASEAN as a diplomatic partner. Tokyo disclaimed any intention of playing a military role in the region, expressed its desire for "heart-to-heart" dialogue and greater cultural exchanges, and sharply increased its development assistance. Japanese firms meanwhile revamped their business practices to expand local participation in their operations. At the same time, mounting trade disputes between Japan and the United States led many of these firms to see Southeast Asia as an attractive platform for offshore manufacturing aimed at the American market. Singapore, Malaysia, Thailand, and Indonesia, which they considered particularly suitable for this purpose, reaped the reward, developing profitable export industries based on Japanese subsidiaries and joint ventures. These countries joined South Korea and Taiwan in looking upon Japan as an economic model, a trend reflected in the "Learn from Japan" campaign of Singapore's Lee Kuan Yew and the "Look East" policy of Malaysian prime minister Dr. Mahathir Mohamad.

U.S.–Japan Tensions

By the 1980s, East Asia was becoming an interconnected economic unit integrated around Japan and whose economies more or less replicated Japan's system of export-led growth. The key to this system was close government–business collaboration. Working hand in glove with big business, Japanese bureaucrats were armed with broad discretionary authority to guide the economy toward goals set by the political leadership. The ruling LDP defined these goals as maintaining a high rate of growth, distributing the benefits equitably, and rewarding its political supporters with subsidies and protection. The Japanese system kept the LDP in power by enabling it to consistently win diet majorities in relatively free and fair elections. It also produced highly efficient export industries that were often able to overwhelm foreign competitors who lacked comparable government backing. But there were some downsides. The system insulated inefficient sectors such as agriculture and retail trade from foreign competition, and Japanese consumers paid the price. Moreover, government–business collaboration lent itself to bribery scandals, to which LDP politicians were notoriously prone.

Japan's system of state-guided capitalism led to acrimonious trade disputes with the United States, its principal trading partner. The Americans, who dubbed this system "Japan Inc.," looked askance at it. In their view, government should act as a referee rather than a coach in a properly run free market economy. Japanese exporters seemed to enjoy unfair advantages over their U.S. competitors. Moreover, Japan's domestic market was largely closed to American manufactured goods even though these were competitive with Japanese products in price and quality. The Americans demanded a "level playing field" while the Japanese advised them to become better players. U.S. and Japanese trade negotiators worked out a series of compromises, which brought temporary relief. But the underlying systemic conflict persisted, giving rise to increasingly shrill mutual recriminations. Some Americans accused Japan of being an economic predator seeking regional and perhaps even global dominance. Japanese denounced such accusations as racist "Japan bashing," and a few nationalists publicly urged that Japan use its high-tech prowess to bring the United States to heel.

Bilateral trade disputes were not new, having recurred virtually nonstop since the late 1960s. What was new in the 1980s, however, was a reviving spirit of national pride and assertiveness among Japanese. One sign of this trend was the vogue of popular books celebrating the theme of "Japan as Number One" (the title of a 1979 best-seller by an American admirer of Japan's political-economic system). Japanese expositors of this theme tended to extoll the superiority of traditional Japanese values of harmony, discipline, and teamwork over the more individualistic values of Westerners in general and Americans in particular. Some observers discerned in such writings the seeds of another nativist and pan-Asianist revolt against the West similar to that of the 1930s. As the political influence of the Left waned, moreover, that of the Right waxed. Conservative nationalists in the LDP, who had been quiescent since the 1960s, became more visible and outspoken. They took the lead in lashing back at American criticism of Japan on trade issues, and denouncing Chinese and Korean interference in the way Japanese chose to remember World War II and their place in prewar Asia.

Prime Minister Yasuhiro Nakasone, the most prominent nationalist of the 1980s, did not subscribe to the anti-American views of the extreme Right. During his 1982–87 tenure, he tried to strengthen the American alliance and increase Japan's role in it. To this end, he advocated building up the Self-Defense Force's capabilities, expanding its maritime patrol responsibilities, lifting the ban on sharing military technology, and setting aside the 1 percent of GDP cap on defense spending. He even hinted at revising Article Nine of the constitution. Nakasone also espoused educational reforms aimed at restoring patriotism and respect for patriotic symbols such as the national flag and anthem, which had sharply declined during the postwar decades. One of his special preoccupations was exorcising what he and other nationalists considered to be an unhealthy sense of national shame over the Greater East Asia War. To dramatize this issue, he became in 1985 the first postwar prime minister to officially pay his respects at Yasukuni Shrine in Tokyo, which commemorates Japan's war dead. Accompanied by a large number of LDP diet members, he made this pilgrimage on the August 15 anniversary of the war's end.

Nakasone's Yasukuni visit provoked vehement protests from Beijing, Seoul, and Japanese leftists, and he did not repeat it. Although he was accused by his domestic and foreign critics of trying to revive Japanese militarism and ultranationalism, his objectives were, in fact, quite different. Nakasone sought to arouse the Japanese people from their pacifist-isolationist reverie

Yasukuni Shrine in Tokyo.

and instill in them an awareness of their international political and military responsibilities as citizens of a major power. But he was unsuccessful in this. Despite his personal popularity with Japanese voters, he ran up against a brick wall of resistance from the LDP leadership, the leftist political parties, and Japan's media. They were willing to tolerate token moves to strengthen military cooperation with the United States in light of the Soviet Union's menacing buildup of its Far Eastern fleet, its intervention in the Indochina conflict, and its 1979 invasion of Afghanistan. But they were firmly opposed to any undertaking that involved the slightest risk that Japanese might have to fight on foreign soil. Japan, in other words, remained unwilling even to consider shouldering collective security responsibilities.

Nakasone was also unsuccessful in addressing the underlying causes of U.S.–Japan trade friction. He endorsed the recommendation of a blue ribbon nongovernmental study group that urged Japan to undertake fundamental reforms to open its market and dismantle impediments to competition. But little came of this recommendation. A more significant initiative was the 1985 Plaza Accord under which Tokyo agreed to sharply appreciate the value of the yen in hopes of curbing Japanese exports to the United States. Although it largely failed to achieve this objective, the Plaza Accord had other important effects. One of these was to create what the Japanese termed a "bubble economy"—a wild asset inflation and speculative boom that was aggravated

Japanese cars unloaded for export, 1990.

by the lowering of domestic interest rates. Another consequence of the Plaza Accord was to stimulate a massive outflow of Japanese capital into South Korea, China, Taiwan, China, and Southeast Asia as Japan's export industries sought to evade the high yen barrier by relocating their production facilities overseas. As a result, East Asia became even more tightly integrated around Japan and dependent on its capital and technology.

As the Cold War wound down in the late 1980s, many Americans wondered if Japan might be replacing the fading Soviet Union as their chief rival in East Asia. Proponents of the "Japan threat" school pointed to the inability of reform-minded leaders like Nakasone to rein in, much less dismantle, Japan Inc. In their view, Japan's mercantilist economic machine was running on autopilot and, in contrast to "normal" liberal democracies, was impervious to control by elected politicians. It seemed programmed to steamroller foreign competitors, amass ever-larger trade surpluses, and extend Japan's economic dominance regionally and even globally. By the late 1990s, however, this alarmist literature was out of date. Indeed, the focus of American commentary on Japan shifted to the systemic weaknesses of its economy, which escaped attention earlier. The Japanese juggernaut of the 1970s and 1980s turned out to have feet of clay. What had been overlooked was the burden of sustaining protected and inefficient sectors. Japan Inc. became increasingly expensive to operate and prone to a breakdown once consumption and investment slackened, which is what happened in the 1990s.

10

Post–Cold War Trends

The unanticipated collapse of the Soviet Union in 1989–91 had less dramatic effects in East Asia than in Europe. While Southeast Asia moved toward unity under ASEAN, the inter-Korean and Taiwan–China standoffs continued. Nevertheless, the removal of the common Soviet threat led to the slow unraveling of the late–Cold War U.S.–PRC–Japan entente. During the 1990s, China and the United States shifted to an uneasy rivalry-cum-partnership, while Sino-Japanese relations steadily deteriorated over territorial and history issues. Buoyed by China's rapidly growing economy, Beijing employed smile diplomacy and soft power in a low-key bid for regional leadership. Japan meanwhile bolstered its faltering alliance with the United States and gradually discarded its Cold War pacifist isolationism in favor of assuming "normal" international political-military responsibilities. Although Japan's "miracle" economy stumbled, East Asia's economic growth and integration proceeded apace in the 1990s, inspiring both Asia-Pacific and East Asian regionalism. By the end of the decade, moves were even under way to turn East Asia into something like the European Community.

The Soviet Collapse

The 1989–91 disintegration first of Soviet satellite regimes in Eastern Europe and then of the Soviet Union itself caught most Western observers by surprise. It seemed incredible that the Soviet colossus could self-destruct, and even more amazing that this process elicited little complaint from the Soviets themselves. The Soviet breakdown was internally generated. Communists had always assumed that the capitalist system would collapse from the weight of its internal contradictions; it never occurred to them that the Soviet system would prove even more vulnerable to such contradictions. Foremost among these was the strain of trying to compete with the United States with an economy that was unequal to the task. As noted in the previous chapter, the Soviet command economy had a built-in tendency toward stagnation and retrogression, which

186

became increasingly apparent during the later stages of the 1964–82 Brezhnev era. Instead of attempting to reform the system, Brezhnev and his colleagues resorted to stopgap measures such as importing grain from the West, and acquiesced in the spread of bribery and corruption among the Communist Party elite or nomenklatura.

Despite growing cynicism and demoralization, the Soviet Union might have staggered on indefinitely. Except for dissident intellectuals, there was no domestic opposition. An efficient security apparatus saw to that, backed by a large, well-armed, and disciplined military. In addition, the Soviets boasted an impressive military-industrial complex that produced state-of-the-art weaponry and sustained a space program rivaling that of the United States. But influential elements within the Soviet Communist Party demanded reform. They were alarmed by the decline of the Soviet economy and increasing corruption. The urgency of reform was underscored by Brezhnev's launching of a "Second Cold War" in the mid-1970s involving expensive new Soviet commitments in the Third World, including the USSR's embroilment in what turned out be a losing war in Afghanistan. Moreover, Brezhnev's challenge elicited a strong reaction from the United States. Under President Ronald Reagan, the Americans sought to roll back Soviet advances in the Third World and threw down the gauntlet for an escalation of the arms race by announcing their intention of building a "Star Wars" missile defense system.

The accession of Mikhail Gorbachev in 1985 brought the reformist wing of the Communist Party to power. Recognizing that the Soviet Union was no longer strong enough to sustain toe-to-toe competition with the United States, he entered into arms control talks with Reagan and began pulling back from Afghanistan, Vietnam, and other Third World battlefields. At the same time, he embarked on a renovation of the Soviet system under the slogans glasnost (openness) and perestroika (restructuring). Like Deng Xiaoping, Gorbachev set in motion a move toward a market economy by lifting restrictions on private enterprise. Unlike Deng, however, he ended the Communist Party's monopoly of power and promoted a shift to electoral democracy in hopes that electoral competition would restore popular faith in the government by making it more responsive and accountable. But the result was political chaos: No one seemed to be in charge of the government or know what to do. Like an organism deprived of its central nervous system, the Soviet behemoth became paralyzed and began to fall apart as power devolved to regional party bosses who controlled personal political machines.

The collapse of the Eastern European satellite regimes followed. It had been apparent since the 1950s that these regimes lacked popular support and could survive only with Soviet backing. When Gorbachev told them that the floundering Soviet Union was no longer able or willing to prop them up,

Scrapped Soviet navy ships near Vladivostok, 1993.

they consequently fell like tenpins, illustrating the domino theory that the Americans had earlier applied to Southeast Asia. Except in Romania, all of them gave up without a fight. East Germany even acquiesced in its dissolution and absorption by West Germany in 1990 to form a reunified Germany. The collapse of the Eastern European communist states was as much moral and psychological as political. Few believed in their legitimacy or viability, including their leaders. The contagion spread to independent Yugoslavia and Albania, which suffered similar crises of legitimacy. As communist rule weakened, long-suppressed national loyalties and feuds reasserted themselves. Yugoslavia broke up into its constituent republics, which soon fell to fighting over territory. Czechoslovakia also split into Czech and Slovak states, but these managed an amicable "velvet divorce."

The Soviet Union, a multinational state composed of ostensibly autonomous republics, was beset by the same centrifugal forces as control by the demoralized Soviet Communist Party broke down in 1990–91. The Baltic republics were the first to spin away, followed by Belarus, Ukraine, Georgia, Armenia, and Azerbaijan. The five largely Muslim and Turkish-speaking Central Asian republics—Kazakhstan, Uzbekistan, Tajikistan, Kyrgyzstan, and Turkmenistan—joined the exodus, also becoming independent nation-states. The core of the Soviet Union survived in the form of the Russian Federation, which inherited Soviet treaty obligations and much of its armed forces, nuclear arsenal, and military-industrial complex. But the Russian Federation, led by President Boris Yeltsin, was a pale imitation of its Soviet predecessor. Its economy was weak and its politics confused as it struggled toward liberal democracy and a market economy. Moreover, Yeltsin's government exercised only tenuous authority in outlying regions, and faced separatist movements such as that of the Chechens in the northern Caucasus area.

Effects in East Asia

In contrast to Eastern Europe, the Soviet collapse did not lead to the disintegration of communist regimes in East Asia. Like Castro's Cuba, these regimes had developed independent sources of legitimacy, enabling them to ride out the storm with little damage. Their strength derived from their success in co-opting indigenous nationalism, which Eastern European communist parties had failed to do. The Mongolian People's Republic, the closest East Asian equivalent of a Soviet satellite, maintained friendly relations with and emulated Yeltsin's economic and political reforms. But other communist states went their own way. North Korea continued to pursue national self-reliance under Kim Il Sung's antiquated but still formidable Stalinist regime. The Chinese Communist Party remained firmly in charge in Deng's China, having found a new raison d'être as the overseer of its transition to market socialism. The Vietnamese Communist Party enjoyed unchallengeable authority as the leader of a successful fifty-year national struggle against the French, Americans, and Chinese. Its Laotian offshoot and follower, the Pathet Lao, basked in the prestige of its Vietnamese mentor.

The demise of the Soviet Union did, however, have important effects in East Asia. Perhaps the most significant of these were the unraveling of the U.S.–PRC–Japan entente and the weakening of American bilateral alliances. In 1990–91, both the Philippine and Japanese alliances showed signs of breaking down, as was reflected in the U.S. military withdrawal from the Philippines and the closure of its bases there. The 1989 Tiananmen Square massacre, in which Deng employed his army to suppress prodemocracy demonstrations, meanwhile introduced new tensions in the U.S.–PRC relationship and led to the imposition of Western sanctions on China. Without the glue of a common Soviet threat to hold them together, relations between Washington and Beijing became subject to sharp ups and downs, while those between Tokyo and Beijing steadily deteriorated. But the end of Sino-Soviet rivalry also facilitated the resolution of conflicts and new forms of cooperation. Yeltsin's Russia moved closer to China, settling long-standing border disputes and becoming its main arms supplier. Moreover, hitherto divided Southeast Asia was finally able to unite under ASEAN.

Toward "One Southeast Asia"

In Europe, the Soviet collapse raised the Iron Curtain and brought together Eastern and Western Europe, as was reflected in the eastward expansion of NATO and the European Community (or European Union as it was called after 1991). A similar process occurred in Southeast Asia, where the end of the Cambodian conflict led to the integration of Indochina into ASEAN. As the Soviets cut back their military and economic aid in the late 1980s, Hanoi concluded that its expensive intervention in Cambodia was no longer sustainable, and signaled its readiness to accept a negotiated settlement. China was amenable, but the problem was devising a peace formula acceptable to the rival Cambodian factions. In 1991, the PRC, United States, and France brokered a deal that called for United Nations–supervised elections to choose a new Cambodian government. Although the Khmer Rouge balked at participating, these elections were held in 1993, resulting in the restoration of the monarchy and the installation of a coalition government. Factional infighting continued into the late 1990s, but a measure of stability was achieved under Hun Sen, a onetime Vietnamese protégé who secured broad backing.

The Cambodian settlement eliminated the chief source of tension between Vietnam and ASEAN, paving the way for its admission in 1995. Vietnam had already begun to integrate itself with its neighbors in the mid-1980s when reformers started to dismantle its command economy and institute PRC-style market socialism under continued Vietnamese Communist Party rule. Hanoi subsequently accepted foreign investment and encouraged the development of export industries. Laos, following hesitantly in the footsteps of its Vietnamese mentor, joined ASEAN in 1997. Cambodia's entry was delayed by its domestic political strife but it, too, became a member in 1999. ASEAN's goal of "One Southeast Asia" was realized with the admission of Burma, or Myanmar, as it renamed itself. But this was a controversial step. Although Ne Win fell from power in 1988, the military dictatorship he had created soldiered on, quashing a prodemocracy movement led by Aung San's daughter and resisting meaningful economic reform or any real opening to the outside world. The Americans and Europeans regarded Burma as an egregious human rights violator and treated it as a pariah state.

Whether the admission of Burma, Vietnam, Laos, and Cambodia would ultimately strengthen or weaken ASEAN was much debated. Its five original members had been able to cooperate in part because they shared similar developmental priorities, concerns over communist subversion, and a preference for soft authoritarianism over liberal democracy. They became more alike politically during the 1970s when Ferdinand Marcos abandoned Philippine democracy and imposed a martial law regime. But the pendulum swung back toward democracy in the 1980s, beginning with Marcos's overthrow in the "People Power" revolution of 1985–86 and the advent of the Corazón Aquino government. In the 1990s, Thailand joined the liberal democratic camp as its army withdrew from politics and elected politicians finally gained the ascendancy after several previous false starts. Indonesia, ASEAN's largest and most influential member, also moved away from military-dominated authoritarian government in 1998 when General Suharto stepped down amid violent popular disorders, and his successors began a slow and painful transition back to liberal democracy, which Sukarno had discarded in the late 1950s.

The enlarged ASEAN of 1999 was more heterogeneous than at any earlier point in its thirty-year history. Politically, its ten member-states ran the gamut from Burma's harsh military dictatorship to the vibrant, albeit struggling, liberal democracies of Indonesia, Thailand, and the Philippines. Brunei was an absolute monarchy, while Vietnam and Laos remained authoritarian one-party states at least nominally committed to communism. Singapore and Malaysia were run by "one-party-dominant " regimes that tolerated dissent and electoral competition. Economically, ASEAN had become equally diverse. It included relatively impoverished and still largely agrarian Laos, Burma, and Cambodia as well as affluent Singapore, which boasted living standards comparable to those of Japan and the United States. Thailand and Malaysia were newly industrialized countries, but the Philippines, Indonesia, and Vietnam lagged behind. Under these circumstances, a key challenge for ASEAN was preserving its unity and finding common ground, a challenge heightened by Southeast Asia's increasing economic integration with its Northeast Asian neighbors into a larger East Asia.

The Korean Deadlock Continues

The end of the Cold War initially seemed to augur progress in breaking the inter-Korean deadlock. The ROK, having made a transition from military rule to liberal democracy in 1987–88, was in a stronger position to push for genuine détente with the North, and the international environment was favorable. German reunification offered an inspiration and model. With the winding down of PRC–Soviet rivalry, moreover, Beijing and Moscow disengaged from the DPRK and courted the economically more attractive ROK. In the early 1990s, they established diplomatic relations with Seoul and facilitated its entry into the United Nations. Kim Il Sung thus found himself diplomatically outflanked by his southern rival. To make matters worse, his moribund economy virtually collapsed as the Chinese and the Soviets reduced their aid and began charging market prices for oil and other vital imports. With his back to the wall, Kim launched another peace offensive toward Seoul. This had the dual objective of destabilizing the ROK government, which he still regarded as a fragile and unpopular puppet regime, and cajoling economic and political concessions from its American and Japanese backers.

In 1990–91, Kim and the South Korean president agreed on economic cooperation, family reunification visits, a nonaggression pact, and the denuclearization of the peninsula. In 1992, however, the peace process foundered amid mutual accusations of bad faith. As on previous occasions, Kim called it off because he judged that it had served its propaganda purpose and had failed to elicit sufficient concessions from the United States. He then resolved to get by brinksmanship what he could not get by conciliation. He attracted Washington's attention by waving the red flag of his nuclear weapons program and rejecting International Atomic Energy Agency (IAEA) inspections. This precipitated a U.S.–DPRK confrontation in 1993–94 that came close to war. However, both sides drew back and worked out an "Agreed Framework" in 1994 under which the United States undertook to supply nuclear reactors and fuel oil in return for Pyongyang's acceptance of IAEA inspections and suspension of its weapons program. To sweeten the deal, Washington dangled the prospect of eventual diplomatic recognition and the lifting of trade restrictions contingent on North Korea's good behavior.

Kim's actions underscored the fact he was unwilling to fold his tent and concede defeat despite diminished support from Moscow and Beijing and the breakdown of his economy. Some observers concluded that Kim and his son Kim Jong Il, who succeeded him upon his death in 1994, were "irrational" and would respond only to force. Others supposed that the Kims felt themselves threatened by the United States and would become reasonable if this threat was lifted. In fact, they were eminently rational actors by their own rights. Their ultimate objective remained ejecting the Americans and reunifying the peninsula under North Korean rule. They believed that this objective was attainable as long as the North stayed the course and held true to its Juche principles. In their view, the DPRK still held some strong cards, including a loyal million-man army, a regimented and indoctrinated population, and a military-industrial complex capable of turning out ballistic missiles and nuclear weapons. As mass starvation loomed in North Korea in the late 1990s, many assumed that Kim Jong Il's regime was on the verge of imploding into anarchy or civil war. But this assessment underestimated the DPRK's resilience.

In 1999–2000, ROK President Kim Dae Jung undertook a more determined peace initiative toward the North than any contemplated by his predecessors. This initiative, which he called the "Sunshine Policy," aimed at melting North Korean suspicion and hostility through unprecedented offers of economic assistance. It was based on the assumption that North Korea, now on external life support by China and other foreign donors, would exchange regime survival for peaceful coexistence. Kim Jong Il responded favorably, leading to the first-ever inter-Korean summit in Pyongyang in 2000. ROK food, fuel, and fertilizer poured into the North, accompanied by throngs of South Korean tourists and investors. Critics noted that Kim Jong Il made no move to reduce his army or pull it back from the demilitarized zone. Nor did he permit many North Koreans to visit the South. But a new era of peace and reconciliation seemed to be dawning. The Clinton administration, intrigued by Kim Jong Il's tilt toward moderation, hinted that it might be willing to trade diplomatic normalization for curbs on his ballistic missile program, and Clinton himself was ready to visit Pyongyang as his term ended.

South Koreans were divided over the question of whether Kim Jong Il had, in fact, abandoned his father's dream of retaking the South and become willing to accept peaceful coexistence with Seoul. This debate was conducted partly along generational lines. Those who were old enough to remember the provocations of the Cold War era tended to be skeptical. But the younger generation, particularly the student peace and democracy activists of the 1970s and 1980s, were inclined to give Kim Jong Il the benefit of the doubt. Now in positions of power and influence in the ROK, they insisted that the Sunshine Policy should continue. However, the United States shifted to a hard-line toward stance toward Pyongyang after 2000. The Bush administration was critical of what it considered to be Clinton's willingness to submit to North Korean nuclear blackmail, and suspected that Pyongyang was cheating on its promise in the Agreed Framework to freeze its development of nuclear weapons. Washington's decision to confront Pyongyang on this issue in 2002 led to a second U.S.–DPRK nuclear crisis and growing tensions with Seoul, which favored a more conciliatory approach in line with its Sunshine Policy.

The Taiwan Issue Reemerges

One might expect Taiwan to have been a prime candidate for reunification with the PRC under Deng's "one country, two systems" formula. Its ROC regime was an early Cold War anachronism. It claimed to be the legitimate government of China, temporarily based in Taiwan pending its recovery of the mainland. Although Chiang Kai-shek never had a realistic chance of re-taking the mainland, this claim provided a useful rationale for U.S. efforts to prop him up during the 1950s and 1960s as a counter to Mao's China. After the U.S.–PRC rapprochement, however, the ROC became an embarrassment to Washington. As noted in the previous chapter, the Americans were loathe to completely discard Chiang, but they acquiesced in his expulsion from the United Nations in 1971 and de-recognized him as did every other major power.

By the 1980s, the ROC could no longer credibly claim to be a sovereign state much less the legitimate government of China. It seemed to have no raison d'être as a political entity except as a sanctuary for the mainlanders who had fled with Chiang to the island in 1949, but they were beginning to pass from the scene through old age and death.

The rise of Taiwanese nationalism gave the ROC a new lease on life and changed the dynamics of cross-strait relations. As a recently settled frontier province, Taiwan had a distinctive character even during Qing times. Fifty years of Japanese colonial rule accentuated differences between Taiwanese and mainlanders, and implanted among the former a consciousness that they were a separate people. Chiang's regime unintentionally politicized this feeling of separateness into a budding sense of nationhood by drawing Taiwanese into the army, government, party, and business, where they largely displaced mainlanders. Many native Taiwanese, joined by second-generation mainlanders born in Taiwan, began to look upon Taiwan as their national homeland, not a province of China, and celebrated its growing economic success even as it lost international legitimacy. In the late 1980s, moreover, Taiwan underwent a peaceful transition from authoritarian one-party rule to liberal democracy under Lee Tung-hui, its first native Taiwanese president. Lee felt confident enough to lift Chiang Kai-shek's ban on contact with the mainland, permitting a surge of Taiwanese investment and travel in the PRC.

Despite growing cross-strait economic ties, Taiwanese nationalists wanted no part of political reunification with Deng's PRC, which they regarded as backward, corrupt, and despotic, as well as a separate nation. Like all nationalists, they craved international recognition of their nation as a sovereign state and pressured Lee's government to mount a diplomatic campaign to achieve this goal. The prospect of the emergence of an internationally recognized Taiwanese nation-state was anathema to Deng and his colleagues. They could not acquiesce in such a development without betraying the Chinese Revolution of 1911, which had aimed at creating a strong and united China, including Taiwan. Moreover, their acceptance of Taiwan's independence would give a green light to Tibetan and Uighur separatists, further threatening the integrity of the Chinese nation-state. Beijing was consequently determined to employ military force to block Taiwan from moving toward de jure independence. But this raised the possibility of intervention by the United States, which was on record as opposing the use of force and continued to extend an informal security guarantee to Taiwan.

The explosive potential of the Taiwan issue was demonstrated in the 1995–96 Taiwan Strait Crisis. In the runup to Taiwan's presidential election, President Lee Tung-hui crossed Beijing's red line by visiting the United States to drum up support for independence. Since Washington's willingness to receive him came close to official recognition, the PRC resolved to punish the Taiwanese and dissuade them from electing Lee. To these ends, it mobilized its forces and conducted "missile exercises" around the island, paralyzing shipping and creating panic. The United States responded by sending two carrier battle groups toward the Taiwan Strait, a clear signal of its determination to protect Taiwan and keep shipping lanes open. Having themselves crossed Washington's red line by resorting to force, the Chinese backed off. They were not prepared for a war with the United States. Besides, they believed they had succeeded in their primary objective, which was to deter further Taiwanese independence moves. Although Lee won reelection, he became more circumspect. So did the Clinton administration, which sought Beijing's cooperation and had no desire for another confrontation over Taiwan.

The ROC–PRC standoff continued into the 2000s with no end in sight. Beijing was willing to tolerate Taiwan's de facto independence, anticipating that growing cross-strait economic ties would eventually bring pro-reunification leaders to power in Taipei. But how long the PRC's patience would last was an open question, and it emphasized that the military option was still on the table. Lee's successor, Chen Shui-bian, an even more ardent nationalist, considered promulgating a new constitution as a veiled declaration of independence. But he retreated from this provocative step in the face of Chinese warnings and the withering of his domestic political support. Taiwanese public opinion was cautious and ambivalent. Only small minorities favored either immediate independence or reunification, the majority preferring an indefinite continuation of the status quo. But pro-reunification sentiment rose as the U.S. security guarantee was perceived to be less certain. Although President George W. Bush came into office in 2001 pledging strong backing for Taiwan, he soon shifted to a more evenhanded position as securing Beijing's cooperation in his Global War on Terrorism became a high priority.

China's Rising Power and Influence

One of the most important question hanging over East Asia at the end of the Cold War was the future of the relationship between China and the United States, on which its order and stability largely depended. With the removal of the common Soviet threat, the two seemed fated to again become geopolitical rivals. The modern Chinese nationalist revolution, which Deng Xiaoping and his heirs were committed to carrying forward, aimed at restoring China's past greatness as East Asia's "Middle Kingdom." The United States stood in the way of the achievement of this goal as well as the recovery of what Chinese regarded as the rebel province of Taiwan. Americans, on their part, were appalled at Beijing's repression of prodemocracy activists and alarmed by its

Russian-equipped military buildup, which suggested a willingness to employ force to intimidate its neighbors. The 1995–96 Taiwan Strait Crisis lent credence to American concerns about Chinese bellicosity and pointed to the need for vigilance. So, too, did Beijing's public criticism of U.S. "hegemonism" and its charge that Washington was trying to "contain" China by strengthening the U.S.–Japan alliance and encouraging Japanese "remilitarization."

Expectations of another Sino-American Cold War did not materialize. Deng and his successor Jiang Zemin, who took over the direction of Chinese policy in 1994, considered the United States too strong to make a return to the confrontation of the 1960s a realistic option. The PRC lacked reliable allies, and its military capabilities, although steadily increasing, were outclassed by those of the United States. Moreover, Deng had committed China to economic modernization and interdependence with its neighbors, which required a peaceful and stable international environment. Americans were divided in their assessment of Chinese intentions. Some warned of a rising "China threat," while others argued that China was amenable to cooperation if treated with respect. Bill Clinton inclined toward the latter view, going so far as to call for a U.S.–PRC "strategic partnership" in 1997–98. In practice, U.S. policy exhibited elements of both engagement and containment, with the mix varying according to the ups and downs of bilateral relations and shifts in U.S. domestic politics. In 2001, President Bush spoke of China as a "strategic competitor," but he soon switched to a more conciliatory position.

The most significant change in East Asia's power equation during the 1990s was China's rising political influence and economic importance. Deng's experiment in market socialism proved unexpectedly successful, generating sustained double-digit growth in the 1980s which continued in the 1990s. By 2000, China had a trillion-dollar economy and was a major exporter of consumer goods and other light industrial products, much of them sold in the American market. China's economy was still only about one-fourth the size of Japan's, and its per capita wealth remained far smaller. Still, China was growing rapidly while Japan was mired in a protracted recession. Straight-line projections indicated that China would surpass Japan as East Asia's leading economic power in a few decades and begin to rival the United States. Observers disagreed over whether China could maintain its high growth rate. Mounting energy shortages and environmental problems suggested a slowdown, as did the drag of its large and inefficient state enterprises. On the other hand, Beijing had so far managed to overcome all obstacles, and there was no reason to assume that it would be less able to do so in the future.

China sent mixed signals to its East Asian neighbors on how it intended to use its increasing clout. In 1992, it aroused concerns among Southeast

Table 10.1

U.S. Trade Deficit with China, 1990–2006 (in billions of U.S. dollars)

Year	Exports to China	Imports from China	Deficit
1990	4,806	15,237	−10,431
1991	6,278	18,969	−12,691
1992	7,419	25,728	−18,309
1993	8,763	31,534	−22,770
1994	9,281	38,787	−29,505
1995	11,754	45,543	−33,790
1996	11,993	51,513	−39,520
1997	12,862	62,558	−49,696
1998	14,241	71,169	−56,927
1999	13,111	81,788	−68,677
2000	16,185	100,018	−83,833
2001	19,182	102,278	−83,096
2002	22,128	125,193	−103,065
2003	28,368	152,436	−124,068
2004	34,744	196,682	−161,938
2005	41,925	243,470	−201,545
2006	50,036	263,584	−213,549

Source: U.S. Census Bureau, Foreign Trade Statistics.

Asians by unilaterally asserting Chinese sovereignty over the Spratly Islands in the South China Sea, some of which were claimed by the Philippines, Malaysia, Brunei, and Vietnam. Its seizure of the Philippines-claimed Mischief Reef in 1995 pointed to possible armed clashes, particularly if suspected oil and gas deposits in the area turned out to be present. In the mid-1990s, however, the PRC shifted to a nonconfrontational approach as part of its courtship of ASEAN, which it saw as an attractive economic partner and a vehicle to enhance its influence in Southeast Asia. Although wary of China, ASEAN member countries were impressed by its booming economy and hopeful of converting it to the ASEAN Way. In the early 2000s, Beijing accepted an ASEAN-proposed Code of Conduct in the Spratlys abjuring the use of force. It also signed a Framework Agreement for the creation of an ASEAN–China Free Trade Area, and acceded to ASEAN's 1976 Treaty of Amity and Cooperation, becoming the first non-ASEAN state to do so.

In addition to courting ASEAN, China endeavored to build special relationships with countries it deemed important to advancing its strategic and political interests. Russia was a useful partner, but Moscow was not interested in forming a united front against the United States and was leery of Chinese immigration into its vulnerable Far Eastern territories. Friendless Burma was a more promising target, offering China access to the Bay of Bengal. ASEAN's concerns about Rangoon's growing links with Beijing underlay its decision in

1997 to induct Burma as a member. Thailand, which had established a quasi-alliance with Beijing during the late Cold War period, was another object of Chinese attentions, as were the Indochinese states. Cambodia, historically conditioned to seek counterweights to Thai and Vietnamese dominance, was receptive. The Vietnamese remained suspicious of China, but Hanoi went along with its offers of a rapprochement. ROK–PRC ties burgeoned during the 1990s as South Koreans were gripped by a "China fever" and Beijing employed smile diplomacy to try to wean them from their dependence on the United States and pull them toward China.

The Sino-Japanese History Quarrel

China's Good Neighbor policy excluded Japan. Indeed, Beijing made it clear that it regarded Japan as a rival and a potential threat. For the Japanese, this was an unanticipated and discomfiting development. As noted in the previous chapter, the Japanese had had some success in building a relatively cordial relationship with the PRC in the late Cold War period, and they assumed that this would continue. For a time it did. Tokyo balked at joining the United States in imposing post-Tiananmen sanctions on China, and the Sino-Japanese partnership reached a high point in 1992 with the visit to Beijing of Japan's emperor. Thereafter, however, relations went downhill. The Japanese were dismayed by Beijing's rebuff of their protests against its nuclear weapons testing and alarmed by its saber rattling toward Taiwan and belligerent posture in the Spratlys. Even more worrisome to Tokyo were China's aggressive reassertion of its long-dormant claim to the disputed Senkaku (Diaoyutai) Islands southwest of Okinawa, its refusal to agree on the demarcation of Japanese and Chinese Exclusive Economic Zones in the East China Sea, and its launching of provocative naval probes around Japan.

In contrast to its conciliatory attitude toward South Korea and ASEAN, moreover, Beijing depicted Japan as a dangerous revanchist state. The Chinese found evidence for this claim in the steady buildup of Japan's Self Defense Force's (SDF) capabilities and the reluctance of Japanese to disavow their imperialist and militarist past. Notwithstanding Japan's commitment to pacifism and democracy, there was some basis for the latter charge. Conservative nationalists like Prime Minister Nakasone were unhappy with what they regarded as Japan's excessively apologetic stance toward the war, which, in their view, stood in the way of a revival of national self-respect and patriotism. Right-wing "revisionists" went further, arguing that Japan had done no wrong and was, in fact, the victim of anti-Japanese propaganda and calumnies. Tilting between Japan and China over war guilt issues escalated during the 1990s, fueled by the increasing unwillingness of the Japanese government to extend unequivocal apologies, and lurid new revelations of wartime outrages such as the Japanese army's testing of chemical and biological weapons on Chinese and its dragooning of Asian women into service as military prostitutes.

The Sino-Japanese history quarrel was ultimately less about history than about regional preeminence. Chinese resented Japan's pretensions to be East Asia's "Number One," a position they felt China should rightfully occupy by virtue of its paramount position in the region in the past. For Beijing, holding Japan's feet to the fire on history issues served the double purpose of tarnishing its regional leadership credentials and drawing East Asians toward the new, nonthreatening China. The PRC had some success in realizing these objectives, especially with South Korea, which lined up with China in denouncing manifestations of Japan's supposed revanchist tendencies. In 1998, President Kim Dae Jung tried to end the squabble by agreeing to rein in ROK criticism of Japan in return for a forthright national apology by the Japanese prime minister. But this settlement proved only temporary. Popular suspicion and hostility toward Japan ran too deep in South Korea to make a diplomatic quick fix possible. By the late 1990s, moreover, the center of gravity of Japanese politics and public opinion was shifting in the direction of what conservative nationalists called "becoming a normal country."

Japan Moves Toward "Normalcy"

The end of the Cold War weakened Japan's pacifist-isolationist consensus and triggered a gradual move by the Japanese toward assuming "normal" international political-military responsibilities. The catalyst was the 1990–91 Kuwait crisis. Tokyo rebuffed Washington's request for an SDF contingent, citing the constraints of its Peace Constitution, and had to be coerced into contributing $13 billion to the war effort with the veiled threat of a pullout of U.S. forces from Japan. This episode made Japan the object of international ridicule for its reliance on "checkbook diplomacy." It also called into question the viability of the U.S.–Japan alliance in the post–Cold War context in which Japanese bases were less important to the United States and it expected Japan to do more in the common defense. The fragility of the alliance was again highlighted during the 1993–94 North Korean nuclear crisis when Tokyo dismayed Washington by informing it that the SDF could do nothing to aid the United States in the event of war, since there were no grounds in Japanese law for deploying it in support of American forces. Although a U.S.–North Korean war was averted, the alliance was clearly in serious trouble.

Japan's response was twofold. In 1992, its diet enacted legislation authorizing the SDF's participation in United Nations peacekeeping operations, albeit under highly restrictive conditions that virtually precluded the possibility that it would have to fight or sustain casualties. The SDF's first overseas mission, helping supervise the 1993 Cambodian elections, nearly came to grief when several Japanese peacekeepers were killed by the Khmer Rouge, producing an uproar in Japan that threatened for a time to lead to its withdrawal. Japan's other major initiative was agreeing to revise the SDF's operational guidelines to permit it to provide logistical support to U.S. forces engaged in regional military contingencies "near" Japan, presumably including the Taiwan Strait, although this was not spelled out to avoid unnecessarily antagonizing China. This step, which was announced during the 1996 Taiwan Strait Crisis, angered Beijing but placated American critics of the alliance by demonstrating that Japan was prepared to play a direct military role in helping the United States maintain the peace and stability of Northeast Asia, something it had previously been unwilling to do.

In 1998, North Korea lobbed a missile over northern Japan, spreading panic and consternation among the hitherto complacent Japanese public. This event, more than any other in the post–Cold War era, brought home to the Japanese that they lived in a "rough neighborhood" and that a new approach to national security was needed. Pacifists retreated to the sidelines of Japanese politics, and conservative nationalists moved to the fore. Like Nakasone fifteen years earlier, the latter called for strengthening the American alliance, bolstering the SDF, and promoting patriotism. Unlike Nakasone, however, they enjoyed broad support. Signs that Japan was moving in a new direction multiplied in 1999–2000. These included the passage of diet resolutions urging the display of the national flag and singing of the national anthem; the establishment of a diet committee to study constitutional revision; and moves to modernize the SDF and equip it with power projection capabilities. Japan also agreed to participate in joint missile defense research with the United States, and undertook the development of its own satellite surveillance system to give early warning of hostile missile launches.

The rise of conservative nationalists reflected generational, attitudinal, and political changes. The Japan Socialist Party, the Cold War standard-bearer of the Left, self-destructed in the mid-1990s as a result of its willingness to abandon its advocacy of unarmed neutrality in return for a share of power, a move that discredited it in the eyes of Japanese voters. While leftists and pacifists remained a significant force in Japanese politics, they thus lost their main political vehicle, and fragmented into factions within the Liberal Democratic Party and opposition parties. In the 1990s, moreover, a new generation came into positions of power and influence in Japanese society that had no memories of the Pacific War, the American Occupation, and the bitter ideological struggles of the 1950s. Members of this generation did not share their elders' fear of the military or aversion to patriotic symbols. Nor did they feel a sense of guilt about Japan's descent into what leftists called the "dark valley" of militarism and ultranationalism in the 1930s. They took pride in Japan's postwar accomplishments and its rise to regional and global prominence, and they were receptive to nationalists' calls for a "strong Japan."

The accession of Prime Minister Junichiro Koizumi in 2001 brought to power a charismatic nationalist who had an agenda similar to Nakasone's but who proved more forceful in implementing it. Among his first moves were officially visiting Yasukuni Shrine and approving a nationalistic history textbook, thereby signaling that Japan would no longer bow to Chinese and Korean pressure on war guilt issues. Koizumi also made it clear that he favored forging a closer alliance with the United States, lifting constraints on the SDF and making it a full-fledged military, encouraging patriotism and national pride, and dismantling "Japan Inc." through deregulation and liberalization. While Koizumi thus continued Nakasone's program of making Japan a "normal country," he acted against a different domestic background. Nakasone presided over Japan at a time of booming prosperity, rising national confidence, and growing Japanese influence in East Asia. Koizumi inherited a floundering economy, a mood of pessimism and self-doubt, and an inclination to retreat from the burdens and frustrations of Asian leadership. He offered an antidote to Japan's sense of national weakness and drift.

Japan Tilts Away from Asia

Japan's vaunted economic growth machine sputtered to a halt during the 1990s, defying all efforts to restart it. Its bubble economy of the late 1980s collapsed in the early 1990s with a crash of inflated stock and property values. Business and consumer confidence evaporated in the face of a mountain of worthless investments and bad loans. Tried-and-true government pump-priming measures had little effect in reversing the slump. The situation might have been worse had not Japan's relatively efficient export industries enabled it to maintain sizable trade surpluses. However, these industries weakened under the strain of preserving costly business practices such as lifetime employment, and subsidizing unprofitable but protected enterprises and sectors. It became increasingly evident that Japan's protectionist and mercantilist system was obsolete in an era of globalization, and that a return to economic health would require structural reform. But politically powerful vested interests rallied to block anything more than incremental change. Although Japan Inc. thus limped more or less intact into the twenty-first century, Japanese lost faith in it and many viewed it as a failed system.

In the early 1990s, Japan was hailed as the leader of what the World Bank called the "East Asian miracle." By the end of the decade, however, China had taken its place as East Asia's economic pacesetter, and the future of the miracle itself seemed in doubt. Japan's economic troubles dimmed its appeal as a model, slowed its capital flows into the region, and turned its attention inward. The 1997–98 Asian financial crisis gave the coup de grâce to Japanese leadership aspirations. This was a chain-reaction currency collapse that engulfed much of the region and led to severe recessions in Indonesia, Thailand, and South Korea. Although Tokyo contributed generously to bailouts and currency stabilization efforts, it got little thanks for its assistance inasmuch as it allowed the yen to depreciate, making Japan's exports more competitive with those of its weakened neighbors. Beijing, on the other hand, won accolades by refraining from devaluing its currency, which, not being convertible, was largely unaffected by the crisis. As its economy continued to barrel ahead at double-digit growth rates, China was seen by many East Asians, including Japanese, as toppling Japan from its throne as the regional economic superpower.

In the aftermath of the financial crisis, Japan tilted away from East Asia back toward the United States, a shift that became more pronounced under Koizumi. This reversed the trend of the 1970s and 1980s, and represented the latest manifestation of modern Japan's historical tendency to oscillate between Asia and West. Faced by an unfriendly China, a belligerent North Korea, a suspicious South Korea, and an unappreciative Southeast Asia, the Japanese sought safety in the American alliance. But they did not disengage politically and economically from East Asia. Japan's economy was too closely intertwined with those of its neighbors, and its security was too dependent on them, to make putting all its eggs in the U.S. basket a realistic option even for pro-American nationalists like Koizumi. Despite the souring of political relations between China and Japan, for example, their economic interdependence increased, and each became the other's principal trading partner. Japan consequently continued to see itself as having an important stake in maintaining stable relations with China and the rest of East Asia, and as a major player in emerging forms of regional cooperation.

East Asian Regionalism Revives

As described in the Introduction, the idea of East Asia as a region was revived in the 1980s. Reasons include the late–Cold War dissolution of ideological and political barriers, the economic integration of Northeast and Southeast Asia around Japan, and the demonstration effect of other ventures in regional cooperation, particularly the European Community. But East Asian regionalism also grew out of the pan-Asianist tradition. ASEAN had earlier invoked this tradition to construct a distinctive Southeast Asian cultural identity based on norms different from those of the West. The ASEAN model was available to East Asian region builders, and helped inspire the "Asian Values" movement of the 1990s. It is no accident that the chief proponents of this movement, such as Malaysia's Mahathir Mohamad and Singapore's Lee Kuan Yew, were ASEAN leaders. The Southeast Asian values reflected in the ASEAN Way overlapped with the broader East Asian Values touted by Mahathir, Lee, and others insofar as both were assumed to be rooted in an historically based communitarian ethic opposed to the individualism, rationalism, and materialism of the West.

In 1990, Mahathir proposed the establishment of an "East Asian Economic Group," which he envisioned as a regional trading bloc centered on Japan. But this proposal failed to get off the ground. The United States opposed it and few East Asians were willing to jeopardize their access to the U.S. market which was vital to their export-driven economies. Washington preferred broader Asia-Pacific cooperation and this prevailed, leading to the creation of the Asia-Pacific Economic Cooperation (APEC) forum that encompassed East Asia, Russia, Australia, Canada, Mexico, and the United States. Another venture in Asia-Pacific regionalism was the ASEAN Regional Forum (ARF), which was launched in 1994 with a membership including North America and East Asia plus Russia, the European Union, and later India and even North Korea. The Clinton administration viewed APEC as a vehicle to promote trade liberalization. ASEAN touted ARF as an experiment in multilateral security cooperation based on the ASEAN Way and aimed at advancing from confidence building to preventive diplomacy and conflict resolution in gradual, step-by-step fashion.

In the late 1990s, Mahathir's idea of an East Asian group came to life in the form of the ASEAN Plus Three (APT) forum that brought together China, South Korea, Japan, and the ten members of ASEAN. The main impetus behind APT's creation was the 1997–98 financial crisis, which underscored the need for monetary coordination to forestall another disaster and lessen East Asia's dependence on the U.S.-dominated International Monetary Fund. But APT was not just about financial cooperation. Many of its promoters saw it as the nucleus of an East Asian counterpart of the European Community and pushed for a formal East Asian summit as the first step in moving from a "region of nations to a bona fide regional community." There were, however, obstacles in the path of the proposed East Asian Community, including disagreement over its membership. Some, like Mahathir, insisted that it should be limited to the countries of East Asia, which shared common values, historical experiences, and racial affinities. Others maintained that it should be open to outside powers such as Australia, Canada, and the United States, which played an important role in regional security and prosperity.

ASEAN leaders in 2004.

East Asian regionalism was thus Janus-faced, pointing simultaneously in closed and open directions. Open regionalism promised to complement Asia-Pacific institutions like APEC and ARF and keep the United States engaged in East Asia. Closed regionalism spoke to East Asians' quest for a non-Western identity and their attraction to the pan-Asianist ideal of Asian unity and cooperation. Underlying both of these approaches was the perhaps more fundamental question of whether East Asia had enough cohesion to sustain any form of regionalism. This question was particularly acute for those who favored turning East Asia into a version of the European Community. Western Europe's political and economic integration in the 1950s was based on the reconciliation of France and Germany. But there was little sign that Japan and China, their East Asian counterparts, were prepared to bury the hatchet. Indeed, their rivalry and hostility intensified in the early 2000s as Japan took a more intransigent stand on history issues and China, buoyed by the success of its smile diplomacy and economic initiatives toward Southeast Asia, began to see itself as East Asia's new leader.

11

East Asia's Future

Where is East Asia headed? No one, of course, knows for sure, but the trend lines point to its continued economic growth and integration, which is underwritten by its relative peace and stability. As the region comes together economically, paced by the ongoing rise of China, it is reasonable to expect further moves to build an East Asian "community" around the reviving pan-Asianist idea of shared Asian values. These moves will be offset by the feud between Japan and China, which shows little sign of abating. There is also no early end in sight to the standoffs in the Korean Peninsula and the Taiwan Strait, although the outbreak of war in either place seems increasingly unlikely. The War on Terrorism has highlighted the threat to Southeast Asia posed by Islamic extremists bent on waging "Holy War" against the West and Western ways, and creating fundamentalist Islamic states. But neither these militants nor their pan-Islamic ideology have much of a future in East Asia. With the demise of communism, nationalism and pan-Asianism hold sway, and the question is which will prevail. The outcome of ASEAN's current effort to pull East Asia together around itself may hold the answer to this question.

Growth Prospects

At the dawn of the new millennium, East Asia accounted for about 26 percent of world GDP, putting it close to the levels of North America (30 percent) and Western Europe (32 percent). Forty years earlier, in 1960, the combined North American and Western European share exceeded 75 percent, while that of East Asia was only 13 percent. East Asia, in other words, doubled its weight in the global economy. No other region came close to matching this feat. East Asia's growth was achieved largely by an increase in output per head, which reflected a shift from primary production to high value-added manufacturing. In 2000, East Asia's per capita GDP was still five or six times less than that of Western Europe and North America, but it was much higher than in other parts of the non-Western world. There were, to be sure, wide intraregional

Table 11.1

Per Capita GDP (Nominal) of East Asian Countries, 2005
(in thousands of U.S. dollars)

Country	Per Capita GDP
Japan	35,757
Singapore	26,836
South Korea	16,308
Taiwan	15,203
Malaysia	5,042
Thailand	2,659
China	1,709
Indonesia	1,283
Philippines	1,168
Mongolia	736
Vietnam	618
Laos	485
Cambodia	430
Timor-Leste	352
Burma	219

Source: IMF.

disparities. Japan and Singapore enjoyed per capita income levels and living standards on a par with those of the West. Taiwan, South Korea, Malaysia, and Thailand were not far behind. But China, Indonesia, Vietnam, and the Philippines lagged, and impoverished Laos, Cambodia, Burma, and North Korea were at the bottom.

Will East Asia's economic growth continue, perhaps enabling it to eclipse America and Europe as the world's pacesetter? Straight-line projections based on current trends are notoriously unreliable, since observers as often as not misread these trends, and unforeseen contingencies have a way of intervening. As noted in a previous chapter, many predicted in the 1980s that a rising Japan would seize economic leadership from a declining United States. But it did not happen. This prediction failed to anticipate the revival of America's economy and the stagnation of Japan's in the 1990s. With the wisdom of hindsight, it is easy to see that Japan's bubble economy and creaky mercantilist system pointed toward an economic trainwreck ahead. At the time, however, this was by no means obvious, and pessimists were brushed aside. The World Bank's proclamation in 1993 of an "East Asian miracle" also proved overly sanguine. Four years later, much of East Asia was in the grips of a serious recession, generated in part by speculative excesses encouraged by this and similar prognostications suggesting that regional growth economies could, in effect, walk on water.

Although exercises in futurology are thus inherently problematical, several long-term trends give grounds for optimism about East Asia's growth prospects. Since the late Cold War period, for example, the region's growth has been underpinned by its peace and stability. The last interstate war was fought in 1979 between Vietnam and China, and this was brief and relatively bloodless. While it is true that insurgencies continued in Cambodia, Burma, Indonesia, and the Philippines, East Asia as a whole has been spared a repeat of destructive conflagrations like the Korean and Vietnam wars. Another late–Cold War legacy that favors continued growth is the embrace by most governments in the region of export-led industrialization based on state-guided capitalism, foreign investment, and open markets. This formula has not always worked, as in the case of the Philippines under Marcos and Suharto's Indonesia, where it led to "crony capitalism." But the successes outnumber the failures and the recipe remains today a major source of East Asia's dynamism. Autarkic and anticapitalist Burma and North Korea are the chief holdouts, and they have paid a heavy economic price.

Economists have proposed various models to explain and predict East Asia's growth. A favorite of the Japanese in the 1970s and 1980s was the "flying geese" analogy in which Japan acted as the lead goose in a formation of other East Asian geese at varying stages of economic development and maturity. However, this construct had to be abandoned in the late 1990s when the Japanese leader faltered and began to be overtaken by its erstwhile followers, especially China. A more recent model compares East Asia's economic ascent to that of a multistage rocket. According to this view, Japan functioned as the initial booster in the late–Cold War liftoff stage, but was replaced in the 1990s as the main engine of regional development by "Greater China"—the informal business network linking China, Hong Kong, Taiwan, Singapore, and Overseas Chinese in Southeast Asia. This model sees East Asia's premodern Sinocentric order reasserting itself as the chief driver of its future economic growth. But the United States also acts as a "growth engine" and ASEAN seems likely to emerge as another. There may, in other words, be multiple leaders in East Asia's economic future.

Demographic, socioeconomic, and environmental pressures will shape East Asia's economic future. The region's 2 billion people, one-third of the world's total, are demographically diverse. Japan has a shrinking and aging population, a fate that will also soon also overtake South Korea and Taiwan, meaning that there will be fewer workers and higher social welfare costs in these countries. China and Southeast Asia confront the opposite problem—expanding populations and "youth bulges" that must be provided gainful employment. The stakes are high. Failure to meet rising expectations could result in political instability, social breakdown, and the spread of revolutionary ideologies and movements. This has happened before in East Asia, and it might well do so again in some countries. The quest for development is complicated by worsening environmental problems. Deforestation, soil erosion, and air and water pollution are already adversely affecting livelihoods and imposing significant public health burdens. These problems and costs will increase, forcing governments to pay greater attention to balancing developmental and environmental priorities.

East Asia's growth prospects also depend on oil, gas, iron ore, copper, lumber, and other basic commodities. Consumption of these commodities, particularly oil, has sharply increased in recent years with industrialization and rising living standards, and this trend will continue, barring a major economic downturn. One likely consequence will be heightened competition among major raw material importers like China, Japan, and South Korea. Resource-poor Japan long ago developed a global supply network, and China and Korea have followed suit, moving into Africa, Latin America, and the Middle East. Global resource interests bring in their wake global political interests. Like Tokyo, Beijing and Seoul will be pulled outward by these interests and their foreign policies will increasingly reflect them. In East Asia, the scramble for resources promises to exacerbate rivalry between Japan and China which are already sparring over ownership of offshore oil fields in the East China Sea and competing for access to Siberian gas. But it may also lead to cooperative ventures such as those recently undertaken by China, Vietnam, and the Philippines to jointly explore for oil and gas in the South China Sea.

Economic Integration

There is every likelihood that functional cooperation among East Asian governments will deepen. For one thing, globalization and its associated transnational problems seem to require it. "Globalization," a shorthand term for the flow of goods, people, and information across national borders, is not new. In premodern times, East Asian trade and immigration centered on Imperial China prefigured globalization. Late-nineteenth-century Western expansion, which was powered by steamships, railroads, and the telegraph, accelerated the process, tying East Asia together and integrating it into the Eurocentric world system of the period. But the pace has quickened in recent decades with innovations such as jet travel, satellite communications, and the Internet. While globalization has benefited many, it has also spawned or exacerbated a host of "transnational threats," including drug trafficking, human smuggling, disease pandemics, acid rain, and terrorism. These threats—the dark side of globalization—will no doubt become more acute in the years ahead, requiring cooperative international responses. East Asian governments are already moving in this direction and almost certainly will continue to do so.

One is also on safe ground in forecasting increased East Asian economic cooperation. The region is coming together economically at a rapid clip. Intra-regional trade now accounts for about half of East Asia's total trade, compared to only 30 percent in 1970, and is on the upswing. As in the 1980s and 1990s, the private sector is the principal driver of regional economic integration, but Japanese companies no longer dominate the field. South Korean, Chinese, Hong Kong, Taiwanese, Singaporean, Malaysian, Thai, and other East Asian corporate giants are also setting up production networks and forming tie-ups with local firms. Business-led economic "regionalization" follows no master plan or grand design, being propelled instead by the logic of the marketplace and the quest for profits. There is, however, a natural complementarity between capital-rich and resource-poor Northeast Asia and capital-poor and resource-rich Southeast Asia. The Japanese architects of the 1941–45 Greater East Asia Co-Prosperity Sphere glimpsed this complementarity. Today, their vision of East Asia's economic unification is being realized, although Japan is now only one of many players in the process.

Business-led integration is also under way in Northeast Asia, pulling together Japan, Taiwan, South Korea, and China into an interdependent economic unit that in some ways recalls the Northeast Asian bloc that Japan attempted to create in the 1930s. Despite their political differences, all of these countries are now among each other's most important trading and investment partners, and their economic ties are deepening. North Korea, Mongolia, and the Russian Far East are the odd men out in Northeast Asia's growth and integration. Although Pyongyang has made some token moves toward economic liberalization, it has shown no serious interest in dismantling its autarkic command economy or expanding trade with its neighbors. Thinly populated Mongolia, fearful of Chinese irredentism and uncertain even whether it is part of East Asia, clings to its longtime Russian protector and traditional nomadic and pastoral way of life. The Russian Far East is a backwater largely ignored by Moscow and beset by political bossism, a declining population, and organized crime. Nevertheless, its oil, gas, and timber resources make it a potentially important actor in East Asia.

Most East Asian governments are enthusiastically promoting economic regionalization, and this will continue. The general perception is that lowering trade and investment barriers generates growth, and growth brings prosperity, dampens sociopolitical conflict, and enhances regime legitimacy. This perception is shared by "communist" China and Vietnam as well as liberal democracies like Japan and the Philippines. Open markets are a mantra around which all can rally. The most important expression of this ideal is the movement to establish free trade areas, or FTAs. ASEAN set this train in motion in 1992 by undertaking to establish an FTA, although progress has been slowed by the admission of its new members. The ASEAN–PRC agreement of 2002 to create an FTA encompassing China and the ten ASEAN states marked a major step toward what many hope will be an eventual East Asian common market. Japan has been reluctant to climb on the FTA bandwagon because of resistance from its protectionist agricultural sector. But it has concluded a bilateral agreement with Singapore, and is negotiating or considering others with its East Asian neighbors, including South Korea.

Another form of intergovernmental cooperation that promotes East Asia's economic integration is "growth triangles." These are geographically contiguous areas of three or more states whose governments cooperate to develop their infrastructure in hopes of attracting private investment. A number of such growth triangles have sprung up across East Asia since the end of the Cold War, the most successful being those created by Thailand, Malaysia, Singapore, and Indonesia. Others that have some potential to spur growth and integration include the Greater Mekong Subregion, involving China, Vietnam, Laos, Cambodia, Thailand, and Burma, and the East ASEAN Growth Area, which brings together Brunei, Indonesia, Malaysia, and the Philippines. Political obstacles and funding constraints have so far prevented Northeast Asian growth triangles from getting very far off the drawing board. The most ambitious of these, the Tumen River project, envisions the establishment of port facilities and a free trade zone at the mouth of the Tumen River on the Japan Sea, which would serve as the commercial hub for North Korea, northeastern China, Mongolia, and the Russian Far East.

The Pan-Asianist Revival

Given East Asia's accelerating economic integration, one might conclude that it is only a matter of time before a self-conscious "East Asian Community" emerges and acquires formal institutions. This seems all the more likely because the region is coalescing culturally. Over much of East Asia, a homogenous mass culture has arisen that exhibits similar tastes in pop music, television programs, movies, clothing, and even food. National cultural styles blend with one another and with those from Europe and North America. The major cities of East Asia from Seoul to Singapore have a similar look and feel, being dominated high-rise buildings, elevated expressways, shopping malls, and automobile-choked streets. Middle-class lifestyles and aspirations are virtually identical, whether in Shanghai, Tokyo, or Kuala Lumpur. Satellite television and the Internet make news and commentary on events in neighboring countries instantly available. Tourism, once a pastime reserved for the well-to-do, now involves masses of people who travel to virtually all corners of the region. Cross-national exchanges among nongovernmental organizations, think tanks, and academic institutions are also on the rise.

Although the fact of East Asia's cultural integration is new, the idea that it possesses an underlying cultural unity is not. As described in earlier chapters, one of the most important spin-offs of East Asia's modern encounter with the West was the ideology of pan-Asianism, which asserts that Asians share a common cultural heritage that differentiates them from Westerners and forms the basis for their solidarity vis-à-vis the West. Pan-Asianism has held a recurrent appeal for successive generations of East Asians beginning in the 1880s. Pan-Asianist upsurges occurred in the early 1900s, and again in the 1930s. Japanese militarists exploited the latter movement to gain support for their crusade to liberate Asia from Western dominance in their Greater East Asia War. Pan-Asianism did not die with Japan's defeat. Rather, it revived in the Asian Relations and Afro-Asian conferences of the 1950s, and helped inspire Southeast Asian regionalism as embodied by ASEAN. The ASEAN Way, which draws on putative non-Western Asian values, is a subregional manifestation of the pan-Asianist tradition. It is also the precursor and prototype of the Asian Values movement of the 1990s.

The post-1990 campaign to establish an East Asian Community based on Asian Values is thus the latest in a series of pan-Asianist movements that stretches back for more than a century. This continuity is not necessarily acknowledged by the East Asian journalists, academics, and politicians, who are currently propagating the notion that Northeast and Southeast Asia are united by common values. Indeed, many of these "New Asianists" seem unaware that they are, in effect, reinventing the pan-Asianist wheel insofar as their arguments echo those put forward earlier. This is not, of course, to suggest that pan-Asianism is monolithic or unchanging. On the contrary, it contains diverse strands, not all of which are explicitly anti-Western or posit an unbridgeable cultural chasm between Asia and the West. It has also evolved over time, picking up and discarding themes such as anticolonialism and overt racism. Moreover, its geographical referent has varied with changing definitions of Asia. From the beginning, pan-Asianists differed over what they meant by "Asia," equating it variously with West, South, and East Asia; South and East Asia; East Asia; Northeast Asia; and Southeast Asia.

The Asian Values debate of the 1990s underscored the fact that pan-Asianism is less about a "real Asia" than an imagined one that is juxtaposed against an equally invented image of the West. Like nationalism, it is concerned with establishing collective identity and pride, not providing an objective description of social reality. Most critics of Asian Values missed this point. Their citing of East Asia's obvious cultural diversity and marshaling of survey data to demonstrate that such values do not and, indeed, cannot exist was an exercise in futility akin to trying to convince nationalists that their cherished nations are figments of their imagination. Like ships passing in the night, debunkers and believers were on different wavelengths and talked past each other. Western critics viewed the Asian Values movement as an assault on Western democracy and human rights, and attributed it to the triumphalism of the "East Asian miracle." But this movement was driven by more than just the euphoria of the high-growth years of the late 1980s and early 1990s, and self-serving political leaders seeking to mobilize their populations invented cultural traditions to legitimize antidemocratic practices and institutions.

The current pan-Asianist upsurge in East Asia, like that which occurred in Japan during the 1920s and 1930s, stems from a reaction against a perceived assault by Western individualism and permissiveness on Asian communitarian values. Conservatives like Lee Kuan Yew and Mahathir Mohamad took the lead in denouncing what they took to be the evils of the post-1960s American "counterculture" as manifest in such trends as the relaxation of pornography censorship, rampant street crime, rising divorce rates and family breakdown, and spreading drug use. Western-oriented liberals and cosmopolitan youth in East Asia accepted these trends without complaint, and even deemed some of them worthy of emulation. But many East Asians looked askance at Euro-American libertarianism and resented claims by Westerners that it reflected universal norms before which all should genuflect. Drawing on this widely shared distaste and resentment, the Asian Values movement survived the collapse of the East Asian miracle in the 1997–98 financial crisis. Today, it quietly persists among elites who are largely ignored by the Western media and given serious attention by only a handful of academics.

East Asian Regionalism

Where is East Asia's pan-Asianist revival headed? Writing in 1996, the American political scientist Samuel Huntington predicted a coming "clash of civilizations" between the West, led by the United States, and a resurgent East Asia, led by an increasingly powerful China. Huntington's reference to an emerging "greater China co-prosperity sphere" suggests that he had in mind an analogy with Japan's drive for regional hegemony in the 1930s, which it rationalized as a pan-Asianist crusade to liberate Asia from Western dominance. But this analogy is misleading. Beijing recognizes the anti-Western undertones of East Asian regionalism and seeks to exploit them to diminish U.S. influence and increase its own. However, its prospects for doing so are not promising. In contrast to the 1930s, Southeast Asia is not seething with anticolonial nationalist resentment against the West. Moreover, most Southeast

Asians are leery of China's ambitions and eager to keep the United States in play as a counterweight. So, too, are the Japanese. Although they no longer entertain serious regional leadership aspirations, they are unwilling to roll over and accept a subordinate role in a PRC-dominated East Asia.

These contending interests were much in evidence in the diplomatic maneuvering that led up to the first East Asian Summit in Kuala Lumpur in December 1995. As noted in the previous chapter, East Asian regionalists pushed for such a summit as an important symbolic step to turn the ASEAN Plus Three, or APT, forum into an instrument for creating a "bona fide regional community." When Malaysian prime minister Abdullah Badawi, Mahathir's successor, offered in 2004 to host the proposed summit, APT members agreed. But the devil was in the details of who should be invited. Malaysia and China led an effort to limit the attendees to "East Asian countries," that is, those sharing putative Asian Values and lying within East Asia's accepted geographical boundaries. However, Japan, supported by Singapore and others, insisted that India, Australia, and New Zealand should also be included. Despite Beijing's objections and intensive bilateral lobbying with ASEAN members, these "outsiders" were in the end invited. But China claimed a partial victory with Badawi's announcement that the APT group would remain the primary vehicle for realizing an East Asian Community.

The Kuala Lumpur summit represents a compromise between advocates of open and closed East Asian regionalism, setting up what is, in effect, a double track leading toward different destinations. Annual "East Asian" summits, including India, Australia, New Zealand, and prospectively Russia, are now in train, headed toward the formation of an Asia-Pacific version of the proposed East Asian Community. Meanwhile, APT summits will continue, aimed at establishing a narrower, East Asia–only Community. Hard-line East Asianists like former Malaysian prime minister Mahathir objected to this compromise, arguing that outsiders, particularly pro-U.S. "whites" such as Australians, have no place in any East Asian Community. But more moderate East Asianists, who are in the majority, seem comfortable with the dual track approach, which allows them to forge closer ties with important extraregional players while simultaneously strengthening their East Asian identity and solidarity. For Southeast Asians, another advantage of this approach is that it keeps them in the driver's seat of East Asian regionalism insofar as ASEAN controls the agenda and venue of both summit processes.

The Sino-Japanese Feud

Although one can anticipate ASEAN-led efforts to promote both East Asian communities, the Sino-Japanese feud threatens to slow or even derail such efforts. An indicator of its intensity was the refusal of PRC leader Hu Jintao to talk with Japanese prime minister Junichiro Koizumi at the Kuala Lumpur summit owing to Koizumi's latest visit to Yasukuni Shrine. This raises the question of how any form of "community" can be constructed in a region where the leaders of the two most powerful states are not on speaking terms. The deterioration of relations between China and Japan was a phenomenon of the 1990s, but its roots go back much further. Indeed, a case can be made that they are natural rivals and, as such, fated to collide. Since the late nineteenth century, neither has shown any willingness to defer to the other, and their interaction has been characterized by conflict and tension with only occasional interludes of relative amity such as the 1980s. For Chinese nationalists, Japan is heavily implicated in China's "century of shame" from the Opium Wars to Mao's triumph in 1949, and a full settling of accounts for past Japanese misdeeds has yet to be made. Indeed, for many, closure may never be possible.

To reiterate points made in the Introduction, history is not destiny and nothing is forever. Enemies can become friends, sometimes with startling speed. This book has dealt with many such reversals, such as Japan's opening to the West in the 1870s and the Sino-American rapprochement of the 1970s. Other examples could be cited from European and American history, including the Anglo-American reconciliation of the 1890s and that between France and Germany in the 1950s. While all of these cases are to some extent sui generis, each involved a "paradigm shift," or adoption of a new way of looking at the world in which longstanding enmities and rivalries are seen as counterproductive and obsolete. The impetus for such shifts often comes from a combination of external shocks, the spread of new ideologies, and the emergence of strong leaders willing and able to strike out in new directions. For example, the Franco-German rapprochement after World War II grew out of a shared revulsion against three self-destructive wars, the appeal of new "Europeanist" ideas, and their endorsement by West German chancellor Konrad Adenauer and his French counterparts.

The short-term outlook for such a paradigm shift in Sino-Japanese relations is bleak. The ruling groups in Tokyo and Beijing seem quite content with the current prickly bilateral relationship. Hard-line positions play well with their nationalist constituents, while compromise and accommodation invite charges of weakness. Moreover, Japanese and Chinese opinion leaders view each other through prisms of mutual distrust and resentment, which magnify relatively minor problems into major provocations. Chinese see Japan as reverting to its old militarist and chauvinist ways; Japanese regard China as a menacing and arrogant bully. Their common commitment to East Asian regionalism has not produced any change in this situation. Nationalism is the operative dynamic on the political side of their relationship and will likely remain so for the foreseeable future. One can therefore expect more flare-ups over Yasukuni Shrine, textbooks, territorial disputes, and other issues. The same prognosis applies to ROK–Japan relations for the same reasons, with the added complication that, as a result of Koreans' lingering colonial hangover, Korean national identity is defined in terms of being anti-Japanese.

While Japan and China will remain political adversaries, they will also continue to be economic partners. As previously noted, they have become each other's largest trading partner and their economic ties are deepening, forming a sheet anchor that stabilizes their contentious political relationship. China relies on Japan to keep its high-growth economy operating, and Japan needs China to lift itself out of its protracted recession. Moreover, Tokyo and Beijing share common interests in maintaining stability on the Korean Peninsula and in the Taiwan Strait, and in addressing transnational problems such as acid rain. In addition, Beijing is reluctant to push the Japanese too hard on history and war guilt issues lest its warnings about Japan's revanchism turn out to be a self-fulfilling prophecy. China's worst nightmare is confronting a hostile and heavily armed Japan whose technological capabilities far surpass its own. The Japanese, for their part, have no wish for such a confrontation despite the bellicose rhetoric of some of their politicians. Both sides will therefore try to keep their rocky relationship on an even keel by patching up squabbles and preserving a semblance of cordiality.

Japan's "Normalization"

Japan will likely continue its slow and hesitant transition from its Cold War–era pacifist isolationism toward political-military "normalcy." Prime Minister Koizumi pushed this process forward by seizing on the U.S.-declared Global War on Terrorism to forge a closer military and strategic partnership with the United States. In particular, he secured diet approval for the unprecedented overseas deployment of the Self Defense Force (SDF) to support Operation Enduring Freedom in Afghanistan and postwar stabilization operations in Iraq. Although these moves reflected a new willingness on the part of the Japanese to assume collective security responsibilities, it is worth noting what Koizumi was not able to accomplish. In the mid-2000s, constitutional revision was still a distant prospect and the SDF remained subject to unusual restrictions such as the prohibition of formal military titles and a ban on weaponry considered offensive in nature. Nor had Japan shown any inclination to put its soldiers in harm's way. The SDF's Afghanistan and Iraq deployments were, for example, carefully hedged to insulate it from combat operations and keep it out of situations in which it might have to fight even in self-defense.

The Japanese are betwixt and between on the issue of becoming a "normal country." While still largely in the grips of their postwar pacifist-isolationist mindset, they are willing to tolerate incremental changes in the direction of "normalcy" as long as these are packaged in ways that suggest no sharp break with the past. As described in the last chapter, a modest revival of nationalism is under way, driven by domestic political and attitudinal changes as well as perceptions of a more threatening international environment. But it is easy to exaggerate the significance of this revival. Despite claims by some that the Japanese are predisposed by their culture and history toward ultranationalism and foreign aggression, contemporary Japanese are perhaps the least nationalistic of East Asian peoples and the most averse to the rough-and-tumble world of international power politics. They still see themselves as a nation standing apart from all others, uniquely dedicated to realizing the ideals of their "Peace Constitution." Changes in this national self-image are likely to be gradual, perhaps less because the Japanese are committed pacifists than because they are strongly attached to the status quo.

In the post-Koizumi era, one can expect the continued ascendancy of conservative nationalists, more initiatives to strengthen the U.S.–Japan alliance, and further moves by "normalizers" to chip away at Japan's pacifist orthodoxy. Pending formal constitutional revision, a step most Japanese favor but do not see as urgent, de facto revision will proceed through specific diet legislation incrementally lifting constraints on the SDF's power projection capabilities and deployment in overseas missions. No dramatic change in Japan's military posture will occur as long as the Japanese perceive that the United States remains a reliable guarantor of their security. Nevertheless, they will move ahead with their current plans to convert the SDF into a more mobile force configured for offshore operations, including possible confrontations with the Chinese over territorial disputes in the East China Sea. While disinclined to engage in the sort of overt strategic rivalry practiced by India and China in the Indian Ocean and Southeast Asia, Japan will also quietly continue to cultivate closer security ties with other regional and extraregional powers that harbor doubts about Beijing's long-term intentions.

Taiwan, Korea, and Russia

Northeast Asia's two "flash points" or epicenters of potential military conflict, the Taiwan–China and inter-Korean standoffs, reflect the continuation of civil wars that began in China in the late 1920s and Korea in the late 1940s. They differ from conflicts between nation-states insofar as they grow out of struggles to unify divided nations and involve the question of political legitimacy, or the right to govern. As pointed out in the last chapter, the dynamics of the Taiwan–China conflict have changed since the end of the Cold War with the rise of Taiwanese nationalism. For many, but by no means all, Taiwanese the issue now is not the unification of the Chinese nation, but national self-determination and sovereign statehood for a separate Taiwanese nation. However, the struggle between the two Koreas continues to revolve around the unification of what North and South Koreans perceive to be a single Korean nation that has been artificially divided into two states and systems. Having assumed the role of protector of Taiwan and South Korea, the United States is a central player in both of these conflicts. Washington's policies and attitudes will therefore strongly affect their playout in the years ahead.

Given Koreans' view of themselves as one nation, and the ROK's large and growing economic lead over the DPRK, it is safe to predict that Korea's unification will eventually occur and that it will involve the South's absorption of the North. But when or how this will take place is difficult to foresee. Kim Jong Il's regime has exhibited surprising staying power and is clearly determined to soldier on. Its collapse is possible but unlikely. Despite economic hardships, the discipline of the heavily indoctrinated North Korean people will not break as long as they remain isolated from disruptive outside influences. Moreover, Kim so far has retained the loyalty of the powerful North Korean military, which is perhaps the key to his regime's survival. Meaningful reform is improbable. If Pyongyang had any serious intention of embracing PRC-style market socialism, export-led growth, and integration with the rest of East Asia, it would have done so long ago. For Kim, as for his late father, the name of the game is "system maintenance"—that is, propping up the DPRK's dysfunctional command economy and holding to its Juche ideology in hopes of outlasting the South and finally triumphing in the marathon struggle.

Pyongyang's engagement with the ROK and confrontation with the United States serve Kim's interests in several ways. Playing along with Seoul's Sunshine Policy enables Kim to milk the ROK for economic aid and sow dissension among South Koreans on the wisdom of this policy. His deadlock with Washington over North Korea's nuclear weapons program heightens tensions in the ROK–U.S. alliance and rallies North Koreans against the "American threat." His participation in recent efforts to resolve this deadlock through on-again, off-again six-party talks involving Japan, Russia, China, the United States, ROK, and DPRK creates the impression of moderation and puts the onus of blocking a settlement on the Americans. In fact, Kim has no intention of trading away his "nuclear card" for anything less than a U.S. commitment to subsidize his regime and system. Beijing is a likely winner

Kim Jong Il and admiring North Koreans.

from the U.S.–DPRK stalemate, which highlights Washington's impotence and dependence on China's cooperation. By pushing for a settlement that takes into account "legitimate" DPRK interests, moreover, China scores points with both Seoul and Pyongyang and positions itself to be the godfather of Korean unification.

If the endgame of the inter-Korean struggle is not yet in sight, neither is that of the Taiwan–China standoff. As previously noted, what muddies the waters is the fact that the Taiwanese remain undecided on whether they form part of the Chinese nation or are a separate Taiwanese nation. Working in favor of Taiwanese nationalists are the informal American security guarantee, the aversion of Taiwanese to China's authoritarian political system, and their close links with the United States and Japan. However, the nationalists' goal of formal independence is unattainable inasmuch as Beijing will not stand for it and Washington will not support it. Pro-unification Taiwanese, for their part, benefit from a number of factors, including the pull of a common Chinese culture, the appeal of hitching up to what many see as East Asia's emerging superpower, and the attraction of China's booming economy. Taiwan's prosperity depends on its trade and investment ties with the PRC. Moreover, these ties are deepening, giving Beijing more leverage over Taipei without having to resort to military threats. Ultimately, Taiwan might well opt for autonomy under nominal Chinese sovereignty.

The reduction of tensions in the Taiwan Strait and Korean Peninsula could pave the way for greater international cooperation in Northeast Asia, perhaps leading to the creation of a regional organization along the lines of ASEAN. Some, for example, see the six-party talks on the North Korean nuclear crisis as a possible forerunner of such an organization. But there are problems with this scenario. The six-party talks may or may not continue. In any case, although the major Northeast Asian powers share a common interest in a denuclearized Korean Peninsula, they do not see eye to eye on how to restrain North Korea from developing a nuclear arsenal. Beijing, Moscow, and Seoul favor a conciliatory and flexible approach, while Washington and Tokyo insist on ironclad guarantees from Pyongyang as a precondition for concessions. As suggested above, moreover, China is using the nuclear crisis to regain its historic preeminence on the Korean Peninsula and diminish American and Japanese influence. Rising anti-American sentiment among South Koreans, and continued clashes between Seoul and Tokyo over history and territorial disputes, work in favor of this objective.

Russia is a wild card in Northeast Asia's future. The Russian Federation is a shadow of the Russian Empire and the Soviet Union. The rusting hulks of the Soviet Pacific Fleet in Vladivostok testify to its military weakness and domestic disarray. Under President Vladimir Putin, however, Russia is rebounding and hopes to use its vast Siberian oil and gas resources to make itself an "energy superpower." Moscow is already playing off energy-hungry China and Japan by dangling the lure of preferential access to these resources, and will continue to do so. Putin wants Japanese capital and technology to develop the Russian Far East without having to accede to Tokyo's long-standing demand for the return of the southern Kurile Islands, which Stalin seized in 1945 to avenge the humiliation of 1905. Russia's "energy card" may also give Moscow greater leverage to induce Beijing to rein in ongoing Chinese immigration to the Russian Far East, which threatens to swamp the dwindling European Russian population there. No one has forgotten that the Russian Far East was once part of the Chinese Empire and that Russia forced a weak China to surrender it during an exercise in imperialist power politics in 1858–60.

The War on Terrorism

While Northeast Asia's future will be shaped by Great Power rivalries and national unification struggles, Southeast Asia faces different challenges. Topping the list, in the view of many Americans and some Southeast Asians, is the Global War on Terrorism that President George W. Bush declared in the aftermath of the September 11, 2001, terrorist attacks in New York and Washington. Having never before experienced such an audacious assault on their homeland by a foreign enemy, it is understandable that Americans should endow these attacks with epochal significance, seeing them as marking the end of the post–Cold War interlude and the inauguration of a new era of worldwide conflict with a deadly foe. The immediate enemy is Osama bin Laden's al-Qaeda network, which perpetrated the September 11 outrage and has vowed to carry out similar ones against the United States and its allies. But al-Qaeda is only one manifestation of jihadism, a pan-Islamic religio-political movement that draws on the Koran's injunction to practice Holy War against infidels to legitimize a violent assault on the West and Western ways with the aim of creating theocratic states based on strict adherence to Islamic Holy Law.

Jihadism is a West Asian phenomenon that grew out of the Arab-Israeli conflict, the 1979 Iranian Revolution, and the anti-Soviet guerrilla war in Afghanistan in the 1980s waged by Afghan, Pakistani, and Arab "mujahedeen," or holy warriors of whom bin Laden was one. But its deeper roots lie in a worldwide resurgence of Islamic religiosity, militancy, and solidarity that is linked to widely shared socioeconomic and cultural grievances against the West and Westernization. Jihadism consequently has the potential to spread wherever there are large concentrations of Muslims who are attuned to these broader "fundamentalist" currents. In East Asia, this means primarily Muslim-majority Indonesia and Malaysia. But there are also significant Muslim minorities in Thailand, Burma, Cambodia, Singapore, and the Philippines, as well as China's western province of Xinjiang. Al-Qaeda and affiliated jihadist groups have set themselves the task of infiltrating these populations with a view to recruiting allies, co-opting dissidents, and setting up bases. Like communists in the past, their goals are to radicalize moderate majorities, destabilize governments, split up states, and, ultimately, to seize political power.

Jihadists, many of whom are veterans of the Afghanistan war and alumni of training camps there and in Pakistan, have so far had their greatest success in Indonesia and the southern Philippines. In Indonesia, they have exploited the confusion of its post-1998 democratic transition, benefited from the backing of elements in the army and government, and attracted the support of homegrown Islamic militants. They also enjoy the tolerance of Indonesian political and intellectual elites. Al-Qaeda's principal affiliate in Southeast

Asia, Jemaah Islamiyah (JI), is based in Indonesia and has masterminded a string of bombings and attempted bombings, including the 2002 Bali attack on Australian tourists. JI has close ties with Moro insurgents in the southern Philippines, particularly the Moro Islamic Liberation Front (MILF), a radical Islamic offshoot of an earlier national liberation movement. JI has sympathizers and cells in Malaysia, Singapore, and elsewhere. It may also be seeking to co-opt the Muslim rebellion in southern Thailand, which the heavy-handed response of the Thai government and police converted from a relatively minor disturbance into a bloody civil war in the mid-2000s.

The jury is out on the future of jihadism in Southeast Asia. It seems to be going nowhere in Malaysia, where a strong state presides over a prosperous, Western-oriented society that subscribes to a liberal variant of Islam. Indonesia, however, is a question mark. Although JI has been crippled by the arrest of many of its leaders, its capacity to regenerate itself and mount further terrorist operations is an unknown. Indonesia's weak state, opportunistic politicians, and permissive environment favor JI's survival, as well as that of similar groups. Yet it is difficult to imagine Indonesia going the way of Iran or becoming a hotbed of jihadism like Pakistan. Jihadists are too far outside the mainstream of Indonesian politics and its tolerant, syncretistic brand of Islam to have a long-term future. They are, in all likelihood, a temporary by-product of its difficult democratic transition. Jihadists are also unlikely to find a permanent home in the southern Philippines. While they have inserted themselves into the long-running Moro insurgency, they have little chance of capturing it. The Moros are divided into autonomists and nationalists, with Islamic radicals responsive to jihadist appeals forming a small minority.

Regardless of setbacks and obstacles, jihadists will no doubt continue their proselytizing activities, focusing on disaffected Muslim minorities in the Philippines, Burma, Thailand, and probably China. Beijing is worried about the loyalty of Muslim Uighurs in Xinjiang, many of whom do not regard themselves as part of the Chinese nation and are drawn to their fellow Turkic coreligionists in neighboring Central Asia. From China's perspective, the post-Soviet emergence of new Muslim-dominated Central Asian states is a destabilizing development, since it whets the appetite of Uighurs for separation or independence. Because three of these states border on Xinjiang, moreover, they are potential bases for jihadist subversion. Border security concerns led China to join Russia and Central Asian republics to form what since 2001 has been called the Shanghai Cooperation Organization (SCO). Moreover, Beijing endorsed the U.S.-led Global War on Terrorism largely to legitimize a crackdown on Uighur resistance to an ongoing influx of ethnic Chinese immigrants into Xinjiang, its preferred long-term method of smothering breakaway ethnic and nationalist movements both there and in Tibet.

Toward "One East Asia"?

Jihadists will remain a serious security concern in East Asia as elsewhere inasmuch as globalization offers them and other terrorists unprecedented opportunities to ply their murderous trade. However, jihadism itself is unlikely to make much headway in East Asia. Its appeal is limited to Muslims, and only a minority of these are susceptible. In contrast to the more universalistic ideologies that have shaped modern East Asia—pan-Asianism, communism, and nationalism—jihadism lacks the potential to alter the regional political landscape in any significant way. Of these ideologies, communism has dropped out of the running, the victim of its failure to "deliver the goods" that its adherents expected. Communist regimes survive in China, Vietnam, Laos, and North Korea, and a communist insurgency is under way in the Philippines. But with the exception of North Korea, where it has mutated into a national religion involving worship of the Kim dynasty, communism no longer inspires true believers. In China and its emulators, who have embraced capitalism in the guise of market socialism, it has become a perfunctory orthodoxy that serves chiefly to rationalize continued Communist Party rule.

Nationalism, on the other hand, is alive and well in East Asia. Nation-states are the primary focus of identity and loyalty, and there is no reason to expect that this will change. But nation-building is still a work in progress complicated in many cases by ethnic, religious, and other divisions inherited from the colonial and precolonial past. Although Burma is the most extreme example of the crippling effects of these divisions, it is by no means unique. National economic development is another piece of unfinished business; indeed, in countries like Laos and Cambodia it has barely begun. As previously suggested, export-led industrialization based on state-guided capitalism has been successful in East Asia, playing a major role in consolidating nation-states. Economic growth has also facilitated a long-term shift from authoritarianism to democracy by creating a middle class that demands a political voice, notably in Taiwan, South Korea, and Thailand. As indicated by the 2006 Thai military coup, however, adopting democratic institutions does not ensure that they will work, a fact underscored by the troubled history of the Philippines' attempt to combine democracy with oligarchy.

Although Huntington's "clash of civilizations" thesis overstates the case for a coming collision between East Asia and the West, it highlights the importance of culture and identity as shapers of supranational conflict and cohesion. In East Asia, pan-Asianism—the idea that Asians share a distinctive cultural identity that sets them apart from Westerners—has been and will continue to be a potent unifying force among elites. ASEAN's construction of a Southeast Asian identity based on the ASEAN Way is so far the most successful attempt to translate pan-Asianism into a workable form of regional cooperation. To be sure, the enlarged and less cohesive ASEAN of the 1990s has run into problems. Its passivity in the face of the 1997 financial meltdown, the 1999 East Timor crisis, and the chaotic situation in Burma has led some to conclude that its principles of noninterference and respect for national sovereignty are outmoded. But ASEAN is unlikely to fade away. It is the "only game in town" for the relatively weak states of Southeast Asia, which are just as intent on protecting their autonomy and preventing their domination by external powers as when ASEAN was founded.

ASEAN aspires to be the leader of emerging East Asian regionalism. Despite Beijing's "charm offensive" in Southeast Asia in recent years, it has been unable to persuade ASEAN to support its preference for a closed, presumably PRC-led East Asian Community. As was shown by the 2005 East Asian Summit, ASEAN is determined that it, not China, should define and shape this community, and that extraregional powers should not be excluded. It is, of course, possible that ASEAN-led moves to promote East Asian cooperation and unity will founder on Sino-Japanese animosity. Moreover, the ASEAN Plus Three forum, which was created in 1997 to advance such cooperation, has so far accomplished little except to conclude a currency stabilization agreement, and there are no immediate plans for a regional free trade area or common currency. Still, a number of long-term trends point toward a more cohesive and cooperative East Asia. These include the revival of the pan-Asianist idea of shared Asian Values, growing economic integration and interdependence, the emergence of a uniform middle-class culture, and the common challenges posed by transnational threats.

Select Bibliography

Acharya, Amitav. 2000. *The Quest for Identity: International Relations of Southeast Asia.* Singapore: Oxford University Press.

Alagappa, Muthiah, ed. 2003. *Asian Security Order: Instrumental and Normative Features.* Stanford, CA: Stanford University Press.

Anderson, Benedict. 1996. *Imagined Communities: Reflections on the Origin and Spread of Nationalism.* New York: Verso Press.

Arrighi, Giovanni, Takeshi Hamashita, and Mark Selden, eds. 2003. *The Resurgence of East Asia: 500, 150, and 50 Year Perspectives.* New York: Routledge.

Beasley, W.G. 1995. *The Rise of Modern Japan: Political, Economic, and Social Change Since 1850.* New York: St. Martin's Press.

_____. 1991. *Japanese Imperialism, 1894–1945.* Oxford: Clarendon Press.

Bull, Hedley, and Adam Watson, eds. 1985. *The Expansion of International Society.* Oxford: Clarendon Press.

Buruma, Ian. 1995. *The Wages of Guilt: Memories of War in Germany and Japan.* New York: Meridian.

Church, Peter. 2006. *A Short History of South-East Asia.* Singapore: John Wiley and Sons (Asia).

Cohen, Warren. 2000. *East Asia at the Center: Four Thousand Years of Engagement with the World.* New York: Columbia University Press.

_____. 1993. *America in the Age of Soviet Power, 1945–1991.* Cambridge, UK: Cambridge University Press.

Costello, John. 1985. *The Pacific War.* London: Pan Books.

Crowley, James B., ed. 1970. *Modern East Asia: Essays in Interpretation.* New York: Harcourt, Brace, and World.

Diamond, Larry, and Marc F. Plattner, eds. 1998. *Democracy in East Asia.* Baltimore: The Johns Hopkins University Press.

Dower, John W. 1999. *Embracing Defeat: Japan in the Wake of World War II.* New York: W.W. Norton & Company.

Embree, Ainslie T., and Carol Gluck, eds. 1997. *Asia in Western and World History.* Armonk, NY: M.E. Sharpe.

Fairbank, John K., Edwin O. Reischauer, and Albert M. Craig. 1973. *East Asia: Tradition and Transformation.* Boston: Houghton Mifflin.

Fieldhouse, D.K. 1966. *The Colonial Empires: A Comparative Survey from the Eighteenth Century.* New York: Dell Publishing.

Gaddis, John Lewis. 1998. *We Now Know: Rethinking Cold War History.* Oxford: Oxford University Press, 1998.

Goldman, Merle, and Andrew Gordon, eds. 2000. *Historical Perspectives on Contemporary East Asia.* Cambridge: Harvard University Press.

Hobsbawm, Eric. 1994. *The Age of Extremes: A History of the World, 1914–1991.* New York: Pantheon Books.

_____. 1990. *Nations and Nationalism Since 1780.* Cambridge, UK: Cambridge University Press.

Huntington, Samuel. 1997. *The Clash of Civilizations and the Remaking of the World Order.* New York: Touchstone Books.

Iriye, Akira. 1997. *Japan and the Wider World: From the Mid-Nineteenth Century to the Present* London and New York: Longman.

_____. 1993. *The Globalizing of America, 1913–1945* (Cambridge, UK: Cambridge University Press.

_____. 1990. *After Imperialism: The Search for a New Order in the Far East 1921–1931.* Chicago: Imprint Publications.

Jansen, Marius. 2000. *The Making of Modern Japan.* Cambridge: Harvard University Press.

_____. 1992 *China in the Tokugawa World.* Cambridge: Harvard University Press.

_____. 1970. *Japan and China: From War to Peace, 1894–1972.* Chicago: Rand McNally.

Lewis, Martin W., and Karen E. Wigen. 1997. *The Myth of Continents: A Critique of Metageography.* Berkeley: University of California Press.

McNeil, William. 1999. *A World History.* Oxford: Oxford University Press.

Myers, Ramon H., and Mark R. Peattie. 1984. *The Japanese Colonial Empire, 1895–1945.* Princeton, NJ: Princeton University Press.

Osbourne, Milton. 2000. *Southeast Asia: An Introductory History.* St. Leonards, New South Wales: Allen and Unwin.

Pempel, T.J., ed. 2005. *Remapping East Asia: The Construction of a Region.* Ithaca, NY: Cornell University Press.

Roberts, J.M. 2000. *Twentieth Century: The History of the World, 1901 to 2000.* London: Penguin Books.

_____. 1980. *The Penguin History of the World.* London: Penguin Books.

Smith, Anthony D. 1991. *National Identity.* Reno: University of Nevada Press.

Steinberg, David Joel, ed. 1987. *In Search of Southeast Asia: A Modern History.* Honolulu: University of Hawaii Press.

Yahuda, Michael. 1996. *The International Politics of the Asia-Pacific, 1945–1995.* London: Routledge.

Credit Information for
Maps and Illustrations

Every effort was made to identify the owners of the maps and illustrations reprinted herein in order to secure permissions for publication. If any acknowledgment is missing, please inform the publisher so that the omission can be rectified in any future printing.

Maps

p. 5   Johomaps.com.

p. 6   Johomaps.com.

p. 11   Reprinted by permission of the publisher from *China: A New History* by John King Fairbank, p. 10, Cambridge, Mass.: The Belknap Press of Harvard University Press, Copyright © 2000 by the President and Fellows of Harvard College.

p. 121   Chinese Civil War Index, by U.S. Military Academy.

p. 122   M.E. Sharpe, Inc., Armonk, New York.

p. 127   http://commons.wikimedia.org/wiki/Image: WWIIPacific1942.jpg.

p. 153   Chinese Civil War Index, by U.S. Military Academy.

p. 157   U.S. Army.

p. 168   Jacob Van Staaveren, *Interdiction in Southern Laos, 1960–1968,* Washington DC: Center for Military History, 1993.

Illustrations

p. 26   Anonymous court artist. Hanging scroll, color on silk. The Palace Museum, Beijing.

p. 30   http://commons.wikimedia.org/wiki/Image: TokugawaYoshimune.jpg.

p. 37   Photo by Andreas Hörstemeier

p. 49   National Maritime Museum, London.

p. 55   Source: Roger Viollet.

p. 67   http://commons.wikimedia.org/wiki/Image: KING-CHULALONG-KORN.jpg.

p. 68   Library of Congress, Prints & Photographs Division [reproduction number LC-USZ62-5972]

p. 74   Uchida Kuichi, 1873. Albumen silver print.

p. 80   http://commons.wikimedia.org/wiki/Image:Jose_rizal_01.jpg.

p. 93   Ukiyoe nishiki-e by Utagawa Kokunimasa.

p. 96   Courtesy http://process.portsmouthpeacetreaty.org/process/war/images/
43aTsushimaFleetLg.jpg.

p. 98   Courtesy of Okaya Silk Museum.

p. 108   Courtesy of Taisho Romantica Shiryokan.

p. 119   U.S. Government Photograph.

p. 129   Getty Images.

p. 133   U.S. Park Service.

p. 140   http://commons.wikimedia.org/wiki/Image:Mao1938a.jpg.

p. 147   U.S. Army Photograph.

p. 150   Library of Congress, Prints & Photographs Division, U.S. News & World
Report Magazine Collection, [reproduction number, LC-USZ62-134160].

p. 151   Roger Viollet/Getty Images

p. 171   Getty Images

p. 174   Time & Life Pictures/Getty Images

p. 184   Photo by Jani Patokallio.

p. 185   Time & Life Pictures.

p. 188   Agence France-Presse

p. 204   http://www.aseansec.org/12060.htm.

p. 218   Agence France-Presse

Index

About the Author

Dr. John H. Miller holds a B.A. in history from Amherst College, an M.A. in Asian studies from Stanford University, and a Ph.D. in Japanese history from Princeton University. Currently a Visiting Fellow at the East-West Center in Washington, D.C., he has taught at the University of Wisconsin–Milwaukee; Carroll College in Waukesha, Wisconsin; the Armed Forces Staff College in Norfolk, Virginia; and the Asia-Pacific Center for Security Studies in Honolulu, Hawaii. He served as a United States Foreign Service Officer from 1975 to 2000 with tours of duty in Korea, Japan, the Philippines, Canada, and Washington, D.C. He has published extensively on the bearing of East Asian history on contemporary security concerns.

CPSIA information can be obtained
at www.ICGtesting.com
Printed in the USA
LVHW010359090821
694848LV00011B/954